The Ottoman Mosaic

Ottoman Empire 1451–1683

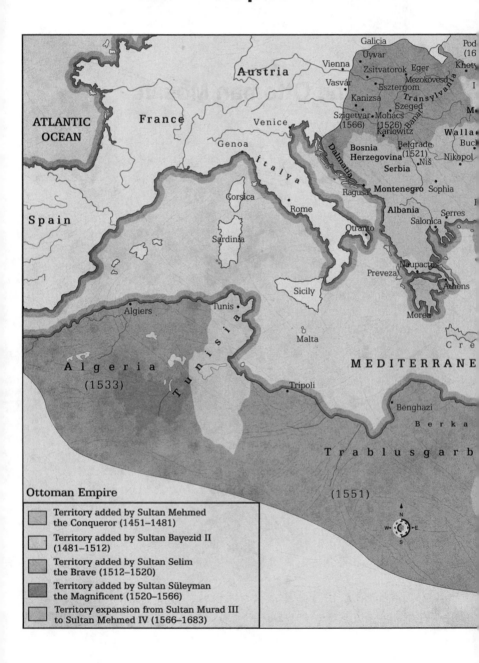

Galicia
Pod
(16
Uyvar
Vienna
Zsitvatorok Eger
Khot
Austria
Mezokövesd
Vasvár
Esztergom
I
Kanizsa
Transylvania
Szeged
M
France
Szigetvar Mohács
Venice
(1566) (1526)
Walla
Karlowitz
Buc
ATLANTIC
Genoa
Bosnia Belgrade
OCEAN
Herzegovina (1521) Nikopol
Italya
Serbia
Niš
Corsica
Ragusa Montenegro Sophia
Rome
Spain
Albania Serres
Salonica
Sardinia
Otranto
Naupactus
Preveza
Athens
Sicily
Morea
Algiers Tunis
Malta
Cre
Algeria **MEDITERRANE**
(1533)
Tripoli
Benghazi
B e r k a
Tunisia
T r a b l u s g a r b

Ottoman Empire

(1551)

- Territory added by Sultan Mehmed the Conqueror (1451–1481)
- Territory added by Sultan Bayezid II (1481–1512)
- Territory added by Sultan Selim the Brave (1512–1520)
- Territory added by Sultan Süleyman the Magnificent (1520–1566)
- Territory expansion from Sultan Murad III to Sultan Mehmed IV (1566–1683)

Credit: *The Ottoman Sultans: Mighty Guests of the Throne*, Tughra Books 2010

The
Ottoman
Mosaic

Exploring Models for Peace by
Re-Exploring the Past

Edited by
Kemal Karpat
Yetkin Yıldırım

Cune

The Ottoman Mosaic:
Exploring Models for Peace by Re-Exploring the Past
© 2010 Kemal Karpat and Yetkin Yıldırım
Cune Press, Seattle 2010
First Edition
2 4 6 8 9 7 5 3

ISBN (hardback) 978-1885942289 (10 digit) 1885942281 $34.95
ISBN (paper) 978-1885942272 (10 digit) 1885942273 $21.95

Library of Congress Cataloging-in-Publication Data

The Ottoman Mosaic : exploring models for peace by re-exploring the
past / edited by Kemal Karpat and Yetkin Yıldırım. — 1st ed.
p. cm.
ISBN 978-1-885942-28-9
1. Turkey—History—Ottoman Empire, 1288-1918. 2. Turkey—
Politics and government. I. Karpat, Kemal H. II. Yıldırım, Yetkin,
1974- III. Title.

DR485.O87 2009
956'.015—dc22   2009037852

The map, "Ottoman Empire 1451–1683," originally appeared in *The
Ottoman Sultans: Mighty Guests of the Throne,* Tughra Books, 2010.
Reprinted with permission.
Cover background photo by Mamoun Sakkal.
Promotional materials - photo credit: Courtesy of Tughra Books

Select titles in the Bridge Between the Cultures Series:
Steel & Silk: Men and Women Who Shaped Syria 1900 - 2000 - by Sami Moubayed
A Pen of Damascus Steel: The Political Cartoons of an Arab Master - by Ali Farzat
The Road from Damascus: A Journey Through Syria - by Scott C. Davis
Kisses from a Distance: An Immigrant Family Experience - by Raff Ellis
Syria - Ballots or Bullets?
Democracy, Islamism, and Secularism in the Levant - by Carsten Wieland

www.cunepress.com | www.cunepress.net

Contents

Foreword

by Dr. Dimitri Kitsikis

THE PRESENT VOLUME IS AN INVALUABLE contribution to the scholarly study of the Ottoman Empire. Having clarified the concept of Ecumenical Empire in my works, I consider that this collective study not only puts in a proper perspective this Empire of Empires, one of the two Ecumenical Empires of our planet throughout History according to my definition (the other one being the Chinese Empire), but it also gives a wealth of information on the Ottoman model of government that has become increasingly relevant in this present world of globalization.

Hard facts are hard facts. They do not need any interpretation. Propaganda is propaganda. But people listen to propaganda as if it were factual. Nationalist propaganda claimed that the Ottoman Empire was an inadequate state construction that should be dismantled in favor of building up from its ruins a great number of nation-states. Naturally, any state construction could be improved, and criticism is necessary for the development of the state. However, the aim of the anti-Ottomanists was not to correct the short-comings of the Ottoman State, but rather, to tear it down.

Muslims are told that the failure of the Empire can be attributed to the Christians, but Christians blame the Muslims. Each version of the story comes with its own psychological boasting, "Be proud to be Turk" or, "Be proud to be Greek." "A Turk never commits crimes and should hate the 'criminal' Greeks," or vice versa. The propagandistic explanations have political agendas, "Republicanism is good," or, "Monarchy is bad." "Western democracy is better than Eastern despotism." Propaganda includes religious injunctions, "The separation of Church and State is good, anything to the contrary is religious fanaticism." Or, "Secularism is superior to the religious nation (millet) system." Then there is economic propaganda, "Libre-échange preserves individual liberty against the monopolies of the state." Or perhaps international morality will weigh in to explain that in the First World War, the good guys were the Allies and the bad guys were the Central Powers. Consequently, the Ottoman Empire should have sided with England, not with Germany. So, if the Empire was defeated, it was solely responsible and therefore, should be punished. International morality says that territory cannot be offered to the defeated, although it is perfectly legitimate to give a victorious state a piece of land that once belonged to a defeated state. This reasoning was applied at international conferences after the end of wars, during which the treaties like the Sèvres Treaty of 1920 were signed.

But let's discuss facts. In 1453, there was a change in the royal dynasty of Constantinople. Dynastic changes have happened many times in the 1500 year-long history of the Roman Empire, and they have always occurred through violence, coup d'état, insurrection or war. This happened in the fourth century AD, when a Christian dynasty replaced a dynasty that followed the Olympian gods. This occurred again in the 8th and 9th centuries AD, when two iconoclastic dynasties (a Christian heresy that destroyed the icons) replaced dynasties that respected the icons. Again, in the fifteenth century and up to 1453, the Christian Orthodox Palaiologos dynasty joined with the Pope and became Roman Catholic. One should understand that there is not "one" Christianity. The differences between the multitudes of Christian "heresies" are so great that one could argue that Christian Orthodoxy is nearer to Anatolian practice of Islam than to Roman Catholicism. And Arnold Toynbee was of the opinion that Islam was a Christian heresy. Finally, Ottoman dynasty from the house of Osman, which focused on and practiced spiritual dimensions of Islam, replaced the last Roman Catholic Palaiologos.

From a dynastic succession point of view, 1453 was nothing new. The Roman Empire went on as before under the new Ottoman Dynasty, which remained in power all the way into the twentieth century, longer than any previous Roman dynasty.

In 1453, the majority of the Greeks were adamantly opposed to the Palaiologos dynasty, which was accused of supporting Roman Catholicism. The Greeks deserted the churches of Constantinople, especially the Cathedral of Aya Sofya, where the Palaiologos had ordered the clergy to officiate the Catholic creed. Under the spiritual leadership of the monk Gennadios, these Greeks formed an overwhelming majority in support of the Ottomans, who were perceived as liberators from the nobles that had betrayed their creed. Even the prime minister of Palaiologos, the Grand Duke Loukas Notaras, stated that, "I would rather see the Turkish turban in the midst of the City than the Latin mitre." I have insisted myself that every May 29, on the anniversary day of the City's fall, Greeks and Turks should celebrate together the liberation of Constantinople by the Fatih, rather than the present divisive situation where the Turks celebrate the day as a victory and the Greeks commemorate it as a day of catastrophe.

From 1453 to 1912, Greeks staunchly supported the new dynasty. They were the most favored people of the Empire; the Turks were, at this point, primarily a peasant population in a feudal society. The Greeks on the other hand made up the bourgeoisie, living in cities and composing some part of the Ottoman aristocracy. The exceptional stability of a dynasty that lasted 644 years (1280-1924)—the longest in two thousand years between the Roman Empire from Emperor Augustus to the last caliphe Abdülmecit II—won the unfailing support of the Greek millet to the sultan.

In 1821, the rebellion against Ottoman power began in Greece. A small minority of Greek peasants in the Peloponnesos, the most undeveloped part of Western Ottoman lands—a place without cities and without roads, took arms and revolted against the central power of the Sultan. These peasants were organized by the wealthy bourgeois communities of the Greek diaspora in Vienna and Paris, who were under the influence of the French Revolution and the emerging ideology of Nationalism. The wealthy bourgeois communities stirred them up by persuading them that their ancestors were the ancient Greeks, something they ignored, being totally illiterate. They eventually managed to create a small state of 700,000 people, and put at its head a German king! However, the vast majority of Greeks in the Empire refused to follow suit and continued to prosper up until 1912, when the fever of Nationalism had spread across the Ottoman lands, setting up for its collapse. Meanwhile, in the newly formed nation-states of the Balkans and the Middle East (including Turkey, formed in 1923), history was being rewritten to suit the needs of Nationalist ideology.

In 1981, Greece became a full member of the European Union. Even though both Greece and Turkey had been accepted as associated members at about the same time (1961 for Greece, 1963 for Turkey), Turkey was denied full membership. The antagonism of the two competing nationalisms had caught the interested eyes of Western imperialists, and Turkish leaders had to make a choice: either continue this absurd antagonism or re-read history. Özal, the prime minister in 1983, chose to re-read it. So on the 14th of April 1987, he sent a letter to Leo Tindemans, the president of the Council of Ministers of the European Community in Brussels, asking officially for full membership in the European Union. The letter contained the following argument, "I wish to emphasize the European vocation of Turkey and her commitment to European unity".

Now, the problem was that centuries of Western propaganda against the "unspeakable Turk" had persuaded the European public that Turks were an Asiatic, nomadic, barbarian, militant people, incapable of civilized behavior. Özal, knowing well that these accusations were ridiculous, still had to defend the dignity of Turkey in the eyes of the Westerners. So he decided to write a history book!

The incentive for this project came from his collaborator and later ambassador of Turkey in Athens, the late MP Gündüz Aktan (1941-2008). Özal, unlike Aktan, did not know any French. The book was written in Turkish, but it was not published in that language (probably because it was too early for the Turkish public to accept such a pro-Greek book). Instead, the book was translated into French by Aktan and published with the title La Turquie en Europe

(Paris, Plon, 1988, 270 pages). Later, an English expurgated edition was published as Turkey in Europe and Europe in Turkey (Nicosia, Rustem, 1991, 376 pages). In this later English edition, the passages considered overly pro-Greek were deleted. Özal intentionally chose to base his book on two authors that he admired, one Turk, Halikarnas Balıkçısı, and one Greek, myself. The general idea of the book was that Turkish civilization had not been imported, but grew in Anatolia out of the traditions of the Greek Ionian civilization. The conclusion was that as Turkey was Greece and Greece was Turkey, it made no sense to include one half of the whole (Greece) in Europe, and leave the other half (Turkey) outside.

Later, Özal told me that he had named his younger son Efe, from the Greek word *efebos* (*ephebe*, young man), because of the Zeybeks of the Turkish coast of the Aegean. He himself explains in his French book what this meant (In the English edition, these French pages (53 to 57) were deleted as too pro-Greek). Özal writes, "There is a Greek tradition that has survived with us: the one of the efe. The word comes from the Greek ephebos (ephebe) and designates young men who, like the Zeybeks, were trained in the use of arms up in the mountains. After this training, they came down to the cities to participate in martial games in the temple of Dionysos. . . . The institution of the Janisaries (similar to the Efes) conceived by the Ottomans was the nearest model possible of the Republic of Plato" (pg 56-57).

But public opinions, in Turkey and Greece, were not yet ready for such writings. Since 1978, I had myself been strongly attacked in Greece for my books which were considered outrageously pro-Turkish. Greek publishers turned down my offer to translate into Greek the Özal book, considering it to be Turkish propaganda! In Turkey, Özal was telling me that he did not dare to publish his book in Turkish.

Özal understood that as long as the history schoolbooks in both countries were not expurgated of Nationalistic views hostile to the other side, nothing serious could be achieved. He gave instructions to Gündüz Aktan, then ambassador to Athens, to put together a collaborative project between Professor İlber Ortaylı (the son of a

Crimean Tatar) and myself to rewrite both Greek and Turkish history schoolbooks. Aktan invited us for a business lunch in the Hotel Grande Bfretagne, in Athens. We all three decided to go ahead. But, later we realized that as long as there was not an official understanding between the two governments, no real progress could be achieved. Özal died in 1993, and Greeks had to wait until after the Karamanlis government left power in 2004 for any steps toward reconciliation. Already, with my encouragement, my friend Herkül Millas had published his doctoral dissertation in Greek, under the title Eikones Hellenon kai Tourkon. Scholika biblia, historiographia, logotechnia kai ethnika stereotypa (Images of Greeks and Turks. Schoolbooks, Historiography, Literature and National Stereotypes), Athens, Alexandria Press, 2001.

When the Greek ministry of Education finally published the new history books in 2006, the Nationalist reaction of the Greek public was so violent that the Minister of Education, Marietta Giannakou was forced to step down. She was not re-elected in the following national elections, and the incriminating schoolbook was withdrawn from circulation. In the section dealing with the Fire of Izmir in 1922 and the fleeing of the Greek population, the Greek public was furious at the explanation provided in that textbook. The textbook claimed that some of the Greek civilian casualties were not caused by the Turkish troops, but by the crowd that pushed one another on the wharf into the sea out of panic.

In 2009, George Papandreou, a staunch supporter of Greek-Turkish friendship, came to power in Cyprus. Hopes of a Greek-Turkish Confederation between Athens and Ankara that meets a similar disposition from the Turkish side of the Erdoğan-Davutoğlu government, have been raised. Nevertheless, the internal situation in both countries and Nationalistic reactions constitute the main obstacles to the realization of such a rapprochement.

The present survey of Ottoman culture provides valuable insight into the history of this diverse society, and offers a hopeful alternative to the Nationalistic divisions that define much of the contemporary intercultural discourse.

Introduction

**Tolerance and Cultural-Religious
Coexistence in the Ottoman Empire**

by Dr. Kemal Karpat and Dr. Yetkin Yıldırım

I. Conference Purpose and Themes

OVER THE COURSE OF A WEEKEND IN MARCH 2007, a group of scholars from all over the world gathered at the University of Texas at Austin to attend a conference titled, "Exploring Models for Peace by Re-exploring the Past: Diversity in the Ottoman Empire." This conference, which was jointly organized by UT's Center for Middle Eastern Studies, the Raindrop Foundation of Houston, and the Institute of Interfaith Dialog, was devoted to the exploration of interfaith coexistence in the Ottoman Empire.

The purpose of this conference was to show how Ottoman rule in the Middle East and southeastern Europe created one of the most successful models of plural society in the early modern world. As a pre-modern, non-democratic, and non-secular polity, the Ottoman State epitomized peaceful coexistence. Although they assumed the role of the protector and the leader of the Islamic world, the Ottomans did not hesitate to engage in a dynamic relationship with non-Islamic and minority cultures. While maintaining active interest in the artistic, architectural, and technological advancements of other civilizations and establishing strong commercial ties with them, the Ottomans also paid special attention to the safeguarding of legal, political, and cultural mechanisms that ensured the harmonious coexistence of the diverse populations within the empire.

The participants in this conference demonstrated that the Ottoman spirit of tolerance survives in people of many different faiths and backgrounds, Muslim and non-Muslim alike, and it was in this spirit that seventeen papers were presented at the conference, dealing with topics ranging from the Ottoman legacy, cultural interactions, the historical demise of Ottoman diversity, the Ottoman Empire's non-Muslim subjects, to the cultural life in the Ottoman Empire. The nine chapters included in this collection are the result of this exploration. While they may vary in their perspectives—in other words, the way in which they analyze the Ottoman Empire in terms of religious diversity and tolerance, systems of governance, dynamics of multiculturalism, emigration and immigration, culture, family life, and marriage—these chapters are linked by a common purpose: to delve into the specifics of Ottoman history and explore its contemporary relevance, with the ultimate aim of inspiring researchers and practitioners of conflict management to explore new approaches and paths to peace, not only in the Middle East, but on a global scale.

II. Overview of Chapters

The Ottoman Empire was not one nation, but a conglomeration of many nations. The Ottomans did not have one religion; they had many religions. Despite the vast differences between the various ethnic groups within the Ottoman Empire, the Ottomans were one soul, one cohesive body uniting different peoples through their common desire for peaceful coexistence.

Today, the Ottoman Empire is legendary for its history of peace in South Eastern Europe, the Middle East, and North Africa. If we try to understand the Ottomans in the context of their own time, when communication and transportation were very limited, we will find that their lives were overall successful and peaceful. In most of the places where the Ottomans ruled, including the Balkans, the Middle East, and North Africa, they established peaceful coexistence among the residents from different cultures. After their era, significant ethnic tensions festered, some of which turned into the bloodiest events of their times.

In today's world of rapidly increasing globalization and complex cultural-religious conflicts, never has the need for an applicable model of tolerance, multiculturalism, and coexistence been so urgent. With this in mind, historical examples of successful peaceful coexistence must be sought. The history of the Ottoman state and its foundation of tolerance, which is still evident in present-day Turkey, may provide just such an example. Faced with rampant ethno-religious conflict all over the world, the Ottoman Empire demonstrates what multi-religious civilizations can become: a land where people of different religions, cultures, and ethnicities can live together peacefully. An example they set for more than six centuries.

While the scholars whose writings are included in this anthology examined the Ottoman Empire through different lenses — from history to government, law, art, and many other interrelated disciplines—their research ultimately share one common goal: to identify the different factors that led to tolerance in the Ottoman Empire and discuss the benefits that such peaceful coexistence brought to the Empire. The scholars also look at how the Ottoman state is viewed in the present day, analyzing political rhetoric and the works of personalities such as Fethullah Gülen and various other thinkers and artists. They advocate using the Ottomans as an example to improve interfaith relations.

Kemal Karpat's essay, "From the Classical Ottoman Religious Cultural Order to Nation State," focuses on a shift of emphasis from a collective religious identity to individual identity based on citizenship in the unitary state in Turkey. In his chapter, Karpat examines increased modernization in Anatolia over the course of the region's history and the centralization and bureaucratization that accompanied it as a point of "disintegration of the Classical Socio-Cultural arrangement." Karpat believes that this represents the beginning of politicization of religious affiliation and antagonism between groups in the Ottoman Empire. He relates how the nineteenth century brought a great many of these modernizing changes to the Ottoman Empire, describing the situation thus:

> As political elites identified themselves more inti-
> mately with the state and its ideologies and used
> the modern educational system to disseminate
> a particular view of history, society, and cultural
> developments, the rise of communal consciousness
> and the breakdown of the old social order brought
> to the fore differences of faith that previously had
> carried little, if any, political significance.

His essay goes on to show how the association of religious faith with conflict resulted from increasing centralization and the abolishing of the classic millet system over the course of the nineteenth century. He cites the Ottoman Parliament (Parliament) of 1876-78 which adopted the modern idea of Ottomanism: "a common citizenship that would have superseded differences of faith, ethnicity and language." According to Karpat, the Parliament's deputies "consisted mostly of local communal leaders . . . who expressed the religious preferences of their communities" thereby sharpening "religious differences between Muslims and non-Muslims who had co-existed peacefully for centuries."

Karpat then suggests the Berlin Treaty of 1878 as a factor which deepened the separation between Muslims and Christians because it recognized independent statehood for most of the Orthodox Christians in the Balkans and left the Ottoman state a predominantly Muslim body; this politicized the previously religious unity and loyalty of the Islamic faith. He describes that with the Berlin Treaty came massive violent forced migrations which intensified immigrants' "antagonism towards the government of their country of origin" and politicized religious consciousness. Analyzing these developments, Karpat writes, "Islamism was born as a strictly defensive measure," but "the European press of the time . . . perceived and depicted its external manifestation as pan Islamism." Here we see that this brief overview of modernization in the Ottoman Empire leads us to one possible source of the stereotypes of Islam as intolerant and narrow-minded, for during the time of the Berlin Treaty, Western Europeans began to fear that "Muslims under British, French, Dutch and Russian rule [would be incited] to rebel against their European imperial masters." Nevertheless, Karpat concludes with the belief that due to the Turkish society's cultural foundations, it "maintains a basic attitude favoring multi-ethnic diversity and multi-cultural harmony."

Many discussions of the Ottomans begin with the attempt to counter-act previously misguided historical representations of Islam in the Ottoman Empire and the stereotypes that these representations have fostered. In "The Roots of Religious Tolerance in the Ottoman Empire," Abdul-Rahman Salem begins with this very point, writing, "The Ottoman Empire has long been subjected to severe, worldwide criticism. . . . Repression, intolerance, and narrow-mindedness are among the main accusations against the Ottomans." Salem goes on to state that his exploration "into the roots of the Ottoman tolerance . . . with regard to freedom of belief," is motivated by the desire to refute such misrepresentations of the Ottomans.

In his essay, Salem, like Karpat, looks at the Ottoman example through a historic lens. However, rather than mapping out a timeline of events, he seeks to "look into the roots of the Ottoman tolerance, especially with regard to freedom of thought and belief." Salem finds his starting point in the Seljuks, the predecessors of the Ottomans in Asia Minor, "who shared with them the same Turkish descent." He asserts that much of the tolerance in the Ottoman Empire came from these Seljuk Turks, writing that they "exerted a certain degree of influence" on early Ottoman leaders, who "adhered to Sunni Islam," but "dealt with the followers of different religions and sects on equal footing, making no distinction between Muslims and non-Muslims."

According to Salem, the Seljuks, who were known to be tolerant towards Christians, defeated the Byzantines in Asia Minor, clearing the way for the Ottomans. Salem demonstrates that the early sultans were very tolerant of other cultures and religions, encouraged peaceful coexistence, and planted the seeds for later tolerance within the Empire. He also shows how establishments such as Sufi orders and *madrasahs*, (institutions which balance mysticism with scholasticism), and practices such as intermarriage helped to promote tolerance in the Ottoman state. He highlights the sultans' protection of religious buildings for all religions with special focus on Sultan Mehmed II's decision to spare much of Constantinople in 1453. From these examples, Salem concludes, "The phenomenon of religious tolerance in the Ottoman Empire was not superficial, but deeply rooted in the structure of the state."

In "'Upon Them be Peace:' The Ottoman Spirit, Early Modern Models of Toleration, and Contemporary Debates over Multiculturalism," Bernadette Andrea looks at contemporary problems in multiculturalism and tolerance and discusses how the melting pot model in the US has often led to racism and forced assimilation of minority populations. Andrea seeks a more accepting model of multiculturalism, one "premised on the protection of minority cultures, freedom to practice one's religion, and elimination of racism." She points to the Classical Period of the Ottoman Empire, during which "Protestant England . . . looked to the Ottomans for a model of tolerance unavailable in Western Europe or the Americas." Here, Andrea suggests that the Ottoman "multiethnic, multifaith and multilingual mosaic" model of multiculturalism could be used to create a greater autonomy of minority populations.

Though she argues that "the political edifice of the Ottoman Empire cannot . . . be replicated as a model of multiculturalism in our global world," Andrea believes that "we should restore the fundamental principles of seeking common ground with those close to us." Also central to Andrea's argument is the perspective of the Turkish writer and scholar Fethullah Gülen, a figure cited in many of the essays within this anthology and a leading advocate of the "Ottoman Spirit" of tolerance. Particularly appealing to Andrea is Gülen's deeply held conviction that "one need not forego the values of one's religion, nation, and history to 'unite on common ground and shake hands with all'" because this suggestion is a more moderate alternative to the strict assimilation multicultural models. Andrea implores her audience to move beyond the extremes of the "clash of civilizations" and the call to "restore the caliphate" and focus instead on the Ottoman model as a more balanced, practical and just approach to maintaining the rights and cultures of many minority groups with diverse societies. Andrea supports her argument about the need for Protestant England to emulate the Ottoman model for tolerance with John Locke's philosophy of cultural liberalism, an idea inspired by Ottoman religious practices.

In "Diversity, Legal Pluralism and Peaceful Coexistence in the Ottoman Centuries," Ihsan Yılmaz echoes Andrea's concern for the protection of minority groups within Western societies' demands for assimilation. Like Andrea, Yılmaz believes that the Ottoman example can help to forge new solutions to these contemporary problems, but his perspective is uniquely focused on comparing the Ottoman system of law and government (the millet system) to the modern legal system in Britain. In his essay, Yılmaz draws out the implications of these two systems for minority populations in multicultural societies.

Yılmaz begins his analysis with a discussion of legal modernity in which "[territorial laws are] replaced by personal laws; special laws are replaced by the general ones, and customary ones by statute laws." Under this type of modern legal system, "central national power tolerates no rivals by means of law in its sovereignty since uniform law is seen as a 'condition of progress toward modern nationhood.'" As Yılmaz points out, the difficulty here is that "legal pluralism is a fact," a truth which we see clearly in the example of Muslims living in Britain. While Muslims are accountable to British law, they remain subject to Muslim law as well, thus creating "a hybrid unofficial law," whereby matters are often settled in "informal family or community conciliation," in avoidance of the official court system. Muslims living in Britain have conciliated their religion with their environment in this way, but Yılmaz points out some of the difficulties this compromise poses, citing the potential for undue hardship, especially on Muslim women who, in situations of divorce, are required to obtain both a secular divorce, recognized by the state, and a religious divorce, recognized by Islam. Yılmaz writes,

> If the woman is not religiously divorced from her husband, it does not matter that she is divorced under civil law. . . . Sometimes capricious husbands divorce their wives officially but do not want to

> pronounce *talaq* or deliver the *get* to prevent the
> women from remarrying. . . . such men have used
> their power to grant or withhold divorce to negoti-
> ate favourable settlements on the issues of finance,
> property, and children.

With this in mind, Yılmaz asserts that "it is obvious in the English context that legal uniformity is a myth and official not legal plural- ism is a reality. Non-recognition of this multicultural reality is an impediment to peaceful co-existence and it also undermines the respect for the state."

In response to this, Yılmaz turns to an Islamic model and the Ottoman example, where he finds that due to the "four main schools of law" in Islam, as well as their incarnations in daily practice, "there has always been an internal plurality of Muslim laws." What is inter- esting here is the suggestion that interfaith activists such as Gülen echo: that tolerance and plurality are not simply positive values or values relating to the Classical Ottoman Empire, but rather, they are particularly Islamic values. Yılmaz asserts this idea when he writes, "Gülen promotes dialogue based on a historically implanted defini- tion of tolerance. This tolerance is defined as a foundation of the Ottoman Empire, which viewed 'Islam as a flexible and tolerant belief system.'" Unlike the melting-pot ideal, which cannot, in reality, erase the plurality of laws from different value systems, the Ottoman model shows a greater acceptance of other groups' differences and a greater toleration for largely autonomous groups living in the realm of the state. Like several of his counterparts, Yılmaz concludes that "today, the Ottoman legal system may not be plausible . . . [but] their acceptance and tolerance of diversity can be emulated."

While Karpat's essay is aimed at showing how Islamism and the stereotypes which surround it were forced to the foreground with the modernization of Turkey, Linda T. Darling attempts to show that the creation of stereotypes of Islam as an intolerant or violent belief system may go back much further. To a large extent this is the subject of her essay, "Christian-Muslim interaction on the Ottoman Frontier: *Gaza* and Accommodation in Early Ottoman History," in which Darling focuses on the Ottoman Empire as a *gazi* state and explores Paul Wittek's famous "*gazi* thesis." In this chapter, Darling attempts "to historicize the concept of *gaza* in the early Ottoman state" by comparing fifteenth century commentators' descriptions of the fourteenth century with other records of the state. Through historic documents, Darling analyzes how the concept of *gaza* has changed over time, including Historian Leopold von Ranke's description of the *gazi* fighter as one who "knew . . . no lord and father but the grand signor, no will but his . . . no occupation but war in his service, no personal purpose unless it were plunder in this life, and in death the paradise thrown open to him who fought for Islam," a fearful characterization later brought to mainstream by Paul Wittek in his depiction of the Ottomans as "relentless 'Warriors of the Faith, continually incited by fanatical dervishes to force Islam upon the inhabitants of the conquered country." Darling challenges this depiction of Islam, noting that:

> *Gaza* is presented in different ways in different sources: religious works written by *ulema* defined *gaza* as a matter of Islamic piety and obedience to rules, while epic poems described *gazis* as inclusive warriors, winning over Christians by tolerance and generosity and caring more about knightly bravery than doctrinal orthodoxy or even religious identity.

Because of the "contradictions in evidence" regarding how *gaza* was actually conceived in the Classical Ottoman empire, Darling suggests that "*gaza* could have been a foundational concept in Ottoman legitimation, appealing to a wide variety of people, without there having been any agreement as to what it meant or what it demanded from its participants." While this statement may be speculative, it is clear that *gaza* as it was so narrowly and unfavorably defined by Wittek did not accurately encompass the nature of the Ottoman Empire, nor the motivations for its conquests. As an example of this, Darling notes that "the conquest of Constantinople in 1453 is usually presented as the Muslim capture of a Christian capital, and it was, but it was also the reuniting of the former Byzantine lands with their capital city, a conquest devoid of religious motivation." Contradicting Wittek's definition of *gaza*, Darling writes of the ebb and flow of tolerance and "religious antagonism in the history of Ottoman conquest" and refers to the famous *gazi* warrior Osman who "protected the first towns he conquered so well that they became more prosperous than before . . . numerous villages, towns, and individuals joined the Ottomans voluntarily." She emphasizes the common interactions between *gazi* warriors and people of different faiths, noting that many Christians served in the military and that Osman himself did business with Christians.

Although by the middle of the fifteenth century, many people were beginning to see the conquests of the Ottomans in terms of a rivalry between Christianity and Islam, the realities of these conquests did not reflect this religious rivalry as primary. Darling writes, "The initial conquests were made by a combination of Muslims and Christians seeking to gain wealth and territory and political authority, not to spread Islam or even Islamic dominion . . . the confrontational ideology of *gaza* appeared on the popular level, rather than coming from the rulers." Because of these contradictions between reality and popular perceptions, "a historical tension" was created between the Ottomans and the West: "the Ottomans saw themselves as accommodating toward non-Muslims, [but] the West confronted the zeal of the army and interpreted Ottoman religious policies accordingly." With this essay, we have another example of a source of historical misrepresentation of Muslim Ottomans and the general character of Islam which though unsubstantiated, resulted in greater antagonism between different people groups over time.

Like Yılmaz, Akif Aydın, examines the Ottoman Empire through an analysis of Ottoman legal and judicial systems and its treatment of minorities under those systems. Rather than compare this system to modern-day nationalist legal systems as Yılmaz has done, Aydın questions the existence and culmination of a Pax Ottomana, a period of peace and tranquility between individual groups in Ottoman lands, in his essay "The Role of Ottoman Law in the Establishment of Pax Ottomana." According to Aydın, "the Pax Ottomana was achieved through the implementation of a merger of political, legal, social, and economical aspects through multi-directional projects." Aydın outlines the role of Ottoman law as instrumental to Pax Ottomana. In his analysis, Aydın focuses a great deal of his attention on the precedence of justice in implementing Ottoman law, emphasizing how leaders of the Ottoman empire greatly valued equal justice under the law for all people, both Muslims and non-Muslims alike. He writes, "The Ottoman administration was very keen on preventing the military officials from punishing anybody without a court decision, and therefore, made a great effort to prevent arbitrary governance." Aydın describes, also, how the value of religious freedom was upheld not only in practice, but by an imperial edit (*berat*) given by Mehmed II, which laid the foundations for the continued existence of minority autonomy in religious practice. In his discussion of the Ottoman court systems, Aydın points out that in many matters concerning individual communities, such as marriage, divorce and inheritance, non-Muslims had the freedom to choose whether to bring these matters to their own community courts or to the centralized Sharia court system. Examining historical records of non-Muslims in the Islamic court system, Aydın asks, "Did the Ottoman judges discriminate between Muslim and non-Muslim subjects in their judgment?" Based on his brief findings, he remarks that "we see almost no complaints dealing with religious discrimination." This chapter provides strong evidence that Ottoman law and the precedent of justice regardless of religious creed both played an important role in the realization of the Pax Ottomana.

Nisya Allovi's chapter on "The Turkish Jews," celebrates the relationship of tolerance that has existed between Jews and Muslims in the Ottoman Empire and the Turkish Republic for over seven centuries. Allovi writes of the history of Jews in Anatolia from the twelfth century all the way up to present day Turkey, noting many instances in which "an increasing number of European Jews escaping persecution in their native countries settled in the Ottoman Empire." Especially compelling here is Allovi's account of World War II, during which "Turkey served as a safe passage for many Jews fleeing the horrors of the Nazis." Allovi also stresses the benefits of promoting multi-cultural coexistence by noting the ways in which Jews contributed to the Ottoman Empire through the introduction of the printing press and through service as diplomats and court physicians. As she moves into discussions of contemporary Jewish existence in Turkey, Allovi writes of the purpose of the Quincentennial Foundation and the establishment of the Museum of Turkish Jews, writing that these efforts aim "to promote the story of 700 years of harmony between Turks and Jews...and to display the humanitarian spirit of the Turkish Nation." The editors recommend further reading on Jewish-Turkish relations such as Mark Mazower's *Salonica - A City of Ghosts* (2006), Arnold Reisman's *The Modernization of Turkey* (2006) which deals with the refugees from Nazism in the 1930s, and Itzak Shoehof's *Meghillah Oven* (translated in Turkish as *Buda Destani* (2007) which compares the oppression or land massacres of Jews by Austrian army in Buda 1686 with the security enjoyed under Turks.

Tom Gage's chapter entitled "Ottoman Palimpsests: The Past Reviewed in Architecture and Literature" demonstrates how the historical diversity and multiculturalism of Ottoman society is reflected in Turkish literature and architecture. Gage asserts that "in today's global economy, artistic representations are a means of ameliorating external and internal tensions and offer a way for the twenty-first century to sustain the Turkish genius." Gage's paper is essentially an analysis of the work of two contemporary Turkish artists, the Nobel Laureate Orhan Pumuk and the late Celik Gulersoy. Gage views the work of both of these artists through the metaphor of a "Palimpsest."

> Before the appearance of inexpensive Chinese paper, an author could compose only on expensive animal skins and material made from the pith of papyrus reeds. The ancients bleached and recycled these palimpsests many times over. Today, researchers can restore the layered meanings from the texts of the past...Orhan Pamuk and Celik Gulersoy, through representative literature and architecture, have made visible, accessible, and understandable

the dual heritage responsible for Turkey's unique dynamism.

Gage's essay shows that both of these artists represent the history of the Turks in ways that celebrate pluralism and multiculturalism, thereby expunging "any visions of an inherent 'clash of civilizations' between East and West."

According to Yetkin Yıldırım and Maria Curtis's "Analysis of the Millet System in Light of Contact Theory," the Ottoman ethic of tolerance is exemplified in the governmental arrangement of the Classical Ottoman state, whereby groups of "Dhimmis" or non-Muslims were not only allowed freedom to practice their religion, but were also "granted a legal designation separate from the Muslim population." Furthermore, authors write that these separate governmental groups called millets "were granted autonomy, not only over religious matters, but over everyday legal matters, including education, marriage, health, communication, and the collection and distribution of taxes." Authors go on to compare the Ottoman Millet System with Contact Theory, an idea derived from George W. Allport's 1954 study which focused on intra-group relations. The basis for this theory is that contact between members of different groups can improve when certain conditions are present. In outlining these conditions, Authors seek to show how many of these circumstances influenced the implementation of the Ottoman millet system. This chapter also examines the work of Fethullah Gülen, who believed that the Ottoman example could give practical insight for the creation of contemporary models for peaceful coexistence. Gülen placed particular emphasis on the creation of dialogue between groups, and the necessity of tolerance if dialogue is to occur. After examining Ottoman history and the millet system through the contemporary ideas of Contact Theory and Fethullah Gülen, Authors highlight the importance of the Ottoman model in balancing the necessity of unity of "diverse communities under a common identity" while simultaneously "enabling the communities to maintain distinct identities."

Departing somewhat from the themes of tolerance and interfaith cooperation, the final chapter, which was written by Salim Ayduz, deals with the development of the classical Ottoman scientific tradition "based on the Islamic classical scientific tradition." In this chapter, entitled, "Multicultural Science in the Ottoman Empire: Examples from Medicine and Astronomy." Ayduz seeks to show how Turkish scientific activities and institutions "brought about the revival of culture, science, and learning in world civilization." Ayduz celebrates this history as providing many important contributions to the fields of medicine and Astronomy, noting especially the role of the Ottoman *madrasahs*. Ayduz describes the incredibly extensive Sahn-i Saman Madrasah as "the first educational complex built in Islamic civilization which contained all religious and social components of city life."

One section of Ayduz's chapter aptly notes how the multiculturalism of Ottoman society helped to progress Ottoman science. To exemplify this, Ayduz writes that "one of the most famous Jewish physicians of Andalusian descent . . . was appointed as Sultan Suleyman's physician and wrote . . . one of the earliest independent works on dentistry." Furthermore, he writes that "the greatest astronomer" of the sixteenth century, "combined the Egypt-Damascus and Samarkand traditions" writing "more than thirty books in Arabic on the subjects of mathematics, astronomy, mechanics, and medicine." With this analysis, the reader is given a picture of the scientific life of the Ottoman Empire in order to gain insight into how tolerance extended beyond Ottoman systems of governance and into cultural realms of daily life.

The editors regret that various limitations prevented them from including a chapter on Katip Çelebi (Haji Khalfa) 1609-1657, the intellectual giant who defended the free practice of folk traditions and customs without interference by religion or government. He wrote twenty-one books of which only the Cihanunuma, a geography treatise is better known.

III. Coming Together: Shared Concerns and Insights
A brief overview of each chapter allows the reader to draw out some of the central ideas and concerns shared by this group of authors.

Several of the essays presented here take interest in the preservation of minority group autonomy, commenting on the potentially problematic nature of the Western "melting pot" model of multiculturalism. These essays look at the example of the Ottoman Empire as providing a pluralism which allows for greater autonomy than many minority groups all over the world experience today. Andrea and Yıldırım both associate the Ottoman millet system with the preservation of minority freedom and autonomy. Yılmaz and Aydın seek to show how minority religious groups such as Jews and Christians were protected under the Ottoman legal system, which allowed minority groups to make their own laws regarding many domestic matters, while simultaneously offering justice through centralized court systems. Also relevant here is Gage's discussion of multiculturalism in the history of the Ottoman Empire as viewed through works of art.

For many of these authors, the primary foundation for the creation of peace in the Ottoman Empire can be found in the implementation of the millet structure and in the governance of the Ottomans through legal and judicial systems. Yıldırım has offered an in-depth breakdown of the millet system and how it allowed different religious groups to form their own largely autonomous communities within the state; Kemal Karpat supports this idea, writing that the millet system was one of the pillars upon which the Ottoman Empire rested. It allowed for effective government of diverse groups, with the leaders of those groups reporting to the central government. Gage also mentions the millet system as one of the reasons why the Ottoman Empire could be so ethnically diverse, as well as pointing out that the Janissary system allowed for the integration of other ethnicities into the Ottoman state. Al-Katury highlights the different aspects of the individual millets—the Orthodox, Armenian, and Jewish, showing how Protestants and Catholics caused problems for the Armenian millet while Ihsan Yılmaz explores the relationship of the millet to the legal system of the Empire. Both he and Mehmet Akif Aydın—who asserts that the Ottoman legal system had its roots in Islamic law and that the justice of the Ottoman courts offered fair trials to everyone regardless of race or religion—discuss how the legal system of the Ottoman Empire helped foster peaceful coexistence.

Similarly, many of these essays give specific examples of the Ottoman ethic of religious tolerance, showing that it was not a temporary statutory right, but one rooted permanently in the belief system. The state appeared as the defender and guarantor of this right rather than its source. In these essays, specific examples of religious and ethnic tolerance and freedom in the Classical Ottoman Empire abound. In his essay, Kemal Karpat stresses the fact that "under Ottoman rule, all ethnic and religious groups enjoyed extensive religious, cultural and linguistic rights and were governed by their own religious leaders. No group . . . could impose its creed, language and culture on any of the others. Still, individuals could assimilate into another group by marriage or acculturation."

Another commonly cited characteristic of Ottoman tolerance was the regular mixing and intermarriage between Muslims and non-Muslims. Salem attempts to pin down the possible origins of this tolerance by analyzing the history of "the Seljuks" who produced a harmonious society which was "multi-racial, multi-cultural, and multi-religious," in which the majority Sunni Muslims "entrusted [minority] Christians with high positions in the state." Salem asserts that the attitude of tolerance in this early Seljuk society laid the foundation for future tolerance in the Ottoman Empire, in which "early Ottoman rulers, who adhered to Sunni Islam, dealt with followers of different religions and sects on equal footing, making no distinction between Muslims and non-Muslims."

Several authors highlight the benefits that peaceful coexistence brought to the Ottoman state. One may add that Muslims and non-Muslims together could join certain associations such as the *lonca* or craftsmen's guilds. As mentioned, beyond the basic advantage of minimizing conflict, Ayduz discusses how Ottoman science improved as a result of Ottoman multiculturalism. Nisya Isman Allovi also details how Jews enriched Ottoman society by contributing to medical advancement as well as political diplomacy. By listing such benefits, these authors provide motivation for people to pay attention to the lessons of the Ottomans, for the benefits of functional multiculturalism include greater potential for development and cross-pollination among people groups.

Most of these authors also deal with the modernization of the Ottoman Empire. Karpat and Yılmaz show that problems arose when Europeans brought the idea of the ethnicity-based nation-state to the Empire. Groups that were once satisfied under the Ottomans now wanted their independence. Ethnic nationalism was the source of strife and diametrically opposed to the communal organization based on the unity of belief of each community that had been the organizational foundation of the Ottoman state. Karpat demonstrates that the Ottomans had to move toward a Muslim identity to keep the core of the Empire together, and that when new nations were formed from the non-Muslim parts of the Empire, they were not tolerant like the Ottomans. Thus, according to these authors as a group, the Ottoman system was more effective at keeping the peace than the European one which replaced it over the course of the nineteenth and twentieth centuries. In spite of modernization and the rise of nationalism in Turkey, Nisya Allovi's analysis of the heritage of the Ottomans concludes that Jews in Turkey are still benefiting from the historic Ottoman ethic of tolerance. The recent writings dealing with the treatment of Armenians and Greeks in the twentieth century are outside the scale of this work.

Another common view found in these essays is that many of the world's complex conflicts can be improved with the aid of the Ottoman example as a model for coexistence. Andrea shows how Nushin Arbabzadeh counters the claims of people like Huntington by using historical examples such as the Ottoman Empire. Yılmaz argues that the issues with legal pluralism in England could be fixed by using the Ottoman legal system as an example. He uses the writings of Turkish Islamic scholar Ali Bulaç to support his argument. He also points out that politicians in Turkey sometimes refer to the Ottoman Empire as a model for our age. Yıldırım relates Ottoman coexistence to a more modern theory of sociology: contact theory. He shows that the Ottoman system meets the requirements that contact theory posits are necessary for peaceful interactions between disparate groups, thus providing another explanation for the peaceful coexistence of diverse groups in the Ottoman Empire. Hopefully by making these points, the authors of this book will make the

Ottoman Empire a more prominently recognized model for today.

Nearly all of these chapters admit that there were certain limitations to Ottoman tolerance, and that a complete transcription of the Ottoman model of tolerance and multiculturalism would be impossible in contemporary multicultural societies. Yılmaz writes, "Today, the Ottoman legal system may not be plausible, but at least their acceptance and tolerance of diversity can be emulated by so-called developed and progressed humanity." Bernadette Andrea also notes that there were some restrictions on non-Muslims for the Ottoman system to be acceptable by today's standards. Despite these issues, however, many authors still agree that the Ottoman example is not only valuable today, but it also served as a model for tolerance in its own time. Andrea asserts this, explaining that in the seventeenth century, the English, suffering from religious differences at home, looked to the Empire as a model to solve their problems. So while it is clear that we cannot copy the Classical Ottoman model, these authors show that we still have a great deal to learn from the study and embodiment of "the Ottoman spirit."

Several of the authors included in this collection express a desire to overcome misrepresentations of the history of Ottoman conquests and to disprove portraits of Islam as an inherently intolerant or violent belief system. Furthermore, many of them are frustrated with the commonly perceived inevitability of religious conflict, looking to the history of the Ottomans as a way of overcoming these negative misconceptions. Darling's essay, "Christian Muslim Interaction on the Ottoman Frontier," opens with the "European myths about the so-called Terrible Turk" which "were based on the assumption of a perpetual enmity and opposition between Islam and Christianity, and thus between Muslims and Christians." Andrea regards racism and anti-Islamism as major hindrances to peaceful interaction. She also looks at how Samuel Huntington's "clash of civilizations" idea has hurt the movement for peace between East and West.

Both Salem and Darling have attempted to delve more deeply into the origins and historical progression in the stereotypical portrayal of Islam as intolerant; they explore how historical evidence from the Classical Ottoman example often runs counter to these misguided assumptions. These efforts are aimed with great hope at a more complex understanding of Islam, the possibility of peaceful interfaith coexistence as well as potential models for effective multicultural societies. In her efforts to overcome negative views about Islam, Andrea aptly quotes Nushin Arbabsadah who declared, "contrary to common perceptions, living in multiethnic, multifaith, and multilingual societies has always been a part of the experience of Muslims."

Fethullah Gülen, another figure who seeks to redefine Islam in the light of the Ottoman example, is referenced in several of these chapters and discussed in depth by Andrea, Yılmaz and Yıldırım. Gülen, a major proponent of interfaith dialogue, uses the Ottoman Empire to show people that different religions did not always fight as they do now. In doing this, he seeks to give contemporary societies a historical foundation from which to work on.

All of these perspectives attempt to link the Ottoman history of tolerance with present-day conflicts and difficulties in the face of globalization and increasingly multi-cultural, multi-ethnic societies. These authors express an urgent need for understanding and acceptance between different groups. As these essays have demonstrated, the study of Ottoman history and models of governance can offer a path of acceptance and moderation to people today. The Ottoman state existed throughout centuries in a delicate balance struck between religious-cultural identity and national identity. The balance and peace which followed have both been difficult for modern nation-states to replicate. Yıldırım summarizes this idea of balance in Ottoman history, writing "the Ottoman Turks succeeded in uniting diverse communities under a common identity and promoting peace and cooperation among them through promoting common goals and minimizing competition, while enabling the communities to maintain distinct identities."

Though these chapters have looked at Ottoman history and its potential contemporary relevance from many different perspectives, the authors reach consensus on the idea that there is much to be learned from the Ottoman example. The contemporary global community confronts a flood of bleak declarations that current states of religious and ethnic conflict are inevitable. Still, these authors have found in the Ottoman example a basis for hope and change.

Chapter One

From the Classical Ottoman Religious Cultural Order to Nation State

by Dr. Kemal Karpat

THE CLASSICAL OTTOMAN STATE STOOD UNTIL the middle of the eighteenth century on two complementary organizational pillars interconnected in a vital fashion. The downfall of either pillar would modernize, transform and force the other to assume different functions. The first pillar was the state's multi-religious, multi-ethnic communal organization. Indeed the basic Ottoman organizational unit was the religious community as provided in the *kanunnames* (laws) of Sultan Mehmet II (1457-81) which laid the constitutional framework of the state.

According to those laws, all the Orthodox Christians constituted one millet—sometimes referred as Greek—under the Patriarch of Istanbul. Established in 1454, the Orthodox millet was headed by George Scholarios, the leader of the anti-unionist party, which had opposed the church's unity of and submission to Rome. The second was the Armenian one which comprised the Eastern Churches including among others the Syriac and Nestorian. The last millet, established at the end of the fifteenth century, comprised the Jews and was headed by the Chief Rabbi. In reality, however, each Jewish community, which became predominantly Sephardic in the sixteenth century, acted independently.

The heads of the millets were regarded as part of the state

bureaucracy and were exempt from taxation. They were charged with governing all cultural, religious, legal (family) and educational affairs of their communities, assisted by a council or, in the case of the Orthodox Christians, a Synod. The head of the community was formally appointed, following the recommendation of its council, by the Sultan in order to prevent the formation of ecclesiastical dynasties.

Each millet although appearing as one body, actually was in fact divided into ethnic groups, each with its own church, using its own tongues, including Serbian, Orthodox Armenian, Bulgarian, and Syriac. After the eighteenth century, the Slavs' church language known as Slavonic was replaced by local languages in reaction to efforts by the Orthodox Patriarchate to make Greek the language of all the Orthodox Christians. It is not the purpose of this chapter to present a history of the Christians and Jews in the Ottoman state, a topic on which there are numerous excellent studies, but to stress the seminal fact that under Ottoman rule, all ethnic and religious groups enjoyed extensive religious, cultural and linguistic rights and were governed by their own religious leaders. No group, however powerful, could impose its creed, language and culture on any of the others, however small. Still, individuals could assimilate into another group by marriage or acculturation.

Muslims, regardless of language or culture, were regarded as one single group. The dominant elites at its center assimilated a variety of individuals into the ruling ranks by marriage, induction or conversion. The identity of this dominant group, the *askeri* or *devletlu*, was first defined by their association with the state, which conferred upon them its position, income and prestige. Because the language of the state was Turkish, however, the elites inadvertently became "Turkish," a seemingly accidental outcome that acquired political importance only at the end of the nineteenth century.

The legitimacy, power and identity of the ruling elites was recognized and accepted by Muslims and non-Muslims for one principal reason. The chief function of the state and the ruling elites was to defend the status quo of the religious-cultural arrangement of the fifteenth century that had become the constitutional foundation of the

Ottoman state. True, the state was formally Muslim and applied the Shariat, but, in view of the heterogeneous cultural-religious structure of the population, it also used the secular rulings of the sultans (*irade* or *kanun*) and custom (*urf*) as source of law. To the Muslims, the sultan was a bona fide Muslim ruler charged to preserve the Muslim character of the state; to the non-Muslims, he was the dispenser of justice, order and security. The non-Muslims did not serve in the army whose lower ranks were almost exclusively Turkish until the second half of the nineteenth century. Their only obligations to the state were the payment of tax (*harac* and *ciziye*, tithe and head tax) and respect for state security and the social order. Nevertheless, as compact Christian and Muslim majorities in certain areas tended to oppress nearby minorities, the central government charged the Janissaries with the specific duty of preventing one religious group from oppressing the Other.

The relative freedom of belief and social order in the Ottoman state was consciously defined and maintained by the government, which considered itself Muslim although it was fully aware that it was ruling a religiously heterogeneous society and thus functioned as a supra-national entity. Led by practical considerations, the government made all the arrangements necessary to satisfy the religious, cultural and educational preferences of the Muslims and non-Muslims alike. (Education, for example, was financed by communities and usually was provided in churches and mosques by the priest or imam, as the case may be.)

The second foundation of the Ottoman state was an informal administrative arrangement between the central government and the notables in the provinces. This crucially important arrangement has received attention only in the last decades, for Ottoman history long was interpreted from the vantage point of the central government, which had its own biases against the opposition of the countryside notables. According to the initial arrangement, to collect taxes and maintain order, the sultan and the central bureaucracy relied on the local elites, such as *ulema* (religious leaders), families of former functionaries, retired soldiers and various rich families. The sultan provided the immediate personal link between what may be called the public and private spheres, legitimizing the countryside elites' position in society and assuring the collection of taxes for the central authority.

The tax collection obviously was an exceptionally important and complex process. Although directed by the highest official of the central government in a given district, it was carried out by local notables who distributed the state lands to cultivators, usually villagers, and collected the taxes. While *osur*, that is, one-tenth of the production, accounted for most of the tax, there also were avariz, or special taxes that were levied during wars but often became permanent. The central government, it should be emphasized, had no direct control over town and village inhabitants who thus appeared immune to direct political influence from the center. The notables served the government faithfully as intermediaries as long as the sultan legitimized and maintained the notables' position and income and had a strong central army at its disposal.

The central government played a key role in the rise or fall of the country elites although much of the social mobility in the countryside developed according to its own internal dynamics and dialectics. The basic leverage the government exercised over the country notables was its control of the main economic resource, namely, the property title to the land. Indeed, a substantial part of the arable lands in Rumili (possibly eighty percent) and Anatolia were *miri* or state lands, administered and taxed by the central government via the local notables known among as *ayans* Muslims and the Corbaci or Kocabasi among Christians. Important to note is the fact that whereas the juridical status of the religious communities was defined by a written law, the relationship between the government and notables was an ad hoc arrangement subject to change and challenge.

Under the classical land arrangement, known as *timar* and controlled by the state, cultivators had to raise the crops designated by the state and sell them at prices fixed by the same state. Challenged as early as the end of the sixteenth century by the new market forces unleashed by the rising capitalist system of the West, the *timar* collapsed in the second half of the eighteenth century as both village cultivators and their notable supervisors wanted to raise the specific crops demanded by the market and receive the highest price offered according to demand. Gradually, the countryside notables, both Muslims and non-Muslims, began to demand conformity to market forces. At the end of the eighteenth century, after the long Turko-Russian war of 1768-74 had weakened the central government and forced it to borrow money from the *ayans*, the Muslim notables ended up assuming direct control and, eventually for a while, ownership of the state lands.

The *ayans* and the non-Muslim notables were also the civilian heads of their communities. Those who headed their village or *mahalle* (city quarters) were responsible to the central government for enforcing its laws and orders, often by bringing guilty parties before a judge appointed by the center. While these notables were secular leaders, the Christian priests and Muslim imams or *hojas* were religious leaders, officiating at births, weddings, funerals as well as conducting the daily or weekly prayers. Thus the millet system, which was the basic organization of the state, was implemented in the countryside by a combination of local religious and lay leaders working in tacit agreement with the central administrator referred to as *subasi*, or *sancakbey*, among other terms. Such local religious and secular leaders conformed to the directives of the central government as long as that government followed the unwritten practice of not interfering or violating the de facto autonomy of the local leaders.

At the same time, the local leaders represented and maintained the culture, traditions and language of their respective communities, such as Greek, Tatar, Boshnak, Bulgarian, or Turkish. The vernacular was the chief means of communication at the local level although Turkish remained the language of the government, which most of the local leaders learned to speak and write. Under this arrangement a great diversity of ethnic, religious, and linguistic groups could live in harmony as long as the center could maintain in the socio-political arrangement.

The Disintegration of the Classical Socio-Cultural Arrangement or Beginning of "Modernization"

Control of the agricultural finally passed to the *ayans*, late in the eighteenth and early nineteenth century, depriving the state of revenue to finance its bureaucracy and the army. The government consequently sought to gain control of economic resources by centralizing power in its own hands. Beginning with the reign of Selim III (1789-1807), the government attempted to create a new bureaucracy that would assume many of the duties performed previously by local leaders. The bureaucrats, trained in modern schools set up for that purpose, would collect taxes directly, implement new laws and dispense justice in new courts created after 1839. This centralization undermined in a relatively short time the centuries-old division of labor between the center and the provinces by eliminating recalcitrant *ayans* and turning others into docile instruments of the center. The operation and its resulting tensions and conflicts between the central bureaucracy and the countryside spanned a century and a half and continue, albeit in changed forms and ideologies, in present-day Turkey. Initially it produced a series of local revolts varying in intensity from one region to another as the provincial elites tried to maintain their old autonomy and control of the community. The process of centralization enforced by the government also produced a widening gap between the state, where bureaucrats adopted modernization as their ideology of power, and the community whose notables, priests and imams appeared to defend tradition and local culture. Eventually the new bureaucracy and intelligentsia branded the local leaders as "conservatives" and "reactionaries," but the main dispute revolved around the growing power of the central bureaucracy and charges that its ideology of modernism was designed to justify and legitimize its power.

The political and social situation actually was far more complex than may appear from existing scholarly works, the government's statements or contemporary European accounts. As political elites identified themselves more intimately with the state and its ideologies and used the modern educational system to disseminate a particular view of history, society and cultural developments, the rise of communal consciousness and the break down of the old social order brought to the fore differences of faith that previously had carried little, if any, political significance.

The Serbian revolt of 1804 and Greek revolt of 1821-28 were originally communal uprisings protesting the usurpation of Christian peasants' land by Janissaries and money lenders. When they became overnight religious nationalist movements directed against a government described as the tool of Muslim rule and oppression, England and France pressured the Ottoman government into accepting the Reform Edict of 1856. That edict introduced the Western concept of a nation as an aggregation of equal individuals, regardless of their religion, language and race. Soon the Citizenship Law of 1864 turned the subjects of the sultan into citizens of the state and so transformed the old sense of communal identity into an increasingly ethnic and linguistic one.

Ethnic-religious nationalism, coupled with the pan-Slavism promoted by Russia after the 1850s among Serbians and Bulgarians, rejected not only the old Ottoman millet system but also the Patriarchates—now regarded as Greek—that had headed the Orthodox millet in the past. The intelligentsia of the rising Christian nations deemed the rule of the ecclesiasts as being out of tune with the contemporary European civilization seen first as the product of Enlightenment and secondarily as secularist. Under pressure from both the European powers and local Christian intellectuals, by 1865 the Ottoman government finally had abolished all the millets that had managed to keep stability for four centuries. Their place was taken by a series of first nine and then twelve congregations for the various Christian denominations, including Armenians, Orthodox, Catholics, and Protestants. The Patriarchates opposed the abolition of the millets although in the end they acquiesced to the fait accompli by identifying themselves with a specific ethnic group while the Orthodox Greek one still claimed ecumenical (universal) status. Thus, by the time the Berlin Treaty of 1878 recognized the independence of the major Christian groups in the Balkans, the old millet system had disintegrated; only the habits it had formed persisted. The newly established independent states assumed responsibility for assuring freedom of belief to all faiths and ethnic groups, but in reality they discriminated against Muslims, Jews and Christians who did not belong to the titular group holding the political power.

Toward a Muslim Millet

The Berlin Treaty of 1878 created a series of Christian nation states in the Balkans and forced a realignment of the Muslim populations. Throughout the existence of the Ottoman state, the Muslims were regarded as one homogeneous entity despite their division into a variety of ethnic and linguistic groups. The Ottoman censuses recorded the Muslims under one category and registered the non-Muslims as either Christians or Jews until the census of 1881-82 implemented a series of ethnic categories, such as Greek, Armenian, and Bulgarians, for the Christians.

The Parliament of 1876-78 had adopted the idea of individual representation, but in practice it paid special attention to ethno-religious representation. That Parliament embodied the idea of Ottomanism, that is, of a common citizenship that would have superseded differences of faith, ethnicity and language. Its deputies, elected by regional councils, however, consisted mostly of local communal leaders from the proprietied middle class who expressed the religious preferences of their constituencies. As a result, their debates sharpened the religious differences between Muslims and non-Muslims, who had co-existed peacefully for centuries, and turned them into political conflicts. The Muslim deputies defined the government and the state as being "Muslim" and therefore, as "ours." At the same time, they began to regard the Christians as "them," mirroring differences already spelled out by the nationalism of the Balkan Christians.

The Berlin Treaty of 1878 deepened the psychological gap between Muslims and Christians created by the Reform Edict of 1856, by recognizing independent statehood for most of the Orthodox "Greek" Christians and leaving the Ottoman state a predominantly (eighty percent) Muslim body. Because the ultimate fate of the Ottoman state now depended on the unity and loyalty of the Muslims, their religious identification with the state were transformed into a political one. That identification was intensified and spelled out even more clearly by the massive immigration of Muslims forced out of the former Ottoman territories in the Caucasus and the Balkans lost to Russia and the new Balkan states. The migrations had begun after the annexation of Crimea by Russia in 1783, when several hundred thousand Tatars immigrated into the Ottoman lands. Beginning roughly around 1862, the Tatars were followed by the Caucasians, most of whom were not ethnically Turks, and then by the Balkan Muslims, encompassing altogether some seven million people by 1918. The emigration—to repeat—was forced by the killing that preceded or accompanied it. Sometimes the Muslims were killed or ousted simply because of their faith or because of the suspicion that they may not be loyal to their Christian masters, or just to give the titular state's population a comfortable majority within its borders. Regardless of the motive behind it, the process of forced emigration had at least two major consequences, intensifying the immigrants' antagonism towards the government of their country of origin and turning their religious consciousness into a political one. The influx of politicized Muslim refugees compelled the Sultan Abdulhamid II (1876-1909) to look upon Islam not only as a faith but also as an ideology that could consolidate the country's internal unity and mobilize the population to resist further foreign encroachment upon Ottoman territories. Thus, Islamism was born as a strictly defensive measure. The European press of the time, however, perceived and depicted its external manifestation as panislamism, an ideology designed to incite the Muslims under British, French, Dutch and Russian rule to rebel against their Europeans imperial masters although such incitement never occurred. (This issue, important as it is, his outside the scope of this chapter. Suffice it to say that Sultan Abdulhamid never declared the jihad.)

The events of 1876-78 also produced a rather unexpected reaction among Muslims. The Berlin Treaty signed by the Sultan, made the territory the sine non qua condition of statehood for peoples such as the Arabs who were so conscious and proud of their own historical, linguistic, cultural, and territorial identity that they sometimes referred to the Ottomans pejoratively as Turks (al atrak). In 1878 many leading Arab families of Syria approached Abdelkader, the hero of anti-French resistance in Algeria who lived in Damascus at that time, to ask him to proclaim the independence of Syria. Sultan Abdulhamid, in turn, bestowed a variety of privileges on

them, increasing the Arabs' self-esteem and national pride and causing considerable reaction among the Turks. The resulting differences
between the Turks and Arabs did not culminate in a split until 1916
simply because the Arab leaders saw Ottoman power as their best
protection against the imperialist aims of France, England, and Italy.

The Turkish Millet-Nation

The rise of Turkishness, that is a Turkish political ethnicity, was determined to a large extent by the conditions outlined in the preceding
pages. Through rather unique type of nation formation, which will
be outlined below it eventually gave rise to the Turkish national state.

In the Ottoman state, the ethnic Turks formed a majority in
Anatolia and some Balkan areas, but although the language of the
state was Turkish and declared so in the Constitution of 1876, the
Ottoman rulers refrained from defining the state as Turkish. On
the other hand, Europeans and most Arab Muslims called the state
Turkey or Turkiyya. Moreover, the organization of the government,
the prevalence of a special hierarchical order, the understanding of
authority and other features originating in Central Asian Genghisid
traditions and the Seljukid state all possessed some Turkish characteristics. Yet, unlike the Arab and Persian rulers who often glorified
their ethnic origin, the Ottoman sultans refrained from exalting their
Turkish origin. After 1839, in fact, the government's Ottomanist and
Islamist ideologies and policies temporarily pushed the Turkishness
of the government further into the background.

Ottomanism was formally maintained as a state ideology until the
end of the Ottoman state, long after it ceased to be a factor in internal political cohesion and solidarity. Instead, Islamism, which had
turned faith into a political ideology of unity and solidarity, assimilated the Muslim immigrants into the new society that emerged from
the amalgam of the new arrivals and the old inhabitants of Anatolia
fostering a new type of Turkish ethnic consciousness.

Coinciding with the influx of refugees, privatization of the state
lands made the immigrants small land owners, which helped their
integration and also boosted agricultural production and trade.
While the government's economic motives intensified the political

transformation, Sultan Abdulhamid began to make increased use of Islam to consolidate the authority of the Caliphate and downgrade his lay position as sultan. Thus Sultan Abdulhamid used his position as Caliph—or the head of the universal Muslim community—as both a legitimizing office and a reassuring religious presence in order to introduce a series of reforms that radically transformed Ottoman society and laid the foundations for the Republic. Chief among those reforms, a modernized educational system, beginning at the elementary level and culminating in professional schools, expanded literacy and provided an avenue for social mobility that turned the children of the lower and middle classes into agents of change, revolutionaries and ultimately masters of the government through the Young Turk upheaval of 1908.

Between 1880 and 1908 the bureaucracy and the army were reformed, a modern railway system was introduced and contacts with Europe and the United States were expanded. Intellectually, the most effective development during the reign of Abdulhamid may have been the introduction of a modern press and an extraordinary increase in the number of printed books, mostly scientific works translated from European languages or written by native intellectuals. For instance, from 1820 to 1859 the number of books published in literature, the positive sciences and religion totaled just 273; 319; 369, respectively; from 1876 to 1908 the corresponding figures had increased to 2,590; 3,891; and 1,307, respectively, and the number of books on government affairs had grown from sixty-eight to 946.

The literary works included translations from French and English as well as some original short stories and novels written in Turkish. The latter were avidly read by a growing number of people who discovered in them new ways of thinking and living and so began to view their own society and the world beyond through new lenses. Such works consequently became known as the "New Turkish Literature" (*Edebiyat-i Cedide*), clearly a product of the second half of the nineteenth century.

The press also expanded the use of colloquial Turkish which, not only became the language of the press and new literature but also introduced individualized ways of thinking and new ways of seeing oneself and others. A true revolution of identity change and the reformulation of the culture were underway. Just as the influx of immigrants, the sedentarization of tribes, the rise of small landowners and a degree of urbanization had created a new society, the modern school system, the press, and the new literature gave that society its own identity and a modern soul that combined the past and present under the old name of Turk.

It is no wonder that one of the keenest Western observers of Turkey, Arminus Vambery, declared towards the end of the nineteenth century that Ottoman society, which he had studied for four decades, had been totally transformed. Nevertheless European political leaders who were eager to occupy the Turks' lands still accused them of being unable to civilize and therefore condemned to remain forever outside the Western orbit.

The modernization and transformation of the Muslim Ottomans into Turks followed a unique course. The Berlin treaty turned the remaining Christians in the Ottoman Empire into minorities each and granted full religious and educational rights but not the autonomy their millets had possessed in previous centuries. The Christians now were led by lay professionals, not the church. Favored and protected by Europe, the two largest Christian communities in Anatolia, the Greeks and Armenians, achieved high standards of living and education far above those of the Turks. The Jews also achieved a rapid and high degree of modernization but did so on their own, without European support, and remained loyal to the Ottoman government as indicated by their enrollment in the army and numerous declarations of support.

As sketched so far, in very broad lines, a new Turkish society arose and took on in the guise of a national political community, combining its old Islamo-Ottoman identity with modernist political and democratic yearnings. As a result, by 1889 reaction to the sultan's closure of the Parliament and suspension of the constitution of 1876 had become an organized opposition in the form of secret societies established in the professional schools and ultimately in the army, all demanding the restoration of the Constitution of 1876. In more than one way that demand for the restoration of the constitution was a demand for representation in the government that eventually culminated in the Young Turks revolution of 1908 and the ousting of Sultan Abdulhamid.

The Young Turks revolution finally brought to the surface both the myriad problems produced by the rise of a new social order and the need to define the Turks' identity in national, political terms rather than solely in religious ones.

Conclusions

The debates in the newspapers, books, reviews and works of the Islamists, Turkists, and nationalist writers, such as Ziya Gokalp, and Yusuf Akcura, revolved around the one key question of who is a Turk. The answer—or answers—came from two forces that were themselves byproducts of socio-political change. The first was the government, whose vast bureaucracy and intelligentsia had implemented the modernizing reforms and regarded themselves as representatives of modernity and ultimately of Turkishness. Members of both the civil and military bureaucracies, whatever their ethnic and linguistic background, were associated with the state and formed the ruling group. Because their main language of communication was Turkish, they had become de facto Turks and spokesmen of the nation that was emerging. Their ideology, practically shared by all other intellectual groups and described so well by Ziya Gokalp, was *muasirlasma*. The term means contemporaenity or modernization, but every group had its own definition. Some minority groups either excluded religion, that is, Islam from their definitions of the nation and modernity (seen as Westernization). Others regarded the faith as an intrinsic part of the nation's identity and reconcilable with change and modernity seen as a rational, scientific, pragmatic way of thinking. Many leading Islamist scholars, notably, Ismail Hakki Izmirli, wrote extensively on the compatibility of Islam and modernity.

The second force involved in the definition of Turkishness consisted of the large body of commoners, living in villages and modest city quarters, who practiced Turkish customs and traditions and spoke centuries-old Turkish dialects that were similar to each other. Islam was an inseparable part of the identity and values of these "real"

Turks primarily because in Anatolia and Rumili Islam had acquired special characteristics that harmonized local and regional beliefs with the broader tenets of the faith. From the two forces struggling to define Turkishness, there emerged two definitions. The first was a statist political Turkishness, and the second traditionalist, clannish and pious. The first tended to use history selectively, and to regard the Ottoman era as a period of regression and stagnation despite the fact that the proponents of this definition were the product of that same era. The second wholeheartedly embraced Ottoman history as a part of its Islamic past and regarded modernization as an essential condition of progress only so long as modernity accepted the traditional identity. This second traditionalist view found expression in a variety of journals, including *Sirat-I Mustakim, Sebilul Resat, Islam Mecmuasi*, in which intellectuals such as Ahmet Agaoglu sought to reconcile a secular Turkish identity with an Islamic one. There were, of course, also extremist versions, including the positivist, semi-materialistic movement represented by the review Ictihat and the ultra- Islamist publication Beyan-ul Hak.

The Republic made a clear-cut choice by defining Turkishness as a strictly secular and ethnic (blood or lineage) identity originating not in the Turks' immediate Ottoman past but in the remote Central Asian pre-Islamic roots.

The introduction of democracy and the general suffrage in 1945-1946 gave the "real" Turks, now encompassing millions of assimilated immigrant who shared the Ottoman past, an opportunity to show their preferences. In response, the multi- party regime and the political parties exploited the yearning of the lower classes for some recognition of their brand of Islamo-Turkish modern identity. For forty years, however, their demand for religious freedom was either rejected or implemented in a distorted fashion.

The coming to power of the traditionalist, Islamic-rooted Justice and Development Party in the elections of November 3, 2002, reignited discussions about the perennial question: who and what is a Turk?

To summarize the broader historical developments that have brought Turkey to the particular place where it stands today, one can say that modern nation-states were created by elites who took control of the government and used the state's power to shape and reshape old identities and cultures into new ones embodied in a nation. Yet, resulting nations have always retained much of the culture, and history of the societies in which they were rooted. In other words, these new nations were nourished by the traditional and spiritual essence of their old cultures, which created for them a sense of continuity belongingness and security as well as ways to connect with other nations. The French Revolution of 1789 and the Iranian revolution of 1979, for instance, each maintained a sense of cultural and historical continuity and an identity that conformed to its lived past. The absolute belief in the power of the state to shape human identity according to predetermined blueprints ignores the society's basic culture, identity and orientation. As a result, the Turkish society today maintains a basic attitude favoring multi-ethnic diversity and multicultural harmony despite a variety of contrary opinions.

Chapter Two

The Roots of Religious Tolerance in the Ottoman Empire

by Dr. Abdel-Rahman Ahmed Salem

THE OTTOMAN EMPIRE HAS LONG BEEN SUBJECTED to severe, worldwide criticism. Even Arabs accuse the Ottomans of oppression, intolerance and narrow mindedness. This chapter adopts another point of view. Instead of going through the long Ottoman history and trying to cite the many examples which can refute such accusations, I have endeavored to look into the roots of the Ottoman tolerance, especially with regard to freedom of thought and belief.

The starting point in this regard should be the connection between the Ottomans and their predecessors in Asia Minor; i.e., the Seljuks (al-Salajiqah) who share common ancestry with the Ottoman Turks. The Seljuks dominated the Abbasid caliphate in Iraq from about the middle of the eleventh century AD to the end of the twelfth.[1] One of the most important roles played by this rising power could be seen in the field of Muslim-Byzantine struggle. Indeed, the Hamdanids of Mousil (al-Mawsil) and Aleppo (Halab) and the Fatimids of Egypt preceded the Seljuks in this field after the decline of the Abbasid caliphate, but the role of the Seljuks in this respect was the most outstanding until the rise of the Ottomans, who were destined to take the lead. The famous battle of Manzikert (Malazkird or Malazjird) in Armenia in 1071 AD / 463 AH between the Seljuk Sultan Alp Arslan (1063-1073 AD / 455-465 AH) and the Byzantine Emperor

Romanus IV Diogenes (1068-1071 AD) was a turning point in the history of Muslim-Byzantine struggle in general and that of the Seljuks in particular.[2] As a result of this battle, in which the Byzantine army was annihilated and the Emperor himself was taken captive, the Seljuks dominated Armenia and began to penetrate into Asia Minor. These Seljuks, as Professor Hitti put it, "laid the basis of the Turkification of Asia Minor."[3] Soon after this battle, the Sultanate of the Rum Seljuks (Salajiqat-al-Rum) was established, and Iconium (Quniyah or Konya) became its capital.[4] Yaqut describes Iconium as "one of the greatest Muslim cities in the land of the Rum."[5]

Although the Seljuks were stubborn fighters, they were liberal-minded, tolerant and magnanimous. When Romanus IV was captured, the Seljuks treated him very humanely and released him on easy terms. The Sultan honored Romanus and ordered some of the Seljuk troops to escort him to his country.[6] Some modern scholars rightly maintain that the sense of security of religious life under Muslim rule led many of the Christians of Asia Minor "to welcome the advent of the Seljuk Turks as their deliverers from the hated Byzantine government."[7] The Seljuks encouraged the arts and learning and as a result of their wise government, "the transition of Anatolia from a mainly Christian to a mainly Muslim country was achieved so smoothly that no one troubled to record the details."[8]

The society in Asia Minor in which the "Seljuks of Rum" lived for more than two centuries was multi-racial, multi-cultural and multi-religious. The indigenous inhabitants of Asia Minor at that time were mainly Christians of different races. It is indicative in this context that the Seljuks, who were Sunni Muslims,[9] did not hesitate to seek the administrative help of Christian subjects in their Sultanate. The Seljuks entrusted Christians with high positions in the state, an act which clearly expresses the elevated level of trust and confidence the Seljuks had in their subjects. Furthermore, it is worthy of note here that intermarriage was common between the Seljuk fighters, or *gazis*, and the local population of Asia Minor. Even some of the harems in the palaces of the Seljuk sultans were native Christians.[10] Understandably, this helped to cultivate the spirit of religious tolerance and establish a solid basis for cultural diversity in the Seljuk society of Asia Minor.

Thus, when the Ottomans replaced the Seljuks in Asia Minor, they inherited this dominant spirit of tolerance and social harmony and were able to add new dimensions to it. It should be pointed out that the ancestors of the Ottomans settled in Asia Minor, under the authority of the Seljuks of Rum, some time before the rise of the Ottoman state, but the exact time of their settlement is not agreed upon. Some historians maintain that they began to migrate from their homeland in Central Asia after the aforementioned battle of Manzikert in 1071. This view is derived from recently discovered thirteenth century accounts.[11] The more common view, however, places this migration in the second half of the thirteenth century when one portion of the Qayi tribe of Turkomans left their country under the pressure of the Mongols and sought refuge in Anatolia. Led by Ertughrul, son of Suliaman Shah, they lent their military support to 'Ala' al-Din, the Seljuk Sultan of Konya, against their common enemy, the Mongols.[12] In return for this support, 'Ala' al-Din granted Ertughrul and his people some territory in northern Phrygia along the frontiers of Bithynia between Dorylaem (Eskishehir) and Nicaea (Iznik), with Sogud as its centre.[13]

Whether the ancestors of the Ottomans migrated to Anatolia during the eleventh century or the thirteenth, the fact remains that the Seljuks had settled there first and exerted a certain degree of influence upon them.

Having examined the connection between the Seljuks and the Ottomans in Asia Minor and the impact of the former on the latter in terms of religious tolerance, we should now turn our attention to the period of the first three Ottoman rulers who undertook the heavy task of laying the foundations of the Ottoman state. They are Ertughrul (died c.1281), Osman, or Othman (d.1326) and Orhan or Orkhan (died c.1360).[14] The importance of this period lies in the fact that it presented the basis upon which the succeeding Ottoman rulers were expected to build. Our aim here is to explore the different aspects and dimensions of the Ottoman religious tolerance during the period under discussion.

To start with, when those early founders of the Ottoman state had established themselves in Anatolia, they came into close contact with different religious communities and races. Indeed, the dominant religion was Greek Orthodox Christianity, but there were also Armenian Monophysites and even Paulicians.[15] The early Ottoman rulers, who adhered to Sunni Islam, dealt with the followers of different religions and sects on equal footing, making no distinction between Muslims and non-Muslims. It should be noted here that this tolerant religious policy was observed and even enhanced by many succeeding Ottoman rulers who made it their duty to follow the examples of the early Ottomans. Of special importance in this regard is Muhammad (Mehmet) II (1451-1481) who was the first ruler to introduce the system of the millet into the Ottoman state. According to this system, "Muhammad II granted the Greek Orthodox Church a secure position in the Ottoman state . . . and made it into a pillar of his empire side by side with Sunnite Islam."[16] We may notice, in passing, that the eighteenth and nineteenth centuries witnessed a remarkable revival of Anatolian Hellenism, and the Armenians were referred to in the nineteenth century as "the faithful nation" *(millet-i-sadiqah)*.[17]

It is widely known that Othman, the real founder of the Ottoman state, married the daughter of Edebali, a famous Muslim religious figure. Edebali exerted a strong influence on Othman, spiritually and politically, and acted as his vizier, helping him in the administration of the state.[18] Although Edebali is considered a legendary figure by some modern scholars,[19] there is no real justification for the Ottoman historians to invent such a figure. Regardless, there is no doubt that Othman was strongly influenced by the Islamic ideals of tolerance, mercy and justice. The following prayer, which was used after Othman's death in the religious ceremony on the accession of every Ottoman sultan to the throne, is highly indicative of Othman's special status in this regard: "May he be as good as Othman."[20]

Speaking of the main factors behind the strong spirit of religious tolerance in the early period of Ottoman history, we have to emphasize the important role of *ulema* (Muslim religious scholars; sometimes transliterated as *ulama)*, *madrasahs* (Muslim religious schools; sometimes transliterated as *medresses* or *madrasahs*) and Sufi orders in this respect. Right from the start of their dynasty, the Ottomans appreciated the role of the *ulema,* and sought their advice and guidance. In fact, this became the common practice of the Ottoman sultans throughout the long history of their empire. Those *ulema* were keen to advocate the real Islamic values of tolerance, justice and freedom of belief.

Othman's son and successor, Orkhan, is credited with establishing the first *madrasah* in Iznik (Nicaea).[21] The special attention devoted by Orkhan to his religious foundations is testified by the generous endowments (*awqaf*) which he dedicated to them.[22] According to the testimony of the Ottoman scholar Tash Kopru Zade (d. 968 AH / 1561 AD), the first professor appointed in this school was Davud (Dawood) al Qaysari, who first studied in his own land. He then traveled to Cairo where he studied Qur'anic Exegesis, the traditions of the prophet and principles of jurisprudence. He distinguished himself in the rational sciences and acquired the science of mysticism.[23]

The above-mentioned sciences studied by the first professor in the Iznik school reveal the quality of teachers Orkhan was keen to employ in it. The rational sciences in which professor Dawood al Qaysari distinguished himself include disciplines such as philosophy, logic and mathematics. This may indicate that the medresses of the early Ottomans were not religious in the narrow sense of the word, but rather Islamic in the sense that Islam encourages the study of useful branches of knowledge, whether religious or secular.

The role of Sufi orders is no less important in cultivating religious tolerance in the early period of the Ottoman dynasty. It should be noted here that Sufi movements in Anatolia preceded the rise of medresses and were more popular among the masses. The Ottoman rulers in the period under discussion (especially Orkhan, who himself led a simple life "and did not abandon tents in favor of palaces," as Ibn Khaldun put it) adopted a very sympathetic attitude towards Sufi movements in their dominions.[24] Indeed, Orkhan supported these movements financially and gave great care to the *khanaqahs* (or lodges of the sufis). These lodges played very important religious, social and cultural roles in Anatolian society in the period of the early Ottomans.

On the religious side, these lodges (commonly known as dervish lodges) succeeded in attracting huge numbers of people and presenting Islam to them in a simple way that was suitable for the masses and paid more attention to the spiritual and ethical side of the Muslim faith than to its rituals. One important feature of the character of these dervishes was their tolerance towards the followers of all religions and creeds. Socially, these lodges provided free food and accommodation for wayfarers and the poor, regardless of their race, creed, religion or social status.[25] This Sufi practice firmly established social cohesion and harmony in Anatolia at the dawn of Ottoman history and continued for manys years. Culturally, these dervish lodges were able to assume the role of *medresses* before the emergence of these educational institutions in Anatolia. Here, we must acknowledge that the Sheikhs of these lodges established relations with different types of people who had different experiences and cultures. Needless to say, these relations enabled the guests of these lodges to listen to each other and have a good chance for cultural exchange.[26]

One of the famous Sufi movements which arose in that early period was called "Bektashi Order of Dervishes" after its founder Hajj Bektash Wali. There is much controversy about the historicity of certain anecdotes connected with Bektash, such as his relationship with Orkhan or his role in the conversion of the janissaries to Islam.[27] The truth, however, is that this order had a strong appeal for the masses in the early history of the Ottoman dynasty because of the pious and ascetic life its sheikhs led.[28] Sourcers even suggest that some Ottoman sultans became sympathetic to the order.[29] The early followers of this Order saw themselves as Sunnis, but their Sunni doctrine is said to have been influenced in later times by other creeds and religions.[30]

Strongly connected with the Sufi orders in Anatolia during that early period were the *akhis* brotherhoods. These Brotherhoods consisted mainly of artisans and formed what may be called "artisans' guilds." The social and cultural roles they performed in the Anatolian society were very similar to those performed by Sufi dervishes, but their way of life was closely associated with the habits and manners of the *futuwwa* tradition. In other words, they tried to create a sort of chivalric society which they were keen to guard and support. They had their own lodges where they received passers-by and the needy and entertained them with full enthusiasm and happiness.[31] In their treatment of people, they took no account of their race, creed or religion. It is highly revealing in this context that the early Ottoman rulers encouraged and supported the *akhis* brotherhoods. As a matter of fact, the activities of the *akhis* played a very remarkable role in cementing social ties in the Ottoman state and this, in turn, enhanced its political stability. Orkhan, in particular, devoted much of his attention and support to the *akhis* brotherhoods, as he did to the Sufi orders, realizing the highly important role of both groups in spreading tolerance and supporting the state. As a practical act of support he assigned endowments (*awqaf*) for financing the activities of the *akhis*.[32]

Ibn Battuta (d. 779 AH/ 1377 AD), the famous Arab traveler, gives in his *rihla* (book of travels), a vivid eyewitness account of some of the activities of the *akhis* in Anatolia. Ibn Battuta starts by explaining the etymology of the word *akhis,* which, in his analysis, is the plural of the Arabic word *akhi* (my brother) in the genitive construction.[33] He gives his account the title of *The Akhis of the Futuwwa*, and mentions that those *akhis* can be seen in every city, town or village throughout the Turkomans' dominions in Asia Minor.[34] He remarks that they are second to none in welcoming strangers by extending their hospitality to them and meeting all their needs. At the same time, they express their real pleasure for having the chance to receive them. Ibn Battuta shows his amazement when, on one occasion, he and some of his companions are received by the *akhis* in one of their orchards in a tiny village in Anatolia; even though the hosts who did not know Arabic and the guests who knew no Turkish lacked an interpreter, the *akhis* entertain them for one full day with all pleasure and respect.[35]

On another occasion, while Ibn Battuta and his companions are traveling through Anatolia, they pass by a town where some people in one of its markets see them and go out of their shops to meet them. But, to the astonishment of Ibn Battuta and his companions, those people begin fighting one another, drawing their knives, and shouting; incapable of understanding the language, Ibn Battuta and his companions believe these people are brigands intending to loot and kill them. One pilgrim who witnesses the scene speaks Arabic and is asked by Ibn Battuta about the whole matter. He tells Ibn Battuta that those people represent two groups of the *akhis*. Each group insisted on receiving the guests, and that was the cause behind their fighting. Eventually, the two groups agree to draw lots in order to settle the dispute.[36]

Ibn Battuta's Rihla is full of such interesting stories about the widespread activities of the *akhis* in Asia Minor during the fourteenth century AD.[37] They all emphasize the great role of this group in establishing a strong basis for a tolerant and congenial Anatolian society during that period. As noted above, this satisfied the political needs of the early Ottomans, who provided the *akhis*, as well as sufis, with their care and support.

Speaking of the main factors behind the deep roots of religious tolerance in the Ottoman Empire, we have to examine briefly the role of two more factors in this respect: intermarriage and the Hanafite school of Jurisprudence. Intermarriage, as we have seen, was common in Seljuk society in Anatolia and helped to establish religious tolerance and cultural diversity in that society. This practice remained and even increased after the rise of the Ottoman state and was established throughout the Ottoman society. The early Ottoman rulers were no exception. One of the most remarkable marriages in this regard was that of Sultan Orkhan to Theodora, the daughter of the Byzantine Emperor Cantacuzenus (1347-1354).[38] Theodora remained a committed Christian and devoted much of her life to charitable acts. She gave birth to Emir Khalil Çelebi.[39]

The spread of intermarriage in the Ottoman society had a great impact on the expansion of cultural exchange, religious tolerance and social harmony.[40] The existence of many children who were brought up by mothers belonging to different backgrounds also contributes to the appreciation of cultural diversity within Ottoman society.

As for the Hanafite school of Muslim Jurisprudence, it is known that it was the school of the Ottomans as well as of their predecessors, the Seljuks. Abu Hanifah (d. 150 AH / 767 AD), the founder of this school, is given the epithet of "al-Imam al-A'zam," i.e. the greatest Imam of Muslim Jurisprudence. His school is reputed as being the leading one in employing *ra'y* (personal judgment) and *qiyas* (syllogism).[41] Accordingly, its adaptability to changing times and conditions is one of its main characteristics. Understandably, this helped to give the Ottoman Sharia laws a liberal nature.[42]

In conclusion, the phenomenon of religious tolerance in the Ottoman Empire was not superficial but deeply rooted in the structure of the state. The Seljuks who preceded the Ottomans in Asia Minor played a definite role in that respect. The effect of the multi-racial, multi-cultural, and multi-religious society in which the early Ottomans lived contributed a great deal to the enhancement of tolerance, as did the *madrasahs* and religious foundations established by early Ottoman rulers. The role of the *ulema* who propagated the real tolerant spirit of Islam was paramount. Sufi lodges and *akhis* guilds had their important share and were supported and protected by the rulers of the state. Further, these Sufi and *akhis* organizations contributed to the creation of cultural diversity and social harmony. These factors were further supported by the intermarriage between people of different cultures, races and religions. The Sharia laws of the Ottoman state, which were mainly derived from the Hanafite school, were adaptable to different times, places and conditions. Indeed, all these factors were merged together to create a great model of tolerance and cultural diversity in its time.

Chapter Three

"Upon Them be Peace:"
The Ottoman Spirit, Early Modern Models of Toleration, and
Contemporary Debates over Multiculturalism

by Dr. Bernadette Andrea

THIS CHAPTER ASSESSES CURRENT EVOCATIONS of the Ottoman
Empire as an exemplar of multiculturalism, broadly defined as
the peaceful coexistence of diverse religious and ethnic groups within
one polity.[1]

In recent decades, the press and politicians in the Turkish Republic
have evoked the Ottoman example of "multiculturalism" under the
rubric of "neo-Ottomanism."[2] European scholars seeking to challenge the biases of Orientalism, identified as "a Western style for
dominating, restructuring, and having authority over the Orient,"[3]
similarly have claimed that "Ottoman statecraft, for all its apparent
flaws, provides in many respects an exemplary model of meritocratic
multicultural and multinational pluralism that remains unsurpassed
anywhere today."[4]

American scholars have cited Ottoman "autonomy for religious
groups," extrapolated to ethnic and racial minorities, as an alternative to the dominant "melting pot" model.[5] However, other scholars
caution that the Ottoman Empire, while remarkably diverse and
tolerant compared with the West for most of its history, "was not
and never saw itself as a multicultural society" in the contemporary

sense.[6] Some broach the question, "Is the Ottoman millet system, or a modernized version of it, a means by which the state can successfully appease subordinate minorities with cultural autonomy?" Even so, they also point out, "inferior status may be combined with substantial cultural autonomy."[7]

Instructively, these references to the Ottoman example in current discussions of multiculturalism, particularly as it pertains to western liberal democracies, reprise the debate over religious toleration in seventeenth century England, which experienced the devastation of a religiously inflected civil war in the middle of the century.[8] The outcome of this debate arguably determined the model of tolerance, expanded into multiculturalism, characteristic of modern Western European and North American societies.[9] As we shall see, this model was based on the reports of the first English travelers to spend a considerable amount of time among the Ottomans, where they observed a standard of peaceful coexistence unavailable in the western tradition and which they recognized as inherently Islamic. Certainly, as scholars on both sides of the current multiculturalism debate underscore, the political edifice of the Ottoman Empire cannot be replicated in our increasingly globalized era. However, the principle of actively seeking common ground with others rather than simply tolerating diversity, which represents the "Ottoman spirit" at its best, continues to be relevant today.

This chapter concludes with two salient challenges to the "clash of civilizations" thesis, which is diametrically opposed to this principle. Samuel Huntington (1927–2008), a professor of government at Harvard University who previously gained notoriety as a presidential advisor during the US war against Vietnam, popularized this thesis as an explanation for current global conflicts, which he conceptualizes as "the West versus the Rest."[10] Fethullah Gülen (1941–), who numbers among the many "Muslim intellectuals and activists" who seek "two-way communication and exchange" between the West and the Islamic world, contests this deleterious thesis from the perspective of "Turkish Islam."[11] Edward Said (1935–2003), a professor of literature and culture at Columbia University whose *Orientalism* ranks as one of the most influential books of the twentieth century, advances a deeply ethical "secular criticism" to attack the inhumanity of Huntington's worldview. Although their approaches are distinct, both Gülen and Said draw on the long history of productive interchanges between the West and the Islamic world to advance their conviction that dialogue is essential and divisions are not inevitable. Indeed, they are profoundly dangerous in our globalized era, when mass destruction can only be mutual.

I. Contemporary Debates:
Multiculturalism and the Ottoman Empire

Assessing the multicultural societies of the West in a global context, sociologist Peter Kivisto adjudicates between assimilationist and separatist theories to conclude that "multiculturalism . . . is about finding a way to preserve discrete ethnic identities, while at the same time finding in citizenship a countervailing identity that unites the disparate groups within a polity."[12] As he documents, the Canadian federal government, representing a historically Eurocentric settler state whose population became increasingly diverse after immigration reforms of the 1960s, pioneered "official multiculturalism" with legislation in the 1970s. This legislation deemed ethnic diversity not only as inevitable given the demands of the Canadian economy, but as positive for society as a whole. Unlike the American "melting pot," a metaphor for often-forced assimilation into the dominant White Anglo-Saxon Protestant culture, Canada sought to construct a cultural "mosaic" out of its various ethnic communities, albeit one based on the continuing dispossession of indigenous populations.[13]

During the closing decades of the twentieth century, the model of "official multiculturalism" spread from North America to Western Europe, influencing policy in the wake of accelerating immigration from former colonies, including many in the Islamic world.[14] By the opening decade of the twenty-first century, support for multiculturalism in Europe has eroded in response to what has been represented by its opponents as a "resurgence of Islam."[15] The parallel American retreat from multiculturalism illuminates the underlying socio-economic factors that are effaced in the anti-Islamic European discourse: primarily racism, resulting in chronic underdevelopment in immigrant communities from former European colonies.[16] As the recent uprising of French youth of Algerian descent demonstrates, racism and poverty premised what was falsely represented in the popular press as a manifestation of "Islamic fundamentalism."[17] Hence, multiculturalism has become an increasingly fraught term in the West (Western Europe and North America), and has increasingly been associated with an array of misrepresentations of Islam.

The Ottoman Empire, as the premier Islamic power from the end of the fifteenth century to the beginning of the twentieth century, figures centrally in the debate over the so-called "clash of civilizations." In the essay which popularized this phrase, political scientist and policy analyst Samuel Huntington proposes that "the battle lines of the future" will be between "the West versus the Rest," meaning (in his disputed taxonomy) "Confucian, Japanese, Islamic, Hindu, Slavic-Orthodox, Latin American and possibly African civilization."[18] The most crucial battle line for Huntington lies between "Islam and the West," with the West defined as Judeo-Christian and exclusively European.[19] He cites "the historic boundary" between the Habsburgs and Ottomans as dividing Europe economically, politically, and religiously, though he groups Eastern Orthodox Christianity with Islam in this dichotomy. Huntington represents the Ottoman Empire, in its expansion and its decline, at the center of "the fault line between Western and Islamic civilizations."[20] He rejects its legacy of internal accommodation, cultural diffusion, and ethnic mixing, all of which are aspects of contemporary multiculturalism.[21]

Those who challenge Huntington's assertion of a "clash of civilizations" frequently cite the Ottoman example. As Nushin Arbabzadah observes in a widely distributed essay titled "Multiculturalism in Medieval Islam":

> In recent European debates on multiculturalism, Muslims have often appeared as the black sheep of the multicultural family."[22]

As a counterpoint, she argues that, "contrary to common perceptions, living in multiethnic, multifaith and multilingual societies has always been part of the experience of Muslims." Focusing on the Islamic concepts of "*ahl al-dhimma*, the 'people of the pact,' and *ahl al-kitab*, the 'people of the book,'" she asserts that the provisions for fellow monotheists (particularly Jews and Christians) to retain their religious and cultural autonomy under Islamic law represents a singular advance in minority rights. "The Ottoman mosaic," in her view, epitomizes this tolerance. Kemal Karpat, a historian of the late Ottoman Empire, likewise elaborates the Islamic basis for its religious tolerance, which encompassed de facto cultural, ethnic, and linguistic tolerance. By contrast:

> The Christian states...were bound by no biblical reference to Muslims to offer them protection or ensure any rights for them. Because there was therefore no room for non-Christians in the new Christian-dominated territorial states [of the former Ottoman Empire], Muslim communities in the Balkans were destroyed even after the Berlin Treaty of 1878 articulated the principle of minority rights.[23]

However, we must approach such references to "multiculturalism in medieval Islam" with caution. As Arbabzadah herself documents, the tolerance for religious minorities (particularly "people of the book") in past Islamic polities involved restrictions that would be unacceptable in today's multicultural mosaic. As she points out, these dhimmi were required to pay a special tax, *jizya,* in return for the protection of their Muslim governors, though Muslim subjects were required to pay other taxes and to perform military service. While this was an exchange, it was an unequal one. Arbabzadah indicates that during the Abbasid period (750–1258 CE), *dhimmi* "had to obey a number of additional rules that were supposed to govern their public conduct," including "'showing a respectful attitude towards Muslims' or 'when celebrating religious ceremonies, keeping the level of noise low.'" *Dhimmi* were also required to build houses lower than those of their Muslim neighbors, to avoid dressing like Muslims, and to ride on "inferior" animals like mules and donkeys rather than horses. Similar conditions prevailed in the Ottoman millet system, where, according to Suraiya Faroqhi, a historian of the classical Ottoman Empire: "Christian and Jewish religious communities were tolerated" but "their members were not accorded a great deal of respect."[24] Even so, the documentary record shows that English Protestants fared better at the hands of Muslims than of Catholics in the region — and that dissenting English Protestants fared better at the hands of Muslims than of their countrymen from the hegemonic church of England.

Certainly, as Arbabzadah and others have asserted, the level of tolerance in the Ottoman Empire at its height exceeded anything imaginable in Western Europe, notorious as it was for its expulsion of Jews and Muslims, as well as for its persecution of Christians deemed "heretics" by various state churches. The evocation of the Ottoman example in the current debate over multiculturalism consequently must be tempered by a comparative historical analysis of the conditions of tolerance. Whereas "tolerance" and "toleration" are used as synonyms in contemporary discourse, in the early modern English context "toleration" meant various churches are permitted in one state and "tolerance" meant various views are permitted within one state church.[25] John Marshall, in *John Locke, Toleration and Early Enlightenment Culture,* mentions the impact of the Ottoman example on Locke's and other political philosophers' articulation, for the first time, of a model of broad religious toleration within Western Christendom.[26] The next section focuses on those travel writers whose accounts of toleration in the Ottoman Empire premised, and arguably made possible, the views of these political philosophers.

II. Early Modern Models: Toleration and the Ottoman Empire

During the seventeenth century, religious conflicts such as the Thirty Years' War between Protestants and Catholics in Germany, from 1618 to 1648, devastated Western Europe. In predominantly Catholic countries such as Spain and France, persecution of Muslims, Jews, and Protestants continued unabated well into the seventeenth century.[27] Catholics fared no better in Protestant countries, nor did other religious minorities. Like the rest of Western Europe, the British Isles were torn apart by the "politics of religion" that dominated the era.[28] The mainstream genealogy for English colonization of North America accordingly begins in the early seventeenth century with the flight from religious persecution by dissenting Calvinists (Puritans). By the middle of the century, England was shattered by a religiously inflected civil war. At its conclusion, a limited toleration was established, which ironically involved intensified persecution of dissenters such as Catholics and Quakers.

This period, known as the English Restoration, ran from 1660, when monarchy was restored in England after two decades as a republic, to 1689, when the so-called Toleration Act was passed. As Henry Kamen cautions in *The Rise of Toleration,* "For all its importance in granting liberty to non-conforming Protestants, the Act was reactionary in tone and content, and fell far short of contemporary ideals."[29] Catholics and Unitarians (non-Trinitarian Christians) were not protected by the Act. Religious toleration, moreover, did not translate into civil equality for non-conforming Protestants such as Baptists, Quakers, and others. The Act did not address non-Christians.[30] Hence, P. J. Vatikiotis, who has been critiqued for his orientalist prejudices by Edward Said, wrongly celebrates the English Restoration as a prototype for religious tolerance, which Vatikiotis incorrectly contrasts with the Islamic model.[31]

Two important individuals who sought solutions for England's religio-political crisis in the Ottoman example were George Sandys, who traveled across the empire at the beginning of the seventeenth century, and Paul Rycaut, who traveled therein during the latter half of the century. Each wrote a narrative detailing aspects of the Ottoman system, including its religious toleration: Sandys's *A Relation of a Journey . . . Containing a Description of the Turkish Empire* (1615) and Rycaut's *The Present State of the Ottoman Empire* (1667). Both volumes went through multiple editions. Sandys was writing during an era when Western Europeans considered the expansionist Ottoman Empire "the Terror of the World."[32] Rycaut was writing during an era that witnessed the first decisive defeat of the Ottomans in the Austro-Ottoman War of 1683–97. This defeat resulted in the

Treaty of Karlowitz (1699), which required the Ottomans to cede much of their European territories. Rycaut's views encapsulate this transition from the European image of the Ottoman Empire as "the Terror of the World" to the "Sick Man of Europe," a phrase coined in the nineteenth century.[33]

Sandys was a clergyman, colonizer, and poet. His interest in the Ottoman Empire began with his elder brother Edwin's conviction that the Ottomans enabled the spread of Protestantism by offering a counterbalance to Catholic Habsburg hegemony and by providing a haven for persecuted Protestants.[34] As James Ellison establishes in his intellectual biography of George Sandys, "theories of tolerance, and toleration, generally originated in horror at religious discord and at the hideous spectacle of persecution in the name of Christianity."[35] The Ottoman example of a state amenable to diverse religions accordingly became central to the early modern English debate.

At the same time, English merchants, and to a lesser degree the English crown, initiated forays into global imperialism, most of which were unsuccessful. A prime example is the tenuous colony at Jamestown, Virginia, during the first decades of the seventeenth century, in which Sandys participated. While the English had engaged in an intensified regional colonization during the sixteenth century, incorporating Wales and Ireland, and while imperialist propaganda emerged at the end of the sixteenth century with Richard Hakluyt's *The Principal Navigations, Voyages and Discoveries of the English Nation* (1589; expanded edition 1598–1600), the English were not serious contenders for the western imperialist mantle of "Lords of all the World."[36] Moreover, while the Scottish king who inherited the throne of England in 1603 — James VI of Scotland, who became James I of England — proposed uniting the two kingdoms as "Great Britain," the actual union did not occur for another century.[37] The English at the beginning of the seventeenth century, motivated by "imperial envy," a term coined by literary and cultural critic Gerald MacLean, thus turned to the ascendant Ottoman Empire as a model for their prospective empire.[38]

Whereas Edwin Sandys's travels did not take him into the Ottoman Empire, his more celebrated younger brother, George, traversed its heartland in Anatolia, its Mediterranean territories, and its frontier beyond Egypt. While in Jerusalem, under Ottoman control at the time, the younger Sandys witnessed how "Christians of all kinds were tolerated by that feared and hated regime."[39] But for him, and for other sixteenth and early seventeenth century English writers, the Ottomans were not simply "feared and hated" for their military achievements; instead, they were admired for their religious tolerance, administrative justice, and social manners. Sources Sandys would have consulted emphasized "the Grand Signor's [Ottoman sultan's] justice," as opposed to the inequities of the legal system in Western Europe; "the Ottoman system of meritocracy," as opposed to class-bound Europe; and "the prevailing freedom of religion in the Ottoman Empire," completely absent in the West. While anti-Islamic comments also appear in these accounts, they do not detract from the overall recognition of the Ottoman Empire "as a sovereign state rather than solely as a religious foe."[40]

Sandys, as a staunch Anglican, admittedly tends towards ethnocentrism. However, an overall analysis of his *A Relation* reveals that he was an admirer of the Ottomans, as was his brother, Edwin. While this travelogue anticipates the later orientalist focus on the purported despotism of the Ottoman government, "the fate of the European Protestants, dependent as it is on the continued strength of the Ottoman Empire, is a key sub-text of *A Relation*."[41] Moreover, to nuance this conclusion, the lesson of religious toleration Sandys gained from his encounter with the Ottomans, not simply their countervailing presence vis-à-vis the Catholic Habsburgs, undergirds his endorsement of the Ottoman example. Drawing on his firsthand experience, he confirms that historic Christian churches in the empire "have the free exercise of their Religion: with publicke Temples, and numbers of strong Monasteries."[42] In his discussion of "The Mahometan [sic] Religion," he observes, albeit ambivalently: "Insomuch that if a Christian have deserved death by their law, if he will convert, they will many times remit his punishment. But they compel no man," with the latter phrase echoing the Qur'an.[43] As a point of comparison, Sandys and fellow English travelers evoked the intolerance of the Catholic Inquisition, which punished individuals for their beliefs rather than their acts. He records numerous examples of persecution by other Christians, as when his "Spanish comrad[e]s were very harsh to [him], (for in these parts [the Mediterranean] they detest the English, & think us not Christians)."[44] By contrast, he shows how the Ottoman Muslims "extend their charity to Christians and Jews, as well as to them of their own religion."[45] Even more significantly, Sandys's experience in the Ottoman Empire led him to understand that these principles were Islamic rather than limited to the Turkish case. He cites the second caliph, Umar ("Homar"), as enacting "liberty of Religion" for the defeated Byzantines "in the year 635," thus providing a precedent for the Ottomans after the conquest of Constantinople in 1453.[46]

Sandys, who established the Ottomans as a model to emulate in seventeenth century English debates over toleration, therefore understood the conditions for its multiculturalism derived from the Qur'anic principle that "there is no compulsion in religion" and from the implementation of this principle in the first Islamic state.[47] Notably, Sandys did not have access to an English translation of the Qur'an, first available in 1649, to shape his views.[48] Rather, Ottoman adherence to these principles provided a living example for him to convey into the English tradition.

With Paul Rycaut, English consul in Turkey from 1667 to 1678, we encounter the first glimmers of the shift to the predominantly orientalist views that emerged in the eighteenth century and held sway into the twentieth century. As a transitional figure, Rycaut echoes the praise for Ottoman meritocracy, justice, and toleration we saw in Sandys's earlier works; however, he simultaneously advances the view of "oriental despotism" that would prevail in subsequent centuries.[49] Despite this negative tendency, his emphasis on religious toleration within the multicultural environment of the Ottoman Empire should not be overlooked.

Rycaut hailed from a multicultural background: Protestant Dutch on his paternal side and Catholic Spanish on his mother's side. As Sonia Anderson ventures, "Such a background helps to explain why Paul Rycaut was to grow up with a passionate belief in religious toleration," though such toleration related primarily to Christian unity.[50]

His service in the Levant Company, the English joint-stock company that managed relations with the Ottoman Empire, took him through the Mediterranean and ultimately to Smyrna (Izmir), the gateway for Western European merchants to the empire. He published several works based on these experiences, including *The Present State of the Ottoman Empire* (1667), *The Present State of the Greek and Armenian Churches* (1679), *The History of the Turkish Empire from 1623 to 1677* (1680), and *The History of the Turks from 1679 to 1699* (1700). These works, particularly *The Present State of the Ottoman Empire,* were widely read, resulting in various duplications and refutations.[51]

As the representative of English trading interests in the highly competitive environment of the Ottoman Empire, Rycaut naturally took a more pragmatic view of its operations. When introducing *The Present State of the Ottoman Empire,* he establishes "that a People, as the Turks are, men of the same composition with us, cannot be so savage and rude as they are generally described."[52] Although his analysis is often hostile to Islam, which he deems a "superstition,"[53] the detail of his survey establishes the breadth of toleration in the empire. It therefore oscillates between stereotypes borrowed from medieval polemics to recognition of the basis for religious tolerance in Islamic principles. Rycaut covers multiple constituencies affected by Ottoman policy, including tributary states, eastern Christian subjects, and western Christian converts. He even devotes an entire chapter to the topic, "The Toleration that Mahometanism [sic] in its Infancy promised other Religions; and in what manner that agreement was afterwards observed,"[54] citing the Qur'an and referring to the Prophet Muhammad's treaties with various Christian groups.[55] But, unlike Sandys, he deems the Ottomans to have fallen away from these principles rather than to be their exemplars. This tension is repeated in *The Present State of the Greek and Armenian Churches,* where he documents the "stable perseverance" of these historic Christian churches in the Islamic empire of the Ottomans even as he bemoans their decline from their former hegemony. Even here, he underscores that religious toleration in the Ottoman Empire is "agreeable to Mahomet's Doctrine."[56]

Rycaut concludes *The Present State of the Ottoman Empire* by comparing the empire with Restoration England,[57] though the comparison seems to favor neither the Ottomans nor the English:

> I shall now give an account [of] how busie these
> Modern times have been at Constantinople
> [Istanbul] in hammering out strange forms and
> chimeras of Religion, the better to aquit England
> from the accusation of being the most subject to
> religious innovations, the world attributing much
> thereof to the Air and constitution of its Climate.[58]

This passage, which says that the Ottoman Empire is as full of religious sects as England, indicates an English inferiority complex vis-à-vis the more established civilizations of the East, including the Ottomans.[59] Yet, it also suggests the value of religious tolerance, long associated with the Ottomans, was being demoted as an ideal. It is not surprising that Rycaut was a firm defender of the hegemonic church of England and an obdurate critic of the radical dissenters who toppled England's monarchy in the middle of the seventeenth century. Nonetheless, even as he marks the shift to the full-fledged Orientalism of subsequent centuries, Rycaut retains the earlier recognition of the Islamic basis for Ottoman religious tolerance. This recognition is instructive when evaluating current polemics over multiculturalism, such as Huntington's, which refuse to accept tolerance as a core Islamic principle.

III. The "Ottoman Spirit" and the "Dialogue among Civilizations"

Gerald MacLean, as previously mentioned, argues that the English learned how to be imperialists by studying the Ottomans. In this essay, I have attempted to assess the lessons from the Ottoman Empire at its height through a comparative historical analysis. I have sought to show, thereby extending MacLean's thesis, how the English began to learn religious tolerance, which broadened into contemporary multiculturalism, from the Ottomans.[60] Nonetheless, as we have seen, the structure of the dhimmi system as articulated in pre-modern Islamic

empires, which represented the vanguard of religious tolerance compared with the monocultural realms of Christendom, cannot be
transposed into our era of global multiculturalism. Rather, it is the
spirit of peaceful coexistence, which early modern English travelers
to the Ottoman Empire recognized as inherently Islamic, that must
inform our efforts to challenge the imposition of a "clash of civilizations" with efforts towards a "dialogue among civilizations." This
phrase was introduced by Mohammad Khatami, former President of
Iran, in his 1999 address to UNESCO (October 29); popularized
after the United Nations designated 2001 as the year of "Dialogue
among Civilizations" (November 21); and adopted by international
organizations, such as the Gülen movement, seeking to challenge the
worldview proposed by Huntington.[61] For instance, Thomas Michel
discusses the latter's efforts in terms of "a *dialogue of civilizations*"
(emphasis in the original).[62]

Along these lines, in his influential essay, "The Necessity of
Interfaith Dialogue," Gülen offers several historical precedents for
"dialog among devout Muslims, Christians and Jews," which he
extends to other world religions.[63] He stresses that "Jews always
have been welcomed [by the Muslim world] in times of trouble, as
when the Ottoman State embraced them after their expulsion from
Andalusia (Spain)" in the early modern period.[64] He also references
the late Ottoman Empire's sheltering of Jews from the Holocaust as a
more recent example of this spirit of tolerance. He elsewhere harkens
to the example of the Prophet Muhammad, who insisted on paying
his respects when passing a Jewish funeral. As he continues, "When
reminded that the man being buried was a Jew [some of whom sought
to destroy the nascent Muslim community], Muhammad replied,
'He is still human though.'"[65] Pursuing "A Comparative Approach
to Islam and Democracy," Gülen notes that the Islamic belief in "the
basic unity of all religions . . . explains why both Christians and
Jews enjoyed their religious rights under the rule of Islamic governments throughout history."[66] Any exception to this mass of historical
evidence therefore constitutes an anomaly and even a deviation from
core Islamic principles.

In this spirit, Gülen critiques the reduction of religion to "a harsh political ideology and a mass ideology of independence," tendencies which emerged in response to western imperialism in the modern era.[67] Addressing this politicization of religion, he counters with Islamic principles that, when practiced, resulted in the tolerance characterizing the Ottoman Empire at its height. These principles include truthfulness, justice, freedom of belief, protection of the individual, and consultative government.[68] But he does not call for a return to the structures of this empire, acknowledging that "modern transportation and mass communication have turned the world into a global village in which every relationship is interactive." As he continues, "The West cannot wipe out Islam or its territory, and Muslim armies can no longer march on the West. Moreover, as this world is becoming even more global, both sides feel the need for a give-and-take relationship."[69] Michel concurs that Gülen's influential "educational vision," related to his views on interfaith and intercultural dialogue, "is very different from reactionary projects which seek to revive or restore the past."[70] As he elaborates:

> Denying that the education offered in the schools associated with his name is an attempt to restore the Ottoman system or to reinstate the caliphate, Gülen repeatedly affirms that: "If there is no adaptation to new conditions, the result will be extinction."[71]

This rejection of the "restoration of the caliphate" and the "clash of civilizations" theses, both of which have been bruited by powerful policy makers and politicians, clearly pertains to the call for a "dialogue among civilizations" in our increasingly global age.[72] As such, Gülen, in "Regarding the Information Age and the Clash of Civilizations," responds to the first term in Huntington's formulation:

> In truth, no divine religion has ever been based on conflict, whether it be the religions represented by Moses and Jesus, or the religion represented by Muhammad, upon them be peace.[73]

Ali Ünal and Alphonse Williams explain that "in any publication dealing with the Prophet Muhammad, his name or title is followed by the phrase 'upon him be peace and blessings,' to show our respect for him and because it is a religious obligation."[74] By extending this respect to Judaism, Christianity, and other world religions, Gülen rejects the inevitability of any "clash."

Edward Said from the standpoint of his "secular criticism," which he defines as "life-enhancing and constitutively opposed to every form of tyranny, domination, and abuse," addresses the insufficiency of Huntington's second term, "civilizations."[75] Civilizations — or, more precisely, cultures — are neither homogeneous nor unchanging. Rather, they are constructed through "an astonishing variety of currents and counter-currents," for which Said adduces the contemporary Islamic world as an example against the assumptions of "tendentious Orientalist scholars for whom Islam is an object of fear and hostility or by journalists who do not know any of the languages or relevant histories and are content to rely on persistent stereotypes that have lingered in the West since the tenth century."[76] All cultures, including the classical Greek culture that forms the basis of Western culture in the most traditional view, are constituted by "borrowings and overlappings."[77] Culture by definition is fluid. "But the truly weakest part of the clash of civilizations thesis," Said concludes, "is the rigid separation assumed among civilizations, despite the overwhelming evidence that today's world is in fact a world of mixtures, of migrations, of crossings over."[78]

As this chapter has sought to show, what Gülen identifies as "Islam's universal call for dialog" informed the solutions for the seemingly intractable problem of religious intolerance in early modern England.[79] These solutions, as we have seen, derived from seventeenth century Englishmen's firsthand experiences in the Ottoman Empire. This "Ottoman spirit," as they recognized, ultimately involves seeking common ground with others rather than simply tolerating diversity. To follow Said, it thereby presents a model for addressing contemporary debates over multiculturalism that may not be as foreign to the western tradition as Huntington and his ilk would have us believe.

Chapter Four

Diversity, Legal Pluralism, and Peaceful Co-Existence in the Ottoman Centuries

by Dr. Ihsan Yılmaz

M ANY REGARD THE OTTOMAN STATE AT THE HEIGHT of its prosperity and success as a symbol of harmony. The State incorporated ethnic and religious differences into its system of rule in ways that gave formally subordinate groups relative autonomy in their cultural, religious, economic, and political affairs (the millet system), and allowed some of their members to rise to positions of power and eminence.

The main premise of this study is very simple: it endeavours to emphasize that even in an area as strict and sensitive as law when clashes between Muslim and non-Muslim states were widespread, the Ottomans maintained a culturally, religiously, ethnically and even legally pluralist order for centuries where ethnic, cultural and religious differences were cherished; even in the realm of private law, non-Muslim minorities were allowed to apply their own ethno-religious laws.

This is not a detailed study of history, but a multidisciplinary examination of law, politics and sociology to see if lessons can be drawn for today's society. From a comparative perspective, we will briefly look at today's uniformity-centric hegemonic legal modernity paradigm. In the English context, we will try to analyze whether legal modernity can successfully accommodate cultural and religious pluralism. After looking at the legal modernity paradigm and testing it in a multicultural setting, we will proceed to see how Islamic law theory deals with diversity and how this theory was put into practice by the Ottomans. I aim to show that Ottoman diversity was not an accident of history, but a result of Islamic law's fundamental nature of accepting diversity as a virtue. We will then proceed to a brief inspection of the discourses, understandings and practices of today's Anatolian Muslims to emphasise that the Ottoman spirit of tolerance has survived and remains very much alive.

We will thus start with a brief discussion of the theory of legal modernity, which espouses uniformity—however unreal—as a virtue, and then proceed to see if legal modernity and legal uniformism effectively work in a multicultural setting.

I. Legal Modernity,
Instrumentalist Use of Law and Limits of Law

Legal modernity has several aspects. It is composed of legal positivism, legal centralism, legal uniformity, instrumentalist use of law for social engineering purposes, and the nation-state paradigm. In legal modernity, the territorial nation-state, rather than mankind, is adopted as the point of reference for law. Laws are applied over wider spatial, ethnic, religious and class areas. Personal law is no longer an issue at stake; they are replaced by territorial laws. Special laws are replaced by general laws and customary laws by statute laws. Secular motives and techniques supersede religious sanctions and inspiration. Law making and its application becomes an area which operates in the name of a central national power. This central national power tolerates no rivals by means of law in its sovereignty, since uniform law is seen as a "condition of progress toward modern nationhood."[1]

The doctrinal study of law—in other words, black-letter law, formalism or legal positivism—evaluates legal rules and cases universally.[2] Legal positivists insist on an analytical separation of law from morality. Thus, they do not deal with "what law ought to be," instead focusing on "what law is." They have a so-called "value-free" approach to law.

An absolutist and centralized legalism still prevails in the legal world. Assimilationist assumptions of development and modernity underlie such conceptualisations: Until the heterogeneous structures have been smelted into a homogeneous population which modern states are likely to enjoy, allowances can be made while unification remains as a unique goal.[3]

The ideological role of law is of central importance in legal modernity. Law can be used as an instrument of social control and as a mode of organizing beliefs and values. Law is viewed in legal modernity in utilitarian terms as a tool, "an amoral and infinitely plastic device of government."[4] According to this instrumentalist mentality, "all legal goals consist of specific end results realizable at some particular moment in time."[5] Instrumentalists take the social space between legislator and subject implicitly as a normative vacuum. In other words, they implicitly assume that the legislator is more or less autonomous from the social context in which the rule is to have its effects, the subjects of the rule are atomistic individuals, and the legislator's command is uninfluenced by the social medium.[6]

Socio-legal studies have shown that the legal positivist ideal is only a myth and an ideological standpoint, not a reality. Social engineering through law is a highly contentious matter. Despite the claims of legal modernity, socio-legal studies have repeatedly discovered that there are alternative normative orderings in society and that resistance to official law is always an issue at stake. As one writer comments: "the 'reach' of state power and state law is subject to specific conditions and always falls short of its ideological pretensions."[7]

At times, state law can be seen as unnecessary, avoidable, and remediable by the people or society. Laws do not work effectively if they are not congruent with their social context. It is evident that no law can ultimately compel action. All the law can do is "try to induce someone, by order or by persuasion or by suggestion, to a certain course of action."[8]

Official laws are not always absolutely effective. Official law alone cannot deal with social problems, and it has a limited capacity to enforce social change. States should acknowledge that there are limits and resistance to official laws in the community, where their sovereignty is not absolute, and that legal pluralism is a fact. However, this does not mean that unofficial laws always exist in direct opposition to the official law. The process is more complex and dynamic.[9] Now, let us look at how—despite the claims of legal modernity—unofficial legal pluralism operates.

2. Discrimination of Muslims and Unofficial Legal Pluralism in England

There are about two million Muslims in Britain. Islam is now the second religion of the country in terms of the number of adherents. As a result of the process of "chain migration," it has become possible for Muslims to more or less reconstruct their traditional milieus in Britain. In the context of English law, Muslim law as a religious law can have the status of moral but not legal rules, in civil as well as in public law.[10] Muslims are therefore subject to the same rules as all other inhabitants of the country concerned.[11] This has resulted in unofficial legal pluralism for Muslims in England, where the co-existence of unofficial Muslim law and official law is a reality. Much was Christian (non-official) and Muslim (official) laws. Although it has been established through the case law that members of Judaism and Sikhism are fully protected under the Race Relations Act, no such protection exists for members of other faiths.[12] As a result, there has been widespread alienation from the state among Muslims. The lack of responsiveness from the English system to the expectations of Muslims "may to a very large extent have been responsible for the now commonly observed phenomenon of 'avoidance reaction.'"[13]

Unofficial Muslim law is often applied in non-dispute situations in the everyday lives of Muslims. Many disputes among Muslims in Britain are settled in the context of informal family or community conciliation and never actually come before the official courts. Senior members of families or community leaders take the place of official courts in these informal conciliation processes.[14] The existence of unofficial laws among Muslims is starkly observable in the field of family law, especially in marriage and divorce issues.

Similarly to other Asian communities, Muslims adapted to English law in such a way that concern for their traditional obligation systems has not been abandoned altogether. They managed to build the requirements of English law into their traditional legal systems. At the same time, they also see the necessity of following the *lex loci*. Now, a new hybrid unofficial law has been emerging as a result of the dynamic interaction between English and Muslim laws. Muslims, consciously or not, developed this new hybrid rule system, which amalgamates the rules of Muslim law and of English law. Therefore, this new hybrid law has become the new Muslim law on English soil.[15]

Islamic law does not distinguish between civil and religious marriages. However, the state of England wishes to supervise the actual process of civil marriage in order to prevent fraud. Should a religious ceremony take place in England without fulfilling the preliminary civil requirements, the official law will not recognize this marriage as legally valid. If a civil ceremony in an English register office is followed by a religious ceremony in an unregistered building, the religious ceremony does not supersede or invalidate the civil ceremony and is not registered as a marriage in any marriage register book.[16] In other words, the civil ceremony is the only marriage which English law recognizes. An unregistered Muslim marriage will be void, even if the parties knowingly and wilfully contracted the marriage.[17] However, it is not clear what the law's approach will be when the parties marry in this form believing that they are contracting a valid marriage according to both their religious tradition and English law.[18]

Islamic law does not distinguish between civil and religious marriages. However, the state in England wishes to supervise the actual process of civil marriage. Should a religious ceremony take place in England without fulfilling the preliminary civil requirements, the official law will not recognise this marriage as legally valid. If a civil ceremony in an English register office is followed by a religious ceremony in an unregistered building, the religious ceremony does not supersede or invalidate the civil ceremony and is not registered as a marriage in any marriage register book. In other words, the civil ceremony is the only marriage which English law recognises. An unregistered Muslim marriage will be void even if the parties knowingly and wilfully contracted the marriage (Yılmaz 2005a: 71-72).

Solemnization of marriages according to Muslim law in Britain was so evident that social scientists started to observe this phenomenon in the late 1950s. This early research showed that Muslims in Britain had three types of marriages: legalized British marriages, the Muslim form of marriage, and common-law marriages.[19] In these years, couples started to observe both English and Muslim laws for two reasons—first, some Muslim couples who had already been married by a registrar also submitted to a *nikah* later for religious reasons. Secondly, spouses who only had a *nikah* might ask that the union be ratified by an official marriage as well, so as to safeguard the family's and prospective children's status. After an initial period of insecurity, when some unregistered Asian marriages in Britain were abused, communities quickly learned the *lex loci* and constructed their new rules in these matters. If the man wanted to leave and walked away, the woman would have no rights whatsoever before the courts under the official law. After losing her virginity, which is very important in Muslim culture, she would have to face difficulties in getting remarried. Even worse, if she had a baby from the previous relationship, the remarriage options would be more difficult.[20]

Virtually all Asians have now "learnt the law" and register their marriages in accordance with English law. The registration ceremony of English law has been built into the customary South Asian pattern of marriage solemnization in such a way that it constitutes something like an engagement in the eyes of the communities. The spouses might be married under the official law, but they will not be counted as married in the eyes of the community and will abstain from sexual intercourse until they get married religiously as well. Only after the religious marriage will they be able to consummate their marriage. Otherwise, their marriage would be regarded as sinful and illegitimate from a religious and cultural perspective. This indicates that it is the religious marriage that determines the nature of the relationship and is perceived as dominant; the official one is only seen as a mere formality which is imposed by the state.[21]

Now, most Muslims in England register their marriage first, knowing that the couple are not actually fully married until the completion of the religious marriage. In that way, they prevent the groom's possible abuse of the socio-legal situation of the Muslim minority by just walking away after the first night. The overall picture is that under this British Muslim law, if a Muslim couple wants to marry, they will actually marry twice. Thus, they meet the requirements of both Muslim law and the English law. In addition, they fortify the strength of *nikah* by incorporating official legal rules into their unofficial laws.[22]

In Muslim law, divorce can be obtained in a number of extra-judicial ways. *Talaq* is a unilateral repudiation by the husband. *Khul* is the divorce at the instance of the wife with or without the husband's agreement and on the basis that she will forego her right to dower. *Mubaraat* is divorce by mutual consent. However, in English law there is merely one way of divorce, which is through a decree granted by a court of civil jurisdiction on the grounds that the marriage has irretrievably broken down.[23] It has been laid down explicitly since 1973 that no extra-judicial divorce shall be recognized in English law.[24] Yet, it is becoming increasingly apparent that the traditional patterns of divorce have not been abandoned by Muslims in England. Secular divorce is not regarded as sufficient to dissolve a marriage in the eyes of Muslims.[25]

In short, having married twice, Muslims have also learnt to divorce twice. This process is facilitated by the increasingly informal nature of English divorce law itself. Almost 98% of all divorces in English law are undefended and effected by means of what is called the "special procedure." This flexible procedure has allowed Muslims in Britain to maintain their customary procedures of divorce almost unmodified. Yet, the British state's hesitation to recognize the socio-legal reality of Muslim legal pluralism has caused a number of problems for the community.[26]

Talaq is still very important for the Muslim mind and for the community.[27] If the woman is not religiously divorced from her husband, it does not matter that she is divorced under the civil law—in the eyes of the community, her remarriage will be regarded as adulterous and any possible offspring will be illegitimate, since it is not allowed under the religious law. So, in reality, until the religious divorce is obtained, the civil divorce remains ineffective because one party is unable to remarry.[28]

In that context, the main problem is the occurrence of limping marriages, which are recognized in some jurisdictions as having been validly dissolved, but in other jurisdictions as still subsisting. Sometimes, capricious husbands divorce their wives officially, but do not want to pronounce *talaq* or deliver the get to prevent the women remarrying.[29] These unscrupulous husbands sometimes blackmail their wives; knowing the value placed on a religious divorce by their wives, such men have used their power to grant or withhold divorce to negotiate favourable settlements on the issues of finance, property and children.[30] Badawi highlights the problem of limping marriages among Muslims in Britain:[31]

> A common problem was that you get a woman seeking a divorce in the courts and obtaining it. She becomes therefore eligible for re-marriage in accordance with the civil law, but her husband has not given her a *talaq*, which is the prerogative of the husband within an ordinary contract of marriage so that the woman becomes unmarried according to the civil law but still married according to the Sharia law. The man could remarry according to the civil law and according to Sharia law as well, since it is open to him to have a polygamous marriage.[32]

It has been largely accepted that limping marriages cause hardship to women and "the potential for great bitterness between the spouses."[33] The ultimate outcome is "acute misery and frustration."[34] It is abundantly clear that the state's non-recognition does not prevent the discriminatory practice.[35] Having recognized that the official legal system has hesitated to solve their disputes in the context of Islamic family law, Muslims have established informal conciliation mechanisms. The Islamic Sharia Council (ISC) is such an example of the concerted efforts to face challenges by the life.[36]

It is obvious in the English context that legal uniformity is a myth and official or not legal pluralism is a reality. Non-recognition of this multicultural reality is an impediment to peaceful co-existence and also undermines the respect for the state.

Having looked at the legal modernity paradigm and tested it in a multicultural setting, we will now look at the theory of Islamic law vis-à-vis cultural & religious diversity. We will then discuss how this theory was practiced by Ottomans to see if it was more realistic in terms of taking into account the heterogeneous and multicultural realities of life and thus achieving social harmony more successfully.

III. Islamic Legal Pluralism, Ottomans and Non-Muslims

Unlike the legal modernity paradigm, diversity has been accepted as a fact by Islamic law, and Islamic law is itself legitimately diverse. In its spirit of respect and tolerance towards non-Muslim faiths, Islamic law proscribes strict non-interference with anything within the realm of the special religious beliefs of non-Muslims. There has always been a kind of internal plurality of Muslim laws and customs due to three main reasons. First, there are four main schools of law (*madhhabs*) and other sects, which all have slightly different views on certain non-fundamental practices of Islam. Second, written law (high Islam) does not completely coincide with people's practices (custom). Third, there are some differences between the state's Islam and folk Islam or local Islam. From a legal pluralist viewpoint, Muslim law is not only the law stated in the Muslim law books, but also what Muslim people apply in everyday life.

Sharia is the divine law whose principles are embedded in the Qur'an and Sunna. It is a territory of textual complexity, for there is no simple set of rules that constitute the Sharia, but rather a body of texts, including the Qur'an, *hadith*, and legal texts of various genres that supply the authoritative base for Islamic legal thought and practice. The science of Muslim jurisprudence within the first two centuries of Islam devised both the sources of law (*usul al-fiqh*) and substantive law itself (*furu al-fiqh*). *Fiqh* is the product of human understanding that seeks to interpret and apply the Sharia in space-time. When faced with new situations or problems, scholars sought a similar situation in the Qur'an and Sunna. The key is the discovery of the effective cause or reason behind a Sharia rule. If questions arose about the meaning of a Qur'anic text or tradition, or if revelation and early Muslim practice were silent, jurists applied their own reasoning (*ijtihad*) to interpret the law, thus maintaining the diversity of Islamic laws. Islamic legal culture and Muslim jurists not only experienced legal change, but were aware that change was a distinct feature of the law, and this has brought about more diversity.[37]

In classical Islamic law, non-Muslim religious communities that possessed an accepted, written holy book were granted a covenant of protection, the dhimma, and were considered to be protected people, the dhimmis. In return for this status, they paid a special poll tax, the *jizya*. From its nascent days to today, Islamic legal scholarship has always maintained that Islam specifically orders Muslims and their rulers to respect and accommodate other faiths. Muslim leaders throughout history followed this doctrine of Islam. Ottoman legal pluralism was not just an accident of history or a simple result of the Ottomans' mercy or compassion, but a result of their religious duty and obligation. In line with Islamic law, diversity was always cherished and seen as a virtue by the Ottomans.

IV. Legal Pluralism in Ottoman Times: The Millet System

Even five to six centuries ago, when clashes between Muslim and non-Muslim states were widespread, the Ottomans, thanks to Islamic law, maintained a culturally, religiously, ethnically, and even legally pluralist order. Ethnic, cultural, and religious differences were cherished, and in the realm of private law, non-Muslim minorities were allowed to apply their ethno-religious laws.

In the pre-modern Middle East, identity was largely based on religion. Divisions of society into communities along religious lines formed the millet (nation) system. The three leading non-Muslim religious communities—the Jews, the Greek Orthodox Church, and the Armenian Church—were established as recognized dhimmi communities known as millets. Each millet was headed by its own religious dignitary: a chief rabbi in the case of the Jews and patriarchs in the case of the Greek Orthodox and Armenian communities. Different denominations dealt with the ruling power through these millet leaders. Non-Muslims were subject to their own ethno-religious groups in the field of private law, and in public law they were subject to state law. It was also left to the non-Muslims to use their own laws and institutions to regulate behaviour and conflicts under the leaders of their religion. Islamic law was not applied to non-Muslims except in cases where non-Muslims came into litigation with Muslims or where both parties agreed to be judged by Islamic law when their own religious laws were insufficient. Schools, welfare, commercial enterprise, and other social activities were left to individuals or to the millets.[38]

As McCarthy describes it, the Ottomans espoused:

> The religious traditions of the Middle East and Balkans and codified them into laws. Each religious group was named as a millet. . . . Their leaders represented the needs of their people to the sultan's government. Sometimes, as was the case with the Greek Orthodox, the place of the millet was specifically recognized by law. Other millets, such as the Jews, were simply recognized by tradition. As the centuries passed, more sects were officially recognized . . . but the millet system was an essential element of Ottoman government from an early date. Even before individual millets were officially recognized, they had a de facto separate existence.[39]

In the words of Ostrorog:

> . . . in its spirit of extreme liberalism towards non-Moslem creeds, Mohammedan Law prescribes not only tolerance of, but strict non-interference with anything which, in the Mohammedan conception, is considered as being within the province of the special religious beliefs of Jews and Christians; and Family law, as also, under certain reserves, the Law of Wills and Inheritance, are considered,

in Mohammedan Law, as matters within that
province. As a consequence, complete liberty was
granted to Christians and Jews to decide in those
matters according to the tenets of their own Law,
and special jurisdiction to that effect was granted
to their own religious authorities, Turkish authorities only intervening to enforce execution, when
required to do so.[40]

The millet system functioned well until the European concepts of
nationalism and ethnicity filtered into the Ottoman Empire in the
second half of the nineteenth century.[41] The system contributed to
the preservation of a separate identity and, eventually, to the generation of a nationalist consciousness distinct from that of Muslims.[42]
Non-Muslims were susceptible to the ideas of equality and nationalism emanating from the French Revolution. The European powers,
in an effort to interfere in the affairs of the Ottoman State, launched
a competitive race to draw the religious and ethnic minorities to their
side and to place them under their protection.[43] But for centuries,
the millet system facilitated a peaceful co-existence for non-Muslim
minorities.

V. The Survival of the Spirit of Ottoman Tolerance Today
The spirit of Ottoman tolerance is not a thing of the past. Even
though Muslims all over the world have been challenged and
influenced by the juggernauts of modernity, nationalism, western
imperialism and colonialism for the past century, in addition to
being harshly subjected to ignorance, poverty and dissension, many
Muslims still believe that respect for diversity as exemplified by the
Ottomans is a religious obligation.

In the field of academics, the prominent Turkish Islamic scholar
Ali Bulaç claims that even today, a legally pluralist system could be
viable. He refers to the Medina society of the time of the Prophet and
the Medina Constitutional Charter, the first application of a millet
system in Muslim history. In this multi-cultural and legally pluralist project, each religious, cultural or ideological bloc, including

atheists, had their religious, cultural and legal autonomy. They were independent in their internal affairs, especially with regard to family law issues.[44] There are also some other projects offered by Muslim scholars which claim to directly refer to the Qur'an rather than to the historical experience of Muslims.[45]

Not only scholars, like Bulaç, are comfortable with diversity. Political Islamists of Turkey deal with it, too. They even go as far as to suggest that not only could the Ottoman spirit be emulated, but the Ottoman experience could also be copied in this age. Some members of the Welfare Party, the Islamist party in power during the first half of 1997, even ventured to say that law should not be produced by the state, but by individuals and communities; the state must assume the role of a co-ordinator.[46]

The inspiring leader of a well-known Muslim faith-based movement, Fethullah Gülen, reiterates that diversity and pluralism are natural facts, and differences should be admitted and professed explicitly.[47] By referencing the form of Islam practiced by the Seljuks and Ottomans, which he calls Anatolian Islam, and their practice of religious pluralism, he emphasizes that:

> The Muslim world has a good record of dealing with the Jews: there has been almost no discrimination, and there has been no Holocaust, denial of basic human rights, or genocide. On the contrary, Jews have always been welcomed in times of trouble, as when the Ottoman State embraced them after their expulsion from Andalusia.[48]

Gülen also underlines that a legally pluralist system existed in Seljuk and Ottoman times. He is tolerant of internal Muslim legal and cultural pluralism. In this context, for instance, he asserts that "Alawis definitely enrich Turkish culture" and encourages Alawis to transform to a written culture from oral culture to preserve their identity.[49] "Alawi meeting or prayer houses," he stresses, "should be supported. In our history, a synagogue, a church, and a mosque stood side by side in many places."[50] He further states:

. . . different beliefs, races, customs and traditions will continue to cohabit in this village. Each
individual is like a unique realm unto themselves;
therefore the desire for all humanity to be similar
to one another is nothing more than wishing for
the impossible. For this reason, the peace of this
(global) village lies in respecting all these differences, considering these differences to be part of
our nature and in ensuring that people appreciate
these differences. Otherwise, it is unavoidable that
the world will devour itself in a web of conflicts,
disputes, fights, and the bloodiest of wars, thus pre-
paring the way for its own end.[51]

He also argues that:

If one were to seek the true face of Islam in its own
sources, history, and true representatives, then one
would discover that it contains no harshness, cru-
elty, or fanaticism. It is a religion of forgiveness,
pardon, and tolerance as such saints and princes of
love and tolerance as Rumi, Yunus Emre, Ahmed
Yesevi, Bediüzzaman and many others have so
beautifully expressed.[52]

Literally millions are motivated by Gülen's teachings of peace,
education, and dialogue. Through his sermons, teachings, books and
activities, he has inspired a whole generation in Turkey and abroad.
For the peaceful world of the future, Gülen encourages his admir-
ers to establish educational institutions in and outside of Turkey.
Gülen's sympathisers are active participants in their society and
perform public service by establishing schools and hospitals. The
community's enthusiasm for establishing secular schools in both the
Muslim and non-Muslim world, specifically schools serving people
of all faiths and nationalities, is unprecedented, not only among

sufis, but among all faith-based groups and movements, making it socially innovative. Instead of being isolated from the society, they follow Gülen's advice and try to reconcile their spiritual life with their worldly one. The movement's schools are non-denominational and follow the national curriculum of the country in which they are based. Many scholars have observed that the Gülen schools endeavour to combine excellence in teaching with the instruction of good morals.[53] These schools aim to instil universal values, such as honesty, cooperation, freedom, happiness, humility, love, respect, responsibility, and acceptance of the Other, through the good example of teachers, educators, and staff.

Through its schools and outlets, the Gülen movement is spreading an Anatolian Muslimness—a renewed practice of Rumi's Islam and *tasawwuf* that emphasizes love, mutual respect, understanding, socio-cultural activism, education, social innovation, peaceful co-existence, dialogue and cooperation with all for a cohesive society. With the help of schools in about 100 countries in North, East, West and South, all over the world, many people, not only Muslims, are getting a quality education in a multicultural, multi-faith environment. English is the primary language of instruction, so that in the future, students will continue to be open to dialogue and will hopefully attain good socio-economic status within their societies. In line with Gülen's firm belief that the road to justice for all is dependent on the provision of an adequate and appropriate universal education, the movement has pursued non-formal education through television and radio channels, newspapers and magazines, and cultural and professional foundations, in addition to the formal education carried out in schools.[54]

Gülen also pioneered the establishment of the Journalists and Writers Foundation in 1994, the activities of which to promote dialogue and tolerance among all strata of the society receive warm welcomes from almost all walks of life. Fethullah Gülen is the Honorary President of the Foundation. The Foundation also works as a think-tank in related issues. The movement tries to bring together all scholars and intellectuals, regardless of their ethnic, ideological, religious and cultural backgrounds. The Abant Platform is a result of the attempt to find solutions to Turkey's problems by bringing together scholars and intellectuals of all colors. This platform is the first of its kind in near Turkish history, where intellectuals could agree to disagree on such sensitive issues as laicism, secularism, religion, and reason relations. The Foundation organizes Abant Conventions annually. In 2007, the Abant Convention's theme was Alawis in Turkey.

Worldwide interfaith dialogue is on the agenda of the Gülen movement. In the countries where the followers of Gülen reside, utilizing the concept of *dar al-hizmet* (country of service to humanity), they either establish interfaith organizations, associations, and societies, or they are in close contact with the men of faith. Thus, Turkish businessmen in Korea, for instance, take Buddhist priests to Turkey to visit historical places where believers of different faiths have lived peacefully. Or in Thailand, administrators of Fatih College regularly visit Buddhist authorities and priests and report to them the progress of the Thai pupils. In Russia, Romania, Georgia, South Africa, Senegal, and so on, the theme is the same. They all believe that interfaith and intercultural dialogue is a must to reach a general universal peace (*sulh-u umumi*), and that the first step in establishing it is forgetting the past, ignoring polemical arguments, and giving precedence to common points.

To sum up, when we turn our attention away from the media's favorite post-modern neo-assassins—at least for a while—and look at what the overwhelming majority of Muslim scholars and ordinary Muslims think of plurality, diversity, and peaceful co-existence today, we find that the Ottoman spirit has survived—in Turkey, at the very least—and respect for diversity is still seen as a religious obligation.[55]

VI. Concluding Remarks and Relevance of the Ottoman Experience Today

Despite the claims of uniformity held by legal modernity, in almost all communities a number of modes of normative orderings co-exist with the official law. Local, customary, and ethnic minority laws are some of the major factors that influence and impede the effectiveness of law in modern societies. These factors are the sources of incoherence, multiple legal authorities and interpretations, and local interests and concerns. There is usually a continuous competition between these normative systems for the allegiance of those to whom they are addressed. They also affect the degree of respect for the official lawmaker and are a source of justification for popular resistance. The empirical evidence from the English experience supports the theory of legal pluralism. As we have seen, co-existence of official and unofficial laws in England is an empirical reality. The consequences of the state's culturally-blind non-recognition of this unofficial legal pluralism are not very promising, especially as far as vulnerable members, i.e. women, of ethnic minorities are concerned.

The Ottomans did not enforce a change from above by instrumentalist use of law and respected diversity, even at times of conflict with non-Muslim foreign powers. Thus, many ethnic and religious identities were preserved in Ottoman times, helping to maintain social harmony and peaceful co-existence, despite internal and external difficulties and challenges. This is one of the reasons why the Ottoman State was a soft power, and in the words of Prince Hassan of Jordan (the grandson of Sharif Hussein bin Ali, the emir of Mecca who led the Arab revolt against Ottoman rule in 1916), it was a commonwealth, not an empire.[56]

The Ottoman experience of respecting diversity and peaceful co-existence was, of course, not a utopian Alice in the Wonderland scenario. It had its ups and downs and was not perfect. Yet, evaluated in its own temporal-spatial sphere, we can conclude that the Ottoman system of plurality was more humane than many of its contemporaries. Moreover, as we have seen above, despite the claims of progress, even today's legal systems are still far from perfect.

In today's global village, borders have blurred, different cultures have more frequent and more intense contact with each other, and people and societies consciously or unconsciously interact more and more with each other. In order to maintain social cohesion, social mediation and peaceful co-existence, within the context of cultural, ethnic, and religious divisions, hierarchies, rivalries, and conflicts that are grounded in socio-economic and political realities, have become vital necessities of our time. An appreciation of diversity must stand as a main point of reference, paving the way for inter-cultural dialogue vis-à-vis processes of globalization, migration, and the transnationalization of social relations. In order to achieve this, and to build bridges between different cultures, socially innovative projects should be implemented to tackle the problems stemming from migration—specifically, the emergence of transnational and diaspora communities and their role in (inter)national conflicts—as well as the re-emergence of religious groups and identities, the politi-cization of religion, and the rise of religious fundamentalism, in the context of global geo-political and economic coalitions, and hence new conflicts and wars.

Intercultural dialogue refers to the intensification of worldwide social relations and the multiplicity of linkages and interconnections between the states and societies which make up the modern world system. It can be an instrument for alternative dispute resolution and social mediation and is an important socially innovative method in our age of globalization. In our modern world, where nations, reli-gions, and civilizations are intermingled and intertwined, respect for the Other and peaceful co-existence are vitally needed. The Ottoman experience has fundamental lessons for today's world, which is full of post-modern neo-assassin terrorists and students of the "clash of civilizations" paradigm.

Today, the Ottoman legal system may not be plausible, but at least their acceptance and tolerance of diversity can be emulated. The Ottoman experience of diversity and co-existence indeed has a lot to teach today's dwellers of the post-modern global village, where dialogue, acceptance of the Other, tolerance, respect for justice, international legitimacy, protection of minorities, and the rule of law have unfortunately been the first casualties whenever and wherever there is intercultural tension.

Chapter Five

Christian-Muslim Interaction on the Ottoman Frontier: *Gaza* and Accommodation in Early Ottoman History

by Dr. Linda T. Darling

EUROPEAN MYTHS ABOUT THE SO-CALLED TERRIBLE TURK were based on the assumption of a perpetual enmity and opposition between Islam and Christianity, and thus between Muslims and Christians. Wittek's famous "*gazi* thesis" expressed the same idea, stating that holy war was the key to Ottoman expansion and state building.

Recent discussions of the nature of the early Ottoman state have questioned that notion in the light of much contradictory evidence, seeking to determine whether the idea of *gaza* was predominant, or even present, in the early Ottoman enterprise, and if so, what the term must have meant to contemporaries to leave such contradictory traces in the historical record. This chapter seeks to historicize the concept of *gaza* in the early Ottoman state, a task made difficult by the dearth of contemporary sources and the retelling of the history of the fourteenth century by fifteenth century historians writing in a very different context. Thus, the chapter's conclusions depend less on how the fifteenth century commentators describe the fourteenth century than on the relations between *gaza* and state that the records exhibit.

This examination shows that there was a definite ebb and flow of religious antagonism in the history of Ottoman conquest. This alternation is also observable in Ottoman state policies on the employment of Christians in official positions and the adoption of Byzantine organizational practices. These changes in the nature of the Ottoman conquests can be linked to military and political conditions at different dates. The Christian-Muslim relationship on the frontier was not one of undying religious hatred. Rather, depending on the empire's political circumstances, it alternated between periods of greater religious exclusiveness and periods of greater inclusiveness and incorporation.

The Ottoman Empire has been known throughout its history for its religious toleration. Christians in Reformation Europe, persecuted by the Church, looked to the Ottoman Empire as a refuge and as an example where different religious groups lived together in harmony. For Ottoman Muslims, Christianity and Judaism were legitimate forerunners of their own faith of Islam; Christians and Jews were "people of the book," who were to be protected. While there might be a certain amount of social pressure for them to convert to Islam, Ottoman Christians and Jews were not subject to systematic persecution as heretical Muslims were. They had a legitimate place in society—a secondary place, but a secure one. For that period in history, their disabilities were mild, although such a discriminatory system would not satisfy the needs of today's more egalitarian world.

Nevertheless, Ottoman toleration cannot be taken for granted. For there was another side to the Ottoman reputation: that of the so-called Terrible Turk, whose goal was world conquest, the *gazi* fighter described by the historian Leopold von Ranke, who "knew no native land but the serai, no lord and father but the grand signor, no will but his . . . no occupation but war in his service, no personal purpose unless it were plunder in this life, and in death the paradise thrown open to him who fought for Islam."[1] This view of the Turks and the motivation for their conquests was put on a scholarly footing by Paul Wittek, who sought to show that the early Ottomans were "relentless 'Warriors of the Faith,' continually incited by fanatical darvishes to force Islam upon the inhabitants of the conquered country;" he saw *gaza* as the formative impulse of the Ottoman state.[2] Halil İnalcık moderated this position as he described Turkish tribal warriors, who were pushed westward by the Mongol invasion, finding in the ideology of *gaza* a unifying idea that legitimized their raiding of Byzantine territories.[3]

In recent years, the depiction of the Ottoman Empire as a *gazi* state has been criticized on a number of grounds. The lack of early writings by Ottoman authors and the rarity of fourteenth century documents have created an opening for a variety of new interpretations. The traditional story of the rise of the Ottomans comes from chronicles written in the fifteenth and sixteenth centuries, presumably based on oral tradition. The first few articles rethinking the *gazi* myth, written in the early 1980s, objected to the traditional story on the basis of anomalous evidence from the chronicles themselves, such as the presence of Christians in the Ottoman military forces—particularly Köse Mihal, a Christian knight who reputedly accepted Islam only on his deathbed. Trying to explain what Christians were doing in a holy war for Islam, Cemal Kafadar, in *Between Two Worlds,* described so-called *gazis* who cooperated with Christians, fell in love with Byzantine women, and sponsored the building of churches.[4]

Comparing the chronicles with epic poetry on *gazis* and with religious works and catechisms, he found that *gaza* was presented in different ways in different sources: religious works written by *ulema* defined *gaza* as a matter of Islamic piety and obedience to rules, while epic poems described *gazis* as inclusive warriors, winning over Christians by tolerance and generosity and caring more about knightly bravery than doctrinal orthodoxy or even religious identity.[5] These differing approaches to Islam and conquest were held by different groups in fifteenth century Ottoman society who struggled for power and rewrote their history accordingly; the tension between them was reflected in contradictions between the sources. These tensions were the stuff of Ottoman politics; they lay at the heart of the struggle for power between Cem and Bayezid, for whom the chronicles were written, and that struggle determined the empire's history. For Kafadar, the struggle over how to define and pursue the *gaza*, and not *gaza* itself, was the formative impulse in early Ottoman history.[6]

In *The Nature of the Early Ottoman State,* Heath Lowry asserted that documents and inscriptions testify abundantly to the fact that the title of *gazi* was part of the standard titulature for a Muslim ruler and did not reflect any special Ottoman dedication to *gaza.* The use of this title was not incompatible with the employment of Christians and/or their descendants in the state and army.[7] In fact, an edict of Bayezid II for a *gaza* in the fifteenth century ordered his military agents to recruit non-Muslims first; thus, *gaza* must have meant simply raiding the enemy, not holy war.[8]

Ottoman documents and inscriptions of the fourteenth and fifteenth centuries record Christians and Christian converts among those closest to the ruler; revenue surveys show that Christians became frontier guards, irregular troops, garrison soldiers, and even *timar*-holding cavalrymen—not just occasionally, but in great numbers.[9] And the Ottoman conquest of Constantinople in 1453 should be seen as the incorporation of an imperial capital rather than the Muslim obliteration of a longtime Christian foe. Surviving Byzantine aristocrats were taken into the Ottoman palace and became Ottoman governors, functionaries, and wives; most grand viziers between 1453 and 1516 were from Christian noble families.[10] According to Lowry, this incorporation of the Byzantines shows how far the Ottoman state was from being based on *gaza* or any other purely Islamic concept. Finally, he examined a fifteenth century legend, relayed by an Italian educated in the Ottoman palace, that the Ottoman Empire emerged from an agreement among four lords of northwest Anatolia, two Muslim and two Christian, who elected Osman as their leader and forged a state that, although headed by a Muslim, represented an alliance between Christian and Muslim forces against the faltering Byzantine government in Anatolia on political rather than religious grounds.[11]

This chapter does not try to define *gaza* but to situate it in the broader context of the changing culture of the region. Whatever *gaza* stood for in early Ottoman history, it cannot be explained away; we need to understand how fighting for Islam coexisted or interacted with a more accommodating relationship between Muslim Ottomans and their Christian neighbors. The scholarly disagreement about the meaning of *gaza* hinges on contradictions in the evidence: different definitions and descriptions can be drawn from different sources. Kafadar's expansion of the relevant sources, and even Lowry's, were too narrow; Kafadar used only Turkish sources, and Lowry added Byzantine sources. Feridun Emecen and Şinasi Tekin used texts from other western Anatolian *beyliks* to trace the appearance of the title of *gazi* and the concept of *gaza*, but we must look still further abroad than that.[12] My previous study of earlier Muslim frontiers in Central Asia, India, and Anatolia found that the tensions reported by Kafadar among Ottoman proponents of *gaza* existed on all those frontiers; *gaza* meant different things to different people. Tracing three groups in Muslim society—*ulema, gazi* warriors, and rulers—this study showed that the literature addressed to each conveyed an idea of *gaza* that was consistent over time and space but varied widely from one social group to another. Each group held a different concept of *gaza* and its practices, even although all used the same definition derived from the same sources. Thus, *gaza* could have been a foundational concept in Ottoman legitimation, appealing to a wide variety of people, without there having been any agreement as to what it meant or what it demanded from its participants. The *ulema* seemed most concerned to draw dividing lines on the basis of religion, while oddly enough it was the warriors who often appeared most accommodating.[13]

This chapter will suggest a different resolution to these contradictions, but one that could coexist with the first: that the meaning and intentions of Ottoman warfare changed over time, and that different practices of conquest predominated in different periods of Ottoman history. It will examine the conquest practices of the western Ottoman frontier during the first two centuries in order to track the changing relationship between conquest, *gaza*, and accommodation.[14] The starting point is not the fifteenth century Ottoman chronicles' description of a nomadic Turkish tribe carving out for itself a place on the frontier a century or two prior to their composition, but two fourteenth century Anatolian Persian chronicles' depiction of Seljuk-Ilkhanid frontier society in their own time.[15] These Persian chronicles do not discuss *gaza* against the Byzantines, but they do portray the fourteenth century border tribes as being in much closer contact with the Perso-Islamic administrations of the Seljuks and Mongols than do the Turkish chronicles, which describe them as pure nomads far from the corruptions of civilization. On the contrary, from the Persian chronicles we learn that the tribes had many opportunities to become acquainted with governmental structures and regulations and with imperial paperwork and the literate arts, even if they themselves were not literate. They were in contact with the Seljuk administration and were sometimes given administrative responsibilities within it.[16] They had capital cities, buildings, courts, and scribes. Even if the Ottomans were the most distant from these kinds of interactions, there is no need to think that they were ignorant of them. In fact, we know that during Osman's reign they employed scribes who wrote Persian and that by around 1350 they were translating Persian and Arabic documentary vocabulary into Turkish. A few of their documents, those relating to pious foundations (evkaf), have survived in the form of copies. The picture painted by these sources allows us to reinterpret the information in the Turkish chronicles about the Ottomans' early development and ideology.

The Turkish chronicles describe Osman as nomadizing in the region between Karaca Hisar and Bilecik, between the border principality of Germiyan and the Byzantines. The chronicles state that when the nomads migrated to their summer pastures, they left their gear in storage in Bilecik in exchange for meat and cheese; this shows that the nomads had close relationships with the sedentary population of the region, even those they later conquered. Moreover, the quantity of gear, too much to carry, suggests that these "nomads" were already semi-sedentary.[17] Western Anatolia at that time was a patchwork of Turkish-occupied and Byzantine-occupied locations. The Turkish pastoral nomads were the leading edge of a wave of settlement, while Byzantines from settlements left unprotected or abandoned often turned to pastoralism; pastoralists surrounded the surviving towns.[18] Turks and Byzantines with similar lifestyles must have mingled, and no line separated their territories. Keith Hopwood emphasized the Ottomans' inclusive religious and cultural practices and suggested that in the tumultuous frontier environment, bonds of patronage and protection crossed confessional lines to link Turks and Byzantines, Muslims and Christians. He pointed particularly to Köse Mihal as the *nöker,* the client or bond-companion of Osman. In the article, "The Legend of Osman Gazi," Imber cast doubt on the existence of Köse Mihal as an individual, seeing him rather as an origin myth, but he was quite prepared without additional evidence to acknowledge the existence of unidentified "Christian lords who, like Köse Mihal, fought alongside the Muslims and eventually accepted Islam."[19] Even if Lowry's story of the compact between Muslim and Christian lords in Bithynia is false, it could have been invented to explain an observed level of equality between the Ottoman family and these Christian leaders.[20]

The idea of an initial compact between Christians and Muslims gains support from the fact that inscriptions and documents containing the title of *gazi* only began to proliferate in the 1330s, after Osman's death, suggesting a growing Islamization among the Ottomans after Osman's lifetime.[21] This Islamization was doubtless propelled by conversions and the influx of personnel from elsewhere in Anatolia; as soon as the Ottomans began making their conquests, they also began attracting volunteers to their cause. They also co-opted or displaced Byzantines in Anatolia who now had no livelihood but campaigning along with them, which must in turn have slowed the Islamization process. The state that Osman forged, although headed by a Muslim, was more of an alliance between Christian and Muslim forces than either a *gazi* army or a tribe.

The stories of Osman's conquests certainly demonstrate the inclusive nature of his warfare, as he incorporated conquered areas and people into his endeavor to replace the Byzantines as the main political authority in northwest Anatolia. Aşıkpaşazâde reports that Osman protected the first towns he conquered so well that they became more prosperous than before, and Greeks and Turks migrated there in order to live under his rule. We refer to Christians as "the conquered people," but numerous villages, towns, and individuals joined the Ottomans voluntarily, without conquest. Their Byzantine defenders had retreated out of the region, and the Turks easily reverted to their non-military occupations and became neighbors. İnalcık saw the conquest of towns in 1299 as the turning point in Osman's career from the leader of a band of warriors to the ruler of a territory with sedentary subjects. This divide between rulers and subjects was not a divide between Muslims and Christians, as it is often represented; the ruling military and the subjects alike included both Christians and Muslims, and several stories in the chronicles reflect outsiders' surprise at the amicable relations between the two groups.

The chroniclers, writing many years later, laid an Islamic gloss over all of early Ottoman history, but their image of pure Turkish Muslims does not hold up even before their own evidence. Aşıkpaşazâde tells of Osman, when asked about farming the market taxes of a newly conquered town, not knowing what a market tax was. This story was obviously exaggerated in order to make an ideological point about Osman's purity and piety, but it does not reflect who the Ottomans really were.

First, they were much more sophisticated than the story implies; their relations with Bilecik show that they were acquainted with normal commercial behavior and, from the tale of its conquest by warriors hidden in baskets of goods, with its tricks.[22] And as the Persian chronicles showed, the tribes of the frontier were generally in a position to be quite familiar with the administrative practices of the thirteenth century Seljuks and Ilkhanids. Lowry also notes the presence of a eunuch at Osman's court and a slave commander, formerly a Christian, in his army; the use of eunuchs and slave administrators indicates a certain level of courtly sophistication, at least in Osman's later years.[23]

But second, Osman's exclusivist Islamic piety in this story cannot be taken literally. Aşıkpaşazâde placed the story of the market tax immediately after the story of Osman's establishing the Friday sermon in his own name and entitled it "Osman Gazi Makes Known His *Kanun* and *Ahkam*," making the story part of his historical support for claims of Osman's independence as a ruler. Neşri, in the same place in his narrative, put a story of Osman protecting a Christian merchant of Bilecik from a Germiyanid warrior taking his goods without payment, a story that emphasized Osman's governing ability and protection of non-Muslims as qualifications for rule.[24]

Orhan's reign, in direct contrast to Osman's, presents abundant evidence that he considered himself a *gazi* and a Muslim ruler. Inscriptions on mosques and tombstones from the 1330s and after call him "Orhan Gazi son of Osman Gazi;" the construction of Islamic buildings enhanced Muslim worship and identity and attracted religious personnel from the surrounding lands; and the dedication of *evkaf* to sufis and Sufi lodges on the frontier established an Islamic presence in the newly conquered lands and documented the Islamic titles Orhan gave himself.[25] However, he also recruited foot soldiers from the countryside in the 1320s, and peasant youths, presumably Christians, offered bribes to be enrolled in the troop.[26] The army was no longer just a band of mounted companions living off nomadism and booty; it was becoming diversified. Cavalry commanders and groups of foot soldiers were awarded *timars* for their support, necessitating a bigger administration and new revenue sources.[27]

Christians and Muslims together operated the Ottoman tax system, an amalgam of the Seljuk and Byzantine systems. By founding mosques and schools, Orhan employed educated men from elsewhere and also began training his own administrative cadre and lower-level religious functionaries (top-level *ulema* were still trained in Cairo and elsewhere until Mehmed the Conqueror's reign). Surviving documents written after 1360 are much more complex than earlier examples and appear from their Turkish translations to have been written originally in Arabic, which argues for Islamically trained personnel as well as expanded administrative capability.[28] Over the course of Orhan's reign, it may have gotten harder to enter the governing cadre if you were not Muslim. While there were still numerous Christians contributing to the Ottoman conquests, this might have been the beginning of their subordination and demands for conversion; Köse Mihal's children, as far as we know, were all Muslims.

On the other hand, Orhan married a Byzantine princess and allied himself closely with the Byzantine Cantacuzenos family and with the Genoese of Galata, on whose behalf he was certainly not fighting for

Islam. During his reign in particular, the Ottomans served as mercenaries for the Byzantines, which is how they first entered Europe. Only after 1354 did they begin to make conquests in Europe for themselves. This evidence all speaks to a gradual Islamizing of the conquests and of the fledgling empire itself.

Although the ruler still led the army in the field, his interests began to diverge from theirs, and the army's interests from those of the general population. This division of interests becomes visible in Murad I's reign, during which the Ottomans made conquests in both Europe and Asia. The military forces in Rumeli were separate from the population in a way they had not been in Anatolia. The Anatolian population was extremely mixed: for several centuries, Greeks and Turks had lived together, fought with and against one another, shared lifestyles, intermarried and seen their ruling families intermarry. By Osman's time the Anatolians do not seem to have cared who ruled them as long as they were protected and safe, taxes were reasonable, and they were left alone in their religion.

To the European Byzantines, however, the Ottomans were an army of foreigners, and this division heightened the religious aspect of the confrontation, despite the fact that some of the conquerors were Christians. Peacetime occupations were a thing of the past; as the frontier expanded, the conquerors did not settle down but brought in Anatolian settlers to populate the towns and establish mosques, baths, and other institutions of Islamic civilization new to the Europeans. There was a clear distinction between the army and the general population that had not existed in Osman's early days. The chronicles place in Murad's reign the institution of the *pençik;* that story may symbolize a more wholesale adoption of Islamic regulations at this time. His *vakfiyes* reveal a level of complexity and a variety of personnel unknown even in the 1350s under Osman.[29] This period also saw the translation of standard Islamic literature, both religious texts and poetic or practical literature, increasing the Ottomans' connection with classical Islamic civilization.

Moreover, the army in Rumeli was more autonomous than before; Murad at this time designated the first Ottoman *kazasker,* who went on campaigns with the army. Frontier beys had been appointed to command the forces on the borders, and Murad left them to push the front forward while he took care of affairs in Anatolia. While he did so, Amadeo of Savoy captured the port of Gallipoli, and from 1366 to 1376 Murad may have been prevented from crossing from Anatolia to rejoin the army. At least, the chronicles do not record any deeds of his in Europe during this period.[30]

In Murad's absence, leadership would have fallen to the frontier beys, cited in the chronicles as responsible for the conquests of this period, and to the Sufi sheikhs who accompanied the army. Neither group had the legitimacy that Murad enjoyed. To unite the army behind them, they may have appealed to a more exclusive or popular concept of *gaza*, as the fight became more clearly one of Muslims versus Christians. Segments of the army seem always to have held a less accommodationist view of the conquest than Osman and Orhan. The Ottoman forces that captured the archbishop Gregory Palamas in 1354, for example, told him their victory proved that Islam was the true religion.[31] Studies of conversion suggest that if the military was filled with converts, it would certainly have been more zealous and exclusionary.[32]

After mid-century, many people, both in Ottoman territory and outside it, saw the conquest in terms of rivalry between Christianity and Islam. Thus, it may have been in Murad's reign that the Ottoman military generated the stereotype among Europeans of fanatical *gazis* galloping over the hill. Or, as the army became more substantially Muslim with increased migration from Anatolia, it may simply have been that its religious leaders could finally press the orthodox concept of *gaza*. We do not know what happened when the sultan and the army were reunited. Did Murad find a new and more zealous ethos among his men? Did he have to adapt to the army's values to retain his prestige as its commander? The chronicles represent the sultans as following the advice of the *ulema* with regard to the imposition of traditional Islamic practices, and since no complaints or rebellions ensued, we can imagine the army as satisfied by Murad's compliance with Islamic tradition.

The same could not be said about Bayezid I. Although he made conquests, battled Crusaders, and besieged Constantinople, Bayezid

also took a Serbian wife, employed Christian advisors, and introduced Byzantine court practices and sophisticated administrative
techniques. Further, he made war on the other Anatolian beyliks.
Clearly, he was not interested in turning the empire into a purely
Muslim enterprise or a standard-bearer for the faith. Earlier generations may have tolerated this attitude or even shared it, but his
own followers found it unacceptable and refused to support him
against the invasion of Timur in 1402. The Ottoman conquest,
begun as a joint Muslim-Christian enterprise, was clearly no longer
that—now it was a Muslim enterprise that could be tainted by too
close association with Christians. Writers at the beginning of the
fifteenth century—the poet Ahmedi, an anonymous chronicler, and
Yahşi Fakih—all held that it was Bayezid's accommodations with
Christians that caused him to lose God's support and fall to Timur.
These writers presented the entire fourteenth century as a period of
gaza, with Osman as the primary *gazi* hero, a rebuke to Bayezid and
a warning to his successors—and it was their version of history that
became the standard one.

Mehmed I and Murad II were careful not to disturb the popular
notion of the Ottomans as *gazis* for Islam, a notion shared even by
Timur. Although both sultans leaned for success on the continuation
of Bayezid's sophisticated administrative techniques, neither pointed
to them for legitimation purposes, preferring to legitimize themselves as *gazis*. Now, however, they waged *gaza* with a regular army
rather than a warrior band, taming and disciplining the *gazi* impulse
to harness it to the purposes of the state. This *gazi* ideology was not
uncontested; to win over the Balkan peoples, the Ottomans accepted
them into the military without conversion. In some places up to fifty
percent of the *timar* holders and / or all of the garrison forces were
Christian, although they often converted to Islam in the next generation.[33] There were also popular preachers calling for unity, or at least
sympathy, between Christianity and Islam.[34] Mehmed I's credentials
as a warrior were excellent, but he also restored Bayezid's administrative system, awarding *timars* to his followers and having the Ilkhanid
finance manual *Kitab-ı Saadet* recopied in 1412 for his developing
finance administration.[35] Mehmed's institutions—the *gazi* army, the

tımar system, and the bureaucracy—were a far cry from the frontier tribal *gazis* of the chronicles, and one could say that in this period the term *gaza* began to shift its reference from irregular border raiding to the warfare of an Islamic state.

Murad II had greater difficulty than Mehmed I in establishing himself as a *gazi*; he did go on campaign and made conquests, and a book was written about his exploits that called them *gaza*,[36] but in later life, at least, he was more interested in religion than warfare and was a great literary patron besides. He also developed the Ottoman administration beyond its earlier level; *tımar* surveys made during his reign produced the oldest surviving Ottoman finance documents, and the first original secretarial handbooks in Turkish were written for his scribes.[37] Murad made peace with his opponents and resigned the sultanate in favor of his young son Mehmed but was called back to the throne to save the empire from the Crusaders at Varna. In one sense the Ottoman capture of Constantinople in 1453 was the culmination of the religious confrontations that the empire had already faced in the Crusades of Nicopolis and Varna.

In another sense, however, that conquest was an end to confrontation, at least within the empire, and the beginning of a period, perhaps the Ottomans' greatest period, of accommodation. The conquest of Constantinople is usually presented as the Muslim capture of the Christian capital, and it was, but it was also the reuniting of the former Byzantine lands with their capital city, a conquest devoid of religious motivation. Mehmed was well aware that the largest and wealthiest part of the empire was in Europe and over half the population was not Muslim, and his conquests were intended, among other things, to regain all the lands that had once been ruled from Constantinople.

To raise funds for his conquests, Mehmed retrieved all state lands not properly awarded; unfortunately, these included the lands of the early conquerors, the frontier *gazis* and Sufi orders.[38] He resettled his new/old capital of Istanbul with Muslims, Christians, and Jews as a microcosm of his empire, giving them empty houses, building mosques and converting some church buildings, but authorizing churches and synagogues as well.[39] He patronized both Greek and

Persian literature and art and brought Italian artists to his court. Ottoman miniature painting began to develop, with Byzantine and Persian precedents and a lesser influence from the Italians. Byzantine scholars became Ottoman subjects and wrote histories of Mehmed and his times, and Greek musicians played at his court.[40] Mehmed staffed his administration with converts, many of them from the Byzantine and Balkan royal families. Unconverted Christians, while tolerated, could no longer attain the high positions they had held in Osman's day.[41]

Bayezid II renounced his father's inclusiveness by popular demand; once again the Islam of the people seems to have been more exclusive than that of the rulers. The "people" in this case were the military and political forces that had supported Bayezid for the sultanate against his brother Cem. Defeated in the conflict for the throne, Cem escaped to the West and became a hostage to Bayezid's good behavior. Bayezid was therefore unable to win his spurs on the western front until after Cem died, and he was never given the title of *gazi*. To reinforce his Islamic credentials in other ways, he returned the lands confiscated by his father (though not always to those from whom they had been taken), and he sold off his father's Italian artworks and devoted himself to the culture of the Timurids, whose "fifteenth century renaissance" was then in full bloom.[42] Both he and Selim I distanced themselves from the inclusiveness of Mehmed's reign, moving gradually toward a more orthodox Islamic position. Bayezid's religious patronage was devoted to the more orthodox Sufi orders, and Selim favored Sunni Islam of the non-mystical type. Throughout the sixteenth century, nevertheless, rulers were conscious of the need to appeal to the broad spectrum of their subjects. They did so largely through the prism of justice, the idea that the ruler was the arbiter between all his varied subjects, dispensing justice to anyone who petitioned to him.

The picture of the empire as a *gazi* state throughout its history comes from the chroniclers of the fifteenth century. Those writing in Bayezid II's time copied the *gazi* narrative from earlier works, finding it useful as a commentary on Bayezid's political circumstances. They used the image of the great *gazi* sultans of the past to critique

Mehmed's confiscation of the lands of the *gazis* and to lobby Bayezid for their return on the grounds of Islamic concepts of property and the greatness of the *gazis*.[43] To prove that his respect for *gaza* was equal to Cem's, Bayezid was compelled to go along, even though it was to the state's financial disadvantage to return the land revenues. The fact that early Ottoman *gazis* appeared in all the most important chronicles made it appear to be a historical fact, and thus it became part of Ottoman identity, employed in numerous inscriptions and documents.[44] Much later it became part of Republican Turkish identity, crystallized by the award of the title of *gazi* to Mustafa Kemal Ataturk, national hero and fighter against invaders from the West, despite his secular outlook.

The remarkable thing is that an obviously Muslim polity formed by conquest saw itself so strongly as an amalgam of Muslims, Christians, and Jews held together by justice. This reexamination of its early history suggests that it saw itself that way because it originated that way. The initial conquests were made by a combination of Muslims and Christians seeking to gain wealth and territory and political authority, not to spread Islam or even Islamic dominion. Gradually, the dominance of Muslims in this combination became apparent, spurred by the general Crusading context in the eastern Mediterranean, the historical role of the Turks as fighters for Muslim empires, the makeup of the population on the border, and the zeal of some of the fighting forces, especially converts. The confrontational ideology of *gaza* appeared on the popular level, rather than coming from the rulers, who always seemed less enthusiastic about it than the army. Chroniclers supporting the army against the ruler painted a history of *gaza* in order to chide a sultan unsympathetic toward the *gazis*. Thus, the ideology of *gaza* appears as an overlay on an empire founded for other reasons.

The fifteenth century Ottoman sultans apparently went along with the "*gazi* spirit" in order to retain their legitimacy, but they attempted to control it by administration or divert it to the frontier, and they retained a more egalitarian policy at the heart of the empire. The tension between that ideology and those other reasons was a formative element in early Ottoman development, and it continued to shape relations between Ottoman rulers and their subjects over time. It also created a historiographical tension between the Ottomans and the West; while the Ottomans saw themselves as accommodating toward non-Muslims, the West confronted the zeal of the army and interpreted Ottoman religious policies accordingly. Contradictions in the Ottomans' reputation between East and West can thus be explained by changes over time in the role of *gaza* in the Ottoman state.

Chapter Six

The Role of Ottoman law in the Establishment of Pax Ottomana

by Dr. M. Akif Aydın

I WOULD LIKE TO BEGIN WITH THE FOLLOWING QUESTION in order to provide a framework for the views and arguments presented in this chapter:

Is it possible for us to talk about the existence of a Pax Ottomana throughout Ottoman history?

As it is widely known, the Ottoman state emerged in Western Anatolia, expanded its borders geographically at the crossroads of three continents and succeeded in surviving for 625 years.

Although the founding group of the state was a Turkish clan which migrated from Central Asia to the West over time, other Turkish clans joined this principality and after the short period of its emergence, the Ottoman State gained a demographic variety. By crossing into Thrace, Ottoman soldiers first connected the Greco Byzantine people to their empire, then the Bulgarians, Serbians, Greeks, and Albanians. They spread out in equal or even less time than it took to widen the Empire in Anatolia. Although some Serbians, Croats, and Bulgarians (to be known as Bosniaks and Pomaks) and most of the Albanians converted to Islam, some preferred to retain their Christianity. In fact, Christian elements such as the Greek, Armenian and Syrian Orthodox Churches were known to have existed before the Ottomans in Anatolia. These elements, which could be called the "Other" as far as religious affiliation and cultural identity are concerned, continued to exist firmly in the Ottoman state. The Jews who lived in the newly conquered lands (Anatolia and Rumalia) as well as those who emigrated from Spain later also added to this diversity.

On the other hand, towards the end of its expansion in Anatolia, different nations from non-Turkish Muslim origins, such as the Arabs and the Kurds, entered under the Ottoman administration. Thus, in the 16th and 17th centuries, we encounter a state which expanded over a wide expanse of land with a people composed of a very complex array of religions, languages, ethnicities, and cultures. The survival and continuation of the Ottoman state for six centuries with this variety of characteristics indicates the existence of a Pax Ottomana in this region. It was not easily obtained and did not arbitrarily emerge. In my opinion, the Pax Ottomana was achieved through the implementation of a merger of political, legal, social and economical aspects through multi-directional projects. In this chapter, I would like to examine one of the very important dimensions of these projects—Ottoman law.

Today, in social and political science literature, the concept of the "Other" is frequently mentioned and highlighted, and the position of the "Other" is taken into consideration in terms of social, legal and psychological points. The Ottoman experience is significant in showing how the position of the "Other" was considered and how rules were applied in Islamic countries in the past. Analysis of the legal dimension is expected to provide an answer to the question mentioned at the beginning of the chapter.

Paul Wittek writes that the emergence of the Ottoman Empire was in large part due to the ideology of *gaza*—that the commitment of the Ottoman conquerors was linked to their ideology of holy war in the name of Islam.[1] Although *gaza* was not the only factor in the Ottoman expansion, it played a considerable role as an ideologically mobilizing force in motivating early founders of the Ottoman state to expand towards Europe instead of Anatolia where people of their own religion and race lived. During and after these conquests, the legal, social and economic policies of the Ottomans played an important role in the weak resistance of the local powers in the Balkan Peninsula to the Ottoman army and administration.

The policy towards local people and their former feudal leaders was very striking and therefore must be taken into consideration. After the conquest of the Balkan region, the Ottomans employed primarily former local leaders as their new administrators. We know there were many Christian military administrators (*tımarlı sipahi*) in the 15th and 16th centuries in the Balkans. As Halil İnalcık rightly points out, there was no requirement or compulsion to convert to Islam to be accepted into the military administrative hierarchy.[2] However, some or most of those who joined the military ranks voluntarily converted to Islam anyway. Protection of the local leaders, their positions, and some of their privileges under the Ottoman administration in the Balkans became an effective tool in the conquest of some castles and fortress without a serious resistance to the Ottoman army.

As far as the Balkans are concerned, I should mention another factor that helped the Ottomans expand and dominate in the area for centuries without any significant problems. In the formative period of the Ottoman state, as a result of the weakening of Byzantium, the Orthodox Christians were left without protection—not from the Ottomans or Muslims, but from the Roman Catholic Christians who had hostile feelings towards Orthodox Christians. The memory of the destruction caused by Catholic soldiers in the Balkans and in Istanbul during the crusades was still very alive.

Moreover, the crusaders established in the Balkans feudal state, notably in the south, which oppressed the peasant far worse than the old Byzantine system. Therefore, the efforts of the emperor of Byzantium to approach the Roman Catholic Papacy in order to save the state when the risk of Turkish conquest became eminent were not approved of by the Orthodox people. The expansion of the Ottomans in the Balkans without considerable resistance was to some extent due to this fact. In other words, for many Orthodox notables in the Balkans, Ottoman rule was preferable to Catholic administration.[3] Let us remember the famous saying:

"We prefer the Muslim turban to Catholic headgear."

While the Ottoman state pursued a soft policy towards local administrators and granted them some privileges, it also ensured the protection of common people under these administrators. For instance, the Ottomans either considerably mitigated the forced labor that the peasants of the Balkans had been required to carry out for their feudal leaders or, in some cases, completely removed it. In the *kanunnames* (corpus juris), it was explicitly written which services and duties were to be performed for the military administrators, i.e. *tımar* holders.[4] These duties were indeed very easy compared to those that were previously required of the peasants.

Additionally, the ratio of the land tax was reduced, and in order to avoid arbitrary tax levying and collection, rules concerning these processes were determined in the *kanunnames* so that the abuse of the military administrators, Muslims or Christians, would be prevented. Likewise, the arbitrarily implemented punitive authority of the feudal leaders which existed in the past was limited as well; in the *kanunnames,* the crimes and the due punishments were explicitly declared. We should add that the main purpose of editing the *kanunnames* was not to announce to the administrators the legal rules to be applied, but to inform the common people about the rules which were to be applied to them in fiscal and criminal matters. In the foreword of some *kanunnames* this was clearly declared. For instance, in the introduction of the *kanunname* of Sultan Mehmed the Second for the Register of the province, it was briefly said:

> Especially because of abundant oppression occurred for the *reaya* (common people) by confiscating their goods contrary to the register and the accepted kanun and because of numerous accusations took place between the people and the military administrators of *tımar*, i.e. *tımar* holders and in order to know the number of the taxpayers and amount of the tax, I ordered a trustworthy official and a secretary to be sent to each province to record all the taxpayers, rich or poor, and not to leave anyone outside the register.[5]

It is noteworthy that when the arbitrariness of the military administrators was augmented, the first expedient which people resorted to was the request of a *kanunname* from the central government dealing with the legal and fiscal rules to be applied to them. It was said in the *kanunname* of Semendire of 1526 AD / 922 AH:

> Previously, people of Semendire and others came to my threshold and said that the military commander of *sancak* (subdivision of the province) and the *vaivodes* excessively wanted from us by force some goods such as barley, wheat and fodder contrary to the old *kanun* (law) on the pretext that they had been taken since the old time. Moreover, the military commanders and their assistants intimidated, bothered, and slandered the people in multiple ways. People complained of the oppression and were so sad that I was not happy and did not consent to the occurrence of such a thing, with people behaving contrary to Sharia and *kanun* under my administration full of justice. Therefore I ordered that. . . .[6]

The *kanunname* of Kefelonya from the period of Bayezid the Second began in this way:

> "The *ferman* (edict) should be written that the people of Kefelonca island who sent an envoy and complained about the local officials and the others, and because they wanted to be sent a *kanunname* I ordered that..."[7]

On the other hand, the Ottoman administration was very keen on preventing the military officials from punishing anybody arbitrarily without a court decision, and therefore made a great effort to prevent arbitrary governance. In the *yasakname* of Tuzla of Bayezid the Second, it was said:

> Whoever opposes my *kanun,* let my agent catch
> him and bring him to the court and let the judge
> scrutinize according to the noble Sharia. If they are
> proved to have behaved contrary to my order, let
> them be punished through my agent with the deci-
> sion of the *kadi.* But without a court decision let
> my agent not punish anybody.[8]

Thus, the Ottoman state did not consider *kadis* to be responsible
for the judgment of the cases which came before them and to be the
only authorities in charge, but it accepted them as inspectors for the
arbitrary behavior of the local rulers to some extent. In a general
kanunname of Bayezid II (Kitâb-ı Kavânîn-i Örfiye-i Osmânî) it was
said:

> Thereafter let them implement aoccording to the
> mentioned codes (kavanin) and not pass over this
> kanun. Whoever rules contrary to this kanun let
> the *kadis* prevent them. And if they were not pre-
> vented let the *kadi* declare them to my noble lodge.
> Otherwise the *kadis* would be responsible.[9]

It is noteworthy here that the persons who the *kadis* are ordered
to prevent from wrongdoing were not the ordinary people, but local
rulers which were called *ehl-i örf.* Here we observe a goal of establishing a state based on the rule of law if we conceptualize this process
with a modern concept. And this goal embraced all of the people,
should they be Muslim or Christian.

It should be pointed out here that the Ottoman statesmen and
scholars exhibited exemplary views and attitudes in the field of religious freedom which may be regarded as examples of good practice
for the present day. At first, this kind of behavior seems to contradict
the concept of *gaza,* i.e. expansion of Islam to non-Muslim areas,
which it was claimed above that the founders of the Ottoman state

had in mind. If the founders were keen on the expansion of Islamic belief, it would make sense for them to coerce the non-Muslims to convert to Islam. For this issue, let us turn to the analysis of Wittek who argued for the *gaza* theory:

> Immediately after the conquests of Brusa and Nicaea, schools of theology (medresses) were erected in these towns. This proves that the ulema had already acquired a strong position in the Ottoman state. The early intervention of the ulema is also important in another way: together with the old Muslim governmental traditions they brought the principle of tolerance towards Christians and Jews which was closely connected with their financial policy, based on the payment of tribute by the non-Muslims in return for their toleration. Thus they exercised a very necessary influence over the Gazi state.[10]

It is well known that the center of Orthodox Christianity passed to the Ottomans' hands after the conquest of Istanbul. Mehmed II appointed Gennadious as the Orthodox and Hovakim as the Gregorian Patriarchs. An imperial edict (*berat*) dealing with the Christians is known to have been given by Mehmed, but this edict did not survive to the present day. However, we have three important contemporary documents dealing with the position of Christians: the commitment to the clergy of Bosnia, the imperial edict given to Genoese Galatians, and a *berat* for the metropolitans. The Ottoman ruler explicitly declared the following in the *berat* for the metropolitans:

> I ordered thereafter that the metropolitans can and should do whatever their religion wanted them to do according to principle of "let them freely do their religious rituals and practices" (*Utrukûhum fîmâ yedînûn*), and let the ministers, fathers and

the other religious officials as well as the metropolitans do whatever they earlier did and let them use
church, vineyard, garden and field as they earlier
used and let them be exempt from the tax such as
avarız (exceptional tax) and the others.[11]

Here, three points are noteworthy. The metropolitans continued
to carry out their religious mission in the same way they did in the
time of the Byzantines. The "vineyard, garden and field" which they
earlier used remained in their possession and use. They became
exempt from some taxes as they earlier were. These rights and privileges granted to them seem to be equal to those given by Christian
rulers, and we have no information that the metropolitans had more
under the Byzantines.[12]

The rights and privileges granted to Christians under the
Byzantine Empire continued to exist. Churches where the congrega-
tion worshipped were protected, the Christian rituals and religious
services were not interfered with, permission for religious and cultural education was given to parents for their children, and they were
even allowed to apply some parts of Church or Jewish law in their
community courts (*cemaat mahkemeleri*) if they so chose. Muslim
lawyers considered the statute personal, i.e. briefly marriage, divorce,
and inheritance, a part of religion and therefore they accepted the
application of Jewish and Church laws in these matters as a kind of
religious freedom. So, the Jews and Christians had the right to apply
to either the Sharia courts or to the community courts. They also had
the liberty of applying their own religious law until the last period of
the Ottoman state.

I should point out here that this legal privilege given by Ottomans
was not part of an international treaty or its application in the
frame of reciprocity among states, but it was completely an internal arrangement of Islamic and Ottoman law. It is based solely on
the recognition of the religious freedom of non-Muslims. Therefore
the application of the community courts was left to the preference
of non-Muslims. If non-Muslims preferred to apply to the normal
Ottoman court in the designated fields of the law, they could, and

during the history of the Ottomans, many Jews and Christians preferred the Ottoman court. The Sharia court records have numerous
examples of this kind of application.

Non-Muslims, like the other Ottoman subjects, applied to the
normal Ottoman courts for conflicts in areas of law other than
personal status. Arguments so far raise the following question:
Did the Ottoman judges discriminate between Muslim and non-
Muslim subjects in their judgment? To put it differently, did the
kadis give their decision in favor of a Muslim when the other party
was a non-Muslim? A statistical research to clarify this matter has
not been made yet as far as I know. However, complaints sent to
the imperial *divan* (*divanı-ı hümayun*) were kept in the *muhimme*
and *şikayet* registers. In these registers, we see almost no complaints
dealing with religious discrimination. Moreover, the patriarchs and
rabbis frequently brought requests and complaints to the sultan and
to the imperial *divan*. There are no records of complaints of *kadi*
discrimination based on favoring Muslims.

Hayim Gerber's view, though it is based on a limited number of
court registers, supports our argument in this matter.[13] He shows that
in cases of conflicts between Muslims and non-Muslims, rich and
powerful people versus poor ones, men versus women, the weaker
ones won the case seventy to seventy-five percent of the time, and
he compares this number with the results of New England's courts
during the same century. We know that the Ottoman central administration was very keen on just judgment for the *reaya*. At this point,
there is no reason to argue that the Ottomans did not follow a similar
policy as far as non-Muslims are concerned. Indeed, we have some
examples indicating that the Ottoman state made efforts to establish
procedures for just judgments for non-Muslims. For instance, the
criminal cases of ministers and rabbis were not heard in the local
courts, but in the imperial *divans*. The main reason behind this kind
of arrangement, as far as I know, was the wish to avoid a one sided
judgment by the *kadis* of the non-Muslim ministers because of their
religious differences.

Finally, we should take into consideration the freedom of religious
and cultural education that the Ottomans granted to non-Muslims

for their children. The Ottomans neither coerced the non-Turkish community to learn and use Turkish instead of their own native language, nor followed a policy to this end. If they had, Christians who lived uninterruptedly for 400-500 years in Rumelia or 700-800 years in Anatolia under the Ottoman administration would have completely, or at least mostly, forgotten their languages and begun using Turkish instead.

It is noteworthy that when the Albanians, Serbians, Bulgarians, and Greeks acquired their independence at the end of the nineteenth century after 400-500 years of living under Ottoman dominion, they became independent with their own language, religion and culture. Let me mention here an elegant answer of a famous Turkish writer and poet, Necip Fazıl Kısakürek, to an Algerian youth who accused the Ottomans of colonialism in French language. As you know, until recent years, Algeria was or is considered to be among the French speaking countries. Kısakürek responded to the youth, "If the Ottomans were colonialists as you claimed, you would have accused us of it in Turkish not in French."

In conclusion, the Ottoman administration and its legal system, with their moderation toward non-Muslim and non-Turkish people, played important roles in the realization of the Pax Ottomana. Let me finish my chapter with the following observation:

When I look at the Balkans and Middle East during the past 80 years and see what has happened to Muslim minorities in this area, I consider the Pax Ottomana an Ottoman romanticism not based on the political reality of today.

Chapter Seven

The Turkish Jews

By Nisya Ishman Allovi

Editor's Note: The term Turkish Jews *is taken from the work of the scholar Naim Güleryüz. See Chapter Seven Notes for more.*

A T MIDNIGHT ON 2 AUGUST, 1492, COLUMBUS's fleet departed from the relatively unknown seaport of Palos, embarking on what would become his most famous expedition to the New World. In the shipping lanes of Cadiz and Seville on this same night, many Sephardic Jews began similar journeys to unknown worlds, but their departures are full of unhappiness: expelled from Spain by the Alhambra Edict of Queen Isabella and King Ferdinand of Spain, these Jews chose to leave their land, property, and belongings rather than abandon their beliefs, traditions, and heritage.[2] Almost no European country accepted these refugees. Even the 120,000 Jews who crossed the border to Portugal were expelled merely four years later.[3] However, in the faraway Ottoman Empire, one ruler extended an immediate welcome to the Sephardim, the persecuted Jews of Spain: this ruler was the Sultan Bayazid II.[4]

Years later, the General Jewish Association of Paris referenced this event in a petition written in 1892 in celebration of the quadcentennial anniversary of the migration of the Sephardim Jews into the Ottoman State. "Expelled from Spain in 1492," it reads, "the Jews have been exposed to misbehaviour in the world. However, they have always been protected by the Ottoman State."[5] The act of humanitarianism commemorated here was consistent with the goodwill traditionally displayed by the Turkish government and people towards those of different creeds, cultures and backgrounds.

In 1992, Turkish Jewry celebrated not only the anniversary of Bayazid II's gracious welcome, but also the remarkable spirit of tolerance and acceptance which has characterized the entire Jewish experience in Turkey. These events which include symposiums, conferences, concerts, exhibitions, books, films, restorations of ancient synagogues, all commemorate the longevity and prosperity of the Jewish community in Anatolia.

As a whole, the celebration aimed to demonstrate the richness and security of life Jews have found in the Ottoman Empire and the Turkish Republic over seven centuries, and to show that it is possible for people of different creeds to live together peacefully under one flag. Turkey is the model to emulate by any nation which finds refugees from the four corners of the world standing at its doors.

Jews in Anatolia

The history of the Jews in Anatolia started many centuries before the migration of Sephardic Jews. Remnants of Jewish settlements from the fourth century BC have been uncovered in the Aegean region. Textual evidence exists from historian Josephus Flavius relating that famous philosopher Aristotle "met Jewish people with whom he had an exchange of views during his trip across Asia Minor."[6] Even earlier traces of ancient synagogue ruins have been found in sites such as Sardis, Miletus, Priene, and Phocee that date from 220 BC. Other remnants of Jewish settlements have been discovered near Bursa, in the southeast, and along the Aegean, Mediterranean, and Black Sea coasts. Further, a bronze column found in Ankara confirms the rights the Emperor Augustus bestowed upon the Jews of Asia Minor.

Jewish communities in Anatolia flourished and continued to prosper throughout the Turkish conquest. When the Ottomans captured Bursa in 1326 and made it their capital, they found a Jewish community oppressed under Byzantine rule.[7] The Jews welcomed the Ottomans as saviors, and Sultan Orhan gave them permission to build the Etz ha-Hayyim (Tree of Life) synagogue, which remained in service until the 1940s.[8]

After the Ottomans established their capital at Edirne in the mid-fourteenth century, Jews from Europe, including Karaites, migrated there. Similarly, Jews expelled from Hungary, France, Sicily, and Bavaria during the fourteenth and fifteenth centuries found refuge in the Ottoman Empire.[9] In the 1420s, Jews from Salonica, then under Venetian control, fled to Edirne.[10] A letter sent by Rabbi Yitzhak Sarfati (Chief Rabbi from Edirne) to Jewish communities in Europe around 1465 "invited his co-religionists to leave the torments they were enduring in Christendom and to seek safety and prosperity in Turkey."[11] When Mehmet II "the Conqueror" took Constantinople in 1453, he encountered an oppressed Romaniote (Byzantine) Jewish community which welcomed him with enthusiasm. He urged them "to ascend the site of the Imperial Throne, to dwell in the best of the land, each beneath his Dine and his fig tree, with silver and with gold, with wealth and with cattle."[12]

In 1492, Sultan Bayezid II ordered the governors of the provinces of the Ottoman Empire "not to refuse the Jews entry or cause them difficulties, but to receive them cordially."[13] The Sultan's offer of refuge gave new hope to the persecuted Sephardim. According to Bernard Lewis, "The Jews were not just permitted to settle in the Ottoman lands, but were encouraged, assisted and sometimes even compelled."[14] In his book *Nomologia o Discuros Legales*, Immanual Aboab features Bayazid II's famous remark that "the Catholic monarch Ferdinand was wrongly considered as wise, since he impoverished Spain by the expulsion of the Jews, and enriched Turkey."[15] The arrival of the Sephardim was a monumental event which altered the structure of the community for both the Jewish refugees and the Muslim Turks.

Turks and Jews in Compromise

Throughout the sixteenth century, an increasing number of European Jews escaping persecution in their native countries settled in the Ottoman Empire. The Jews expelled from the Italian city of Apulia after it fell under Papal control in 1537 and those expelled from Bohemia by King Ferdinand in 1542 found a safe haven in the Ottoman Empire.[16] In March 1556, Sultan Suleiman "The Magnificent" wrote a letter to Pope Paul IV asking for the immediate release of the Ancona Marranos, whom he declared to be Ottoman citizens. The Pope had no alternative but to release them, fearing the Ottoman Empire which had been a "superpower" in those days. By 1477, Jewish households in Istanbul numbered 1,647, representing eleven percent of the total population. Half a century later, 8,070 Jewish houses were listed in the city.[17] In the three hundred years following their expulsion from Spain, the prosperity and creativity of the Ottoman Jews rivalled that of the Golden Age of Spain. Four Turkish cities—Istanbul, Izmir, Safed, and Salonica—became the centers of Sephardic Jewry.[18]

In return, the Sephardic Jews made many significant contributions to the Ottoman Empire. One of the most significant innovations that Jews brought to the Ottoman Empire, for example, was the printing press. In 1493, only one year after their expulsion from Spain, David and Samuel ibn Nahmias established the first Hebrew printing press in Istanbul.[19] In the free air of the Ottoman Empire, Jewish literature flourished. Joseph Caro compiled the Shulhan Arouh. Shlomo ha-Levi Alkabes composed the Lekhah Dodi, a hymn which welcomes the Sabbath according to both Sephardic and Ashkenazi ritual. Jacob Culi began to write the famous MeAm Loez. Rabbi Abraham ben Isaac Assa became known as the father of Judeo-Spanish literature.

The Ottoman Jewry also contributed heavily to the political stability of the state by serving as diplomats, government advisors, ambassadors, tax farmers, financial agents, scribes, international and interregional traders.[20] One famous diplomat, for example, Joseph Nasi the appointed the Duke of Naxos, formerly Portuguese Marrano Joao Miques, gained much influence serving under Selim II (1566-74). Selim II placed so much dependence upon Nasi that when he did fall from the sovereign's favor, the Jewish community suffered such a blow that the event became known as "a degeneration of the Jewish community at large."[21] Another Portuguese Marrano, Alvaro Mendes, was named Duke of Mytylene in return for his diplomatic services to the Sultan. Other important Jewish figures include Salamon ben Nathan Eskenazi who arranged the first diplomatic ties with the British Empire, and Jewish women such as Dona Gracia Mendes Nasi "La Seniora" and Esther Kyra who exercised considerable influence in the Court.[22]

The Jewish population also advanced the medical field in the Ottoman Empire. Jewish doctors gained acknowledgement in the East long before their expulsion from Spain. In the twelfth century, they were hired by Byzantine emperor Manuel I; in the fifteenth, Komneni of Trabzon looked to them for help. In western Anatolia, Jewish doctors served at the Seljukid court in Konya, as well as the courts of the Turkish emirs as early as the fourteenth century.[23]

In the Ottoman Empire, Jewish doctors gained much prominence. The coveted position of *hekimbaşı*, or the chief doctor of the palace, is restricted to one person at a time; this honor was usually given to exceptional Jewish physicians.[24] Excluding the *hekimbaşı*, there is also a group of some forty to sixty physicians forming part of the imperial household; needless to say, the Ottoman Jewry dominated this group also.[25] Furthermore, Ottoman Jews not only coveted prized positions, they also dominated the field, creating dynasties of medical experts.[26] One of the most famous is the Hamon dynasty of Istanbul which began with Joseph Hamon the Elder and his son Moses (in some texts Moshe) Hamon (d. 1554). Joseph Hamon served under Selim I (1512-20) and his son and successor Moses authored a treatise on dentistry in Turkish.[27] This dynasty lasted many successive generations, extending to early eighteenth century.[28] Other notable physicians include Daniel Fonseca, and Gabriel Buenaventura, to name only a few.[29]

Ottoman Jews in the Nineteenth and Twentieth Centuries

On 27 October, 1840, Sultan Abdülmecid issued his famous *ferman* concerning the cases of blood libel in Rhodes and Damascus, saying, "and for the love we bear to our subjects, we cannot permit the Jewish nation, whose innocence for the crime alleged against them is evident, to be worried and tormented as a consequence of accusations which have not the least foundation in truth."[30] A few years later, in 1856, Sultan Abdulmecid accepted a group of Jews affected by the Crimean War. The original document states, "the Jews migrating from Kerc, to Crimea, and applying for taking refuge have been accepted to Ottoman territories on the condition that their rabbi is appointed from among them, for there are differences with the Jews living in the Ottoman state."[31] Once again, this reflects the spirit of tolerance exhibited over the course of Ottoman-Turkish history, but it also shows the Sultan's concern with maintaining peace between groups within the region.

Under Ottoman tradition, each non-Muslim religious community, or millet, was responsible for its own institutions, including schools. While the Turkish government guaranteed protection and freedom of religious practices, each non-Muslim community must pay annual capitation tax.[32] Yet, the Jews were never singled out for persecution simply because of their religion. They experienced material and spiritual impoverishment because of the general decline of the Ottoman Empire; in fact, they usually enjoyed the status of a favored minority.[33]

A petition written in 1892 by the General Jewish Association of Paris regarding the Jews in the Ottoman Empire reflects a special relationship between the millets as autonomous units and the central government. According to the petition:

> Learning the affection of homeland and the Sultan in the Jewish schools supported by the Jewish Association, the children have been trying to complete their education to serve their country on the area of agriculture, commerce, industry, science, and technology. Our Sultan has always been interested in these schools and supporting them.[34]

In the early nineteenth century, Abraham de Camondo established a modern school, "La Escola," causing a serious conflict between conservative and secular rabbis that was only settled by the intervention of Sultan Abdülaziz in 1864. The same year, the Takkanot ha-Kehilla (by-laws of the Jewish Community) was published, defining the structure of the Jewish community.

Efforts to reform the Ottoman Empire led to the proclamation of the Hatt-ı Humayun in 1856, which made all Ottoman citizens, Muslim and non-Muslim alike, equal under the law. As a result, leadership of communities began to shift from religious figures to secular forces.

World War I brought an end to the glory of the Ottoman Empire. In its place rose the young Turkish Republic. Mustafa Kemal Ataturk was elected president, the Caliphate was abolished, and a secular constitution was adopted. By the time the Treaty of Lausanne was signed in 1923, Turkey accorded minority rights to the three principal non-Muslim religious minorities and permitted them to carry on with their own schools, social institutions and foundations. In 1926, on the eve of Turkey's adoption of the Swiss Civil Code, the Jewish Community renounced its minority status on personal rights.[35]

Mustafa Kemal Ataturk and his minister of education, Resit Galip, decided to invite to Turkey hundreds of refugee scholars and scientists, many of them Jews, who had fled Nazi Germany and Austria. These refugees, whose number included many of the most prominent scholars in their fields, made significant contributions to the development of Turkish universities and scientific institutions, as well as to the fine arts and music. For most of the refugee scholars, the Turkish haven, in return, provided an escape from certain death and an opportunity to continue with their professional careers.

During the tragic days of World War II, Turkey managed to maintain its neutrality. As early as 1933, Ataturk and his minister of education, Resit Galip, invited a number of prominent German Jewish professors to flee Nazi Germany and Austria to settle in Turkey.[36] In the years before and during the war, these scholars, whose numbers included many of the most prominent scholars in their fields, contributed a great deal to the development of the Turkish university system.[37] For most of the refugee scholars, Turkey provided an escape from certain death and an opportunity to further their professional careers.[38] While the Jewish communities of nearby Greece were almost completely obliterated by Hitler, the Turkish Jews remained secure. Several Turkish diplomats made every effort to save the Turkish Jews in the Nazi occupied countries from the Holocaust. In many cases, they succeeded.

Because neutral Turkey was valued by both Berlin and Vichy, it was able to assist Jews who were being persecuted throughout Nazi occupied territories. By maintaining diplomatic representation in Germany and most of the occupied countries, Turkish diplomats and consuls intervened on the behalf of Turkish Jews living in those areas. The Turkish embassy in France, located at Vichy starting in 1941, as well as the Turkish consulates-general in Paris and Marseilles worked hard to extricate Jews often at the risk of their own lives.[39] Ambassador to Vichy, Behic Erkın, Consul at Marseilles Necdet Kent, Paris Consul Cevdet Ergin, and Vice Consul of Paris, Namık Kemal Yolga, are just some among a long list of diplomats who worked to rescue Jews during WWII.[40]

These consuls regularly applied to German and French authories to exempt Turkish Jews from the anti-Jewish laws implemented in German occupied countries and the Vichy Government of France by arguing that citizens of Turkey are not persecuted based on their religious practices.[41] Other times, these consulates-generals worked hard to restore former Turkish Jews their citizenships to expediate their departure from Nazi-occupied lands. Sometimes, diplomats even provided false certificates of citizenship to Turkish Jews who were in imminent danger of being deported to labor and concentration cames.

Salahattin Ulkumen, Consul General at Rhodes in 1943-44, was recognized by the Yad Vashem as a Righteous Gentile ("Hassid Umot ha'Olam") in June 1990. Turkey continues to be a shelter and a haven for all those who have to flee dogmatism, intolerance, and persecution.[42]

Jews in Present Day Turkey

The present size of the Turkish Jewish Community estimates at around 25,000. The vast majority of these live in Istanbul, with a community of about 2500 in Izmir and other smaller groups located in Adana, Ankara, Antakya, Bursa, Canakkale, Kirklareli, etc. Sephardim make up ninety-six percent of the community, with Ashkenazim accounting for the rest. There are also less than 100

Karaites, an independent group who does not accept the authority of the Chief Rabbi. Turkish Jews are legally represented, as they have been for many centuries, by the Hahambasi, or the Chief Rabbi. He is assisted by a religious Council made up of five Hahamim. Fifty Lay Counsellors look after the secular affairs of the Community, and an Executive Committee of fourteen runs the daily matters. Representatives of Jewish foundations and institutions meet four times a year as a so-called think tank to exchange opinions on different subjects concerning the Turkish Jewry.

Synagogues are classified as religious foundations *(vakıfs)*. As has been mentioned, leaders of the central government of the Ottoman State have historically had a very respectful attitude toward Jewish places of worship. This is evident in an official document, which was written by Sultan Abdülhamid Han in 1903. The Sultan wrote, "a room has been arranged as a synagogue for Jews living in Darulaceze (Istanbul) until a [permanent] synagogue is built there. Opening ceremony has been carried out reading Tevrat by rabbis. . . . Necessary attention has also been paid to the days of Jews and their foods."[43] Today there are eighteen synagogues in use in Istanbul. Some of them are very old, especially the Ahrida Synagogue in the Balat area, which dates from the middle fifteenth century. The fifteenth and sixteenth century Haskoy and Kuzguncuk cemeteries in Istanbul are still in use today.

Presently, most Jewish children attend state schools or private Turkish or foreign language schools, and many are enrolled in the universities. Additionally, the Community maintains a school complex including elementary and secondary schools for around 700 students in Istanbul. Turkish is the language of instruction, and Hebrew is taught for a few hours a week. While younger Jews speak Turkish as their native language, the over-seventy generation is more at home speaking in French or Judeo-Spanish (Ladino). A conscious effort is spent to preserve the heritage of Judeo-Spanish through mediums such as the Jewish Press.

For many years, Turkish Jews have had their own press. *La Buena Esperansa* and *La Puerta del Oriente* started in Izmir in 1843, and *Or Israel* appeared in Istanbul ten years later. Now only one newspaper survives: *SALOM* (Shalom), a fourteen to sixteen page weekly in Turkish with one page in Judeo-Spanish (Ladino), and a sixteen to twenty page monthly supplement, *El Amaneser*, also in Judeo-Spanish. A Community Calendar (Halila) is published by the Chief Rabbinate every year and distributed free of charge to all those who have paid their dues (Kisba) to the welfare bodies. The Community cannot levy taxes, but can request donations.

Two Jewish hospitals, the 98 bed Or-Ahayim in Istanbul and the 22 bed Karatas Hospital in Izmir, serve the Community. Both cities have homes for the aged (Moshav Zekinim) and several welfare associations to assist the poor, the sick, needy children, and orphans. Social clubs containing libraries, cultural and sports facilities, and discotheques give young people the chance to meet.

The Jewish Community is, of course, a very small group in Turkey today, considering that the total population—ninety-nine percent Muslim—exceeds 70 million. But, in spite of their number, the Jews have distinguished themselves. There are several Jewish professors teaching at the Universities of Istanbul and Ankara, and many Turkish Jews are prominent in business, industry, liberal professions and journalism.

1992 marked the five hundredth year of the gracious welcome of the Sephardim to Turkish lands. Jewish history is full of sad events that are marked by commemorations and memorial services. But with this anniversary, there was a major event to celebrate. Turkish Jews felt it was both fitting and proper to launch an extensive celebration in Turkey, the United States, and Europe, to celebrate both the five hundredth anniversary of the welcoming of the Sephardic Jews to the Ottoman Empire and the five centuries of continuous peaceful life in Turkey that followed.

The Quadcentennial Foundation—500.Yıl Vakfı—was established in Istanbul in 1989 by a group of 113 Turkish citizens, Jews and Muslims alike. The Foundation embarked on a very ambitious program as befit the greatness of the occasion. They planned a three-year (1990-1992) cultural and academic program both within Turkey and abroad—mainly in the U.S., Canada, and Mexico on the American continent, and France, the United Kingdom, and other countries in Europe. What Turkish Jews lack in numbers they make up for in enthusiasm and commitment, and they realized their vision with great ardor. The program was designed to bring the diverse and rich legacy of Turkish Jewry to a greater audience.

The Quincentennial Foundation established the Museum of Turkish Jews (Türk Musevileri Müzesi), the first and only such museum in Turkey.[44] It was inaugurated on November 25th, 2001, in the former Zulfaris Synagogue (Kal Kadosh Galata), situated in the Karakoy district of Istanbul, not far from the Golden Horn shore. There is evidence that the original Zulfaris Synagogue existed as long ago as 1671. However the building which stands today as the current site of the museum was reerected over its original foundations in the early nineteenth century. It is known that in 1856, a ceremony was held at the site of the synagogue commemorating Jewish soldiers who fought alongside the Ottomans against the Russians during the Crimean War. The building went through renovation and repairs in 1890 and again in 1904 and 1968. The last wedding ever performed in the synagogue occurred in 1983, but it was not until 2001 that Zalfuris opened its doors as a museum with the help of financial contributions of the Kamhi family and the dedication of Vice President, Mr.Naim Güleryüz.[45]

President of the Quincentennial Foundation Jak Kamhi says of the history of Turkey and the museum:

> The basic purpose of humanity is to achieve a permanent state of peace for a better world. It is the aim of the Quincentennial Foundation to inform the wider public of the sanctuary that has been offered to the Jews, who have suffered such a painful history, by Turkish and similar societies through values which represent an example to humanity. Further, and through this great example, proof is given that whatever their ethnic or religious affiliations and origins, peoples can live together in harmony.
>
> The agonies that the Jews lived through in the Iberian Peninsula during the 15th Century, and

the subsequent provision of sanctuary to them in the lands of the Ottoman Empire and the Turkish Republic, where they have always been greeted with tolerance, represents one of this phenomenon's most striking examples throughout history.

Indeed, it is a great misfortune that even in recent history, sometimes for economic motivations, Jews have witnessed terrible tyranny and persecution in societies where they had been thought secure. During these times, some of them were saved by the Turks, with their tradition of opening their arms to the oppressed.

It is our hope that the secular and humanistic culture of Turkey, as an example by which to avert the clash of civilisations, may be assimilated by other countries, and that a more harmonious and stable world be left to future generations.

In exhibiting under one roof past and current examples of coexistence in spite of all these differences, as well as the historical and present life of Jews in Turkish lands, the Quincentennial Foundation Jewish Museum of Turkey conveys all this to future generations, and is a means for the expression of gratitude by our Jewish compatriots.

The museum aims to promote the story of 700 years of harmony between Turks and Jews, beginning with the Ottoman conquest of Bursa in 1326, to show how the two cultures have influenced each other throughout the past seven centuries, and to display the humanitarian spirit of the Turkish Nation. In order to achieve this goal, the Museum of Turkish Jews has been the site of many ambitious activities, events, and exhibits, including multi-media presentations of Sephardic wedding photos taken at the Zulfaris synagogue, open air concerts of Sephardic songs, the publication of a 96 page color album of the Museum of Turkish Jews, an exhibition of forty photos entitled *Glimpses of Jewish Life in Ottoman-Turkish Society* and much more. On May 8th, 2006, The Jewish Museum of Turkey was awarded the Civilization Year Reward for the completion of several projects dealing with social issues.[46] Above all, the Museum's mission is to collect, preserve, exhibit, interpret, and disseminate knowledge about the cultural heritage of the Turkish Jews, so that no one can forget that it is possible for people of different faiths to live together in peace.

Chapter Eight

**Ottoman Palimpsests: The Past Reviewed
in Architecture and Literature**

by Dr. Tom Gage

Throughout a history that extends over more than a half millennium, Turkey has prevailed in maintaining a relatively harmonious multicultural society, largely due to an ingenious ability to reorganize itself. Internally, the dynamism among ethnic Turks and minority communities accounts for much of the nation's protean ability to deal with internal and external pressures. This multicultural dynamism is a result of the millet system, unique cultural institutions like the Sultan's Janissaries, and, for the purpose of this paper, modern artistic representation in various media.

Exacting loyalty to the Ottomans, the millet system allowed confessional communities to regulate its members by means of semi-autonomous legislation, taxation, and use of non-Turkish languages. The Janissaries were composed of the fifth sons of Greeks, Armenians, Thracians, Slavs, and Arabs, who were originally enslaved as the Sultan's cooks. However, this platonic corps soon mastered combat, implemented the Sultan's will, and, like Sinan, created many architectural legacies. But, in time, this pillar of national dynamism crumbled when the Janissaries challenged ethnic Turks.[1]

For over a half millennium, external forces have played a role in this relationship between Turks and minorities. Goffman documents the onset of the English faction in competition with other entrepreneurial representatives from fledgling European states, who relied upon dragoman translators in negotiations with the Sublime Porte.[2] Bayly amplifies how the evolution of these competitive states initiated a globalization process that increasingly heightened the interpenetration of economies and linked minorities in Turkey with co-religionists or tribal relations abroad.[3] Before an influx of Spanish gold from the New World inflated Turkish silver during the sixteenth century, the Ottomans with their Janissaries achieved a zenith of power. But, as the Janissaries acquired prestige, ethnic Turks could not join the elite corps, since members were slaves, and Turks could not be enslaved.[4] Gradually, the Janissaries acquired unlimited power and exhibited an arrogant autonomy that eventually destabilized the social order. By expropriating the authority from Turkish tribal leaders, this military unit caused the demise of several sultans. Finally, the corps itself was abolished in the nineteenth century.

Over the centuries, the increasing hegemony of European nation states caused the Ottoman Empire to rely upon its minorities to utilize their linguistic competencies to contribute to Turkish diplomatic mastery. Though modern nationalization destroyed the 800-year old Holy Roman Empire, Turkey endured and, with modifications resulting from accommodations, has continued through to the twenty-first century.

In the early twentieth century when five of these nation states occupied Anatolia, Atatürk conquered and ejected the invading armies, dissolved the Empire, and initiated a nationalism that resulted in a change of status for the Ottoman minorities.[5] He marshaled the unvanquished into a democratic state, based on one language and one ethnic identity, a nation in which women not only voted but seventeen of whom were elected representatives.[6] To acknowledge the traditional heritage of Turkey, Atatürk preserved some of the values and belief systems of the Ottoman Empire while centering the new government in Ankara, mid-Anatolia.

Parenthetically, when I was born, only three democracies existed among the warring nation states of Europe: Turkey, England, and Ireland—and women in France could only vote after 1945. But later, as the Cold War waned, new tensions surfaced, not just in Turkey but globally. The values and belief systems of the Ottoman Empire augur a variation of the important Kemalist past in order to acknowledge the traditional multicultural heritage of Turkey. The problems that confronted Atatürk, challenges similar to ones faced earlier by the Ottomans when the Janissaries revolted, adumbrate issues that today confront the Kemalist heritage. However, some ethnic challenges threaten secession from the national union, opportunistically in the name of human rights.

In today's global economy, artistic representations are a means of ameliorating external and internal tensions and offer a way for Turkey in the twenty-first century to sustain its genius in adapting to changing conditions. This thesis is explicated through the work of two contemporary Turkish artists, the Nobel Laureate Orhan Pamuk and the late Çelik Gülersoy. Renewing Ottoman multiculturalism augurs a most promising resolution of this perennial tension, a restitution assisted by art.

The art of Pamuk and of Gülersoy serve as palimpsests that utilize representations of earlier Ottoman multiculturalism to address current demands of the nation. "Palimpsest" is derived from the word denoting ancient paper. Before the appearance of inexpensive Chinese paper, an author could compose only on expensive animal skins and material made from the pith of papyrus reeds. The ancients bleached and recycled palimpsests many times over. Today, researchers can restore the layered meanings from texts of the past. By metaphorical extension, palimpsests are also buildings and cityscapes, in which the viewer can discern earlier beliefs and structures surfacing through modern facades. In short, Orhan Pamuk and Çelik Gülersoy, through representative literature and buildings, have made visible, accessible, and understandable the dual heritage responsible for Turkey's unique dynamism.

Both artists draw from the Ottoman past, one to cast in literary texts and in architectural transformations a society in which peaceful co-existence among diverse ethnicities, a society in which a pluralistic consciousness prevails. In his novels *My Name is Red,* set in the sixteenth century, and *The White Castle,* set in the seventeenth century, Pamuk restored for readers an understanding of how the Ottomans endured through the help of minorities in dealing with internal and external threats to the Empire. These threats, though fictionalized, are well documented in scholarly research.

My Name is Red

This novel is a drama of voices ventriloquized by a coffee shop *hakawati*, a performing role harkening back to the rhapsodes of Homer, a palimpsest reaching to ancient Anatolia.[7] The speaker of the novel utters a cacophony of voices that center upon a theoretical issue, the purpose of art as representation to sustain memory, the art of painting in particular.

In the tradition of the Qur'an, truth is conveyed by the black ink of the written word on inexpensive paper, a democratic medium accessible to a vast audience. Writing is no frivolous activity, and in this novel the complementing modes of expression, painting and illustrating are no less honorific. The conviction that writing must convey truth is similar to how Dante envisioned the purpose of rhetoric in his *Vita Nuova* and *The Divine Comedy,* an extended analysis recently advanced by Yale's Maria Rosa Menocal in *Writing in Dante's Cult of Truth: From Borges to Boccaccio.*[8] Incidentally, Pamuk opens another novel, *The New Life,* whose title denotes vita nuova, with the lines, "I read a book one day and my whole life was changed." The artist informs truth not as entertainment but to posit the ineffable wisdom of God. In the Ottoman tradition as well as in Dante, the purpose of writing is to convey truth, not to entertain with falsehoods.

One of several of the *hakawati's* personas is Master Osman who heads the studio populated by other voices that also address the reader.[9] Osman believes that the master artist after years of training and practice achieves a style that embodies substantial truth: that God's glories on earth are celebrated by the master painter's documentation of earthly glories. Believing that exposure to trends in painting and illustrations can only corrupt what has been mastered over a lifetime, the master artist conceives that blindness will retain a career of perfecting his craft. A traditional Islamic theme valorizes not facades, semblances, or fashions, but the substance at the heart of phenomena, a theme discernable in painting and poetry.[10] And I will argue below how Çelik Gülersoy renovated architecture to revitalize Ottoman glory.

The blind seeing most clearly and conceptualizing wisdom better than the sighted is a theme one can trace to the shared heritage of West and East, embodied in blind avatars who reveal Truth like the mythic figure Tireisias or the author of *The Iliad* and *The Odyssey,* and, later, in the eleventh century Abu al-Ala al-Mar'ra, the Syrian poet-philosopher or philosopher-poet, who influenced Dante in his creation of *The Comedy,* an analysis that Miguel Asin Palacio extensively advanced in *Islam and the Divine Comedy.*[11]

The setting of the novel, *My Name is Red,* remembers an historic event, when Sultan Murad III, the "Shadow of God on Earth," commissioned Master Osman to compose the *Surname-i Hümayun* or *The Imperial Celebration,* or as referred to in the novel *The Book of Festivities.*[12] The occasion celebrated the circumcision ceremony of Crown Prince Mehmet in 1582. Today this illustrated book is in Istanbul's Topkapi Museum. A historic Master Osman headed the studio of painters and illustrators that provided Pamuk with his cluster of artists that form a vertical axis for the novel: the fictional Osman, the murder victim Eniste Effendi, Butterfly, Black, Stork, and Olive, who was based on the historic figure Velican, one of Master Osman's painters.

The Surname is made up of text and 500 miniature illustrations of 250 processional scenes viewed from the east of a pageantry marching down the ancient Hippodrome of Constantine. Each scene depicts what the Sultan's subjects provided the Ottoman Empire. This setting incidentally includes points of interest to any visitor today walking down the public park that was once the Roman circus: the Obelisk of Theodosius, the palace of Ibrahim Pasha, the New Obelisk, and the Serpentine Column. Framed between the Aya Sofya and the Mosque of Sultan Ahmet, each of these embodies symbols in a palimpsest of a past, with the renovations of the late Çelik Gülersoy like the Aya Sofya Pensions abutting Topkapi and the Otel Konak on the adjacent street, architectural texts that will be addressed below. The novel's setting celebrated in *The Surname* and in Gülersoy's renovations imbricate Western humanism, Ottoman glory, and multiculturism that ameliorate tensions of today.

Marching north to south across the pages of *The Surname* down the Hippodrome are those who provide the Sultan with his splendor and who, four centuries later, provide Pamuk with prototypes for characters. Pamuk chooses from the array of marching representatives that permeate the horizontal axis of the plot, the love affair and the social frame: cloth peddlers, soldiers, athletes, bakers, janissaries, raw-wool tradesmen, trainers with their dogs, illusionists, horses, felt-makers, musicians and pyrotechnics, archery instructors, Jewish merchants from Galata, Greek bakers, sugar-dealers, sherbet-makers, dervishes of different orders, imams, Sufis, herbalists, Moroccan leather dealers, calligraphers, silk-printers, Simurg-kite flyers, coin-catchers, Qur'anic scholars, prisoners of debt, veiled and unveiled women, and a coffeehouse on wheels. This last float is a metonymy of coffee houses, like the den of iniquity in which the novel's hakawati rehearses narratives of war, satire, and bawdry, where congregate secularists, prostitutes, artisans, and activists.

The title of the novel reveals the hakawati who ventriloquized voices of the principal characters. In this café Pamuk's doppelganger hakawati has animate and inanimate subjects speak to the reader as records of what is and has been happening rather than as reports of what happened. Pamuk's dramatic monologues remind the reader of Faulkner's *As I Lay Dying*, a novel that also covers the action of approximately a week.[13] In both novels the reader encounters a sequence of utterances, not narratives but dramatic monologues that address the reader as if the action is happening rather than having just happened. Faulkner and Pamuk employ mortals speaking, both living and dead, but Pamuk adds non-human life, a painting of a dog and a tree in sketches on the wall, and non-sensate objects, a coin and the color red, all voicing instantaneously what is happening. This ensemble makes for challenging reading. Pamuk's original title was *Love at First Sight*, a title that provides some insight into his thesis, the nature of art. In the Islamic tradition that scorns facades, one doesn't fall in love at first sight if the initial encounter is a representation of the beloved, a painting. There is an ancient tale from Persia that reports of a heroine falling in love with the picture of a beloved found hanging on the branch of a tree but love blossoms only after encountering that picture a third time.

Representation in miniature paintings is stylized in a manner of representing the generic, not the particular. Western painting conveys a realism that makes the title *Love at First* implausible for one from the East, plausible more likely for one from the West. The historical Master Osman served three sultans during a zenith of Ottoman history. In the preceding century, Western art of the Renaissance had made some impact on Ottoman sensibilities, resulting from the Conqueror inviting Gentile Bellini from Venice to his new capitol to paint himself and his subjects. Like today, Istanbul was pivotally east-west; Master Osman, in the novel and in fact, negotiated between Islamic traditions and a new style of art from the West: art negotiating external and internal impingements. This site in Istanbul remains pivotal today for visitors to Istanbul and augurs how Turkey can assuage global tensions through art and fellowship.

Some of the artists in Pamuk's studio worry that others are on the verge of following the Italians in violating the taboo of the second commandment, a violation that will cause conflict and eventually does cause the destruction of the coffeehouse. But even among the hakawati's community there are those present, like the murder victim, the voice opening the novel, whose loyalties belonged to Islam not his craft community. His murderer is more aligned to the secular west. The characters of Black, the Jewess, and Shekure are voiced-witnesses recording the drama happening, without the advantage of knowing what will happen at the end of the episode, like actors in the theater who cannot know what the audience often knows.

In one of his utterances Master Osman elaborates his theory of art. Among the sequestered trove of horded art in the Sultan's treasury of the Topkapi, he is studying works from many traditions and styles—Chinese, Persian, Indian, Venetian, as well as Ottoman. The mentor of painters peruses treasures and deliberates about blindness. He accounts fables and histories of earlier miniature illustrations, while ruminating upon how art embodies Truth. Regarding the intrusive new art from the West, Osman differentiates that in Islam meaning precedes form in painting, while in the West form precedes meaning.[14]

Osman first is aroused by the beauty of drawings of youths in gardens, of curvaceous arms, of horses, and flowers, all that Allah has given this world for human consumption and that He has created as glorious subjects to be painted by the greatest artists. But for the truly great artist who has mastered technique and style, to view the object in real life, or as rendered by another's eyesight, jeopardizes one's own comprehension of Truth derived over years of faith and practice, thus possibly eroding what God has blessed one's genius. Better at life's end to blind oneself and to spend the rest of days on earth remembering facets of that Truth.

Master Osman strikes at the heart of a seemingly Platonic reality, in contrast to Ester the Jew, whose ruminations provide contrasting views. As Master Osman and his painters represent a vertical axis over lorded by the Sultan, Ester the Jew represents a position along the horizontal axis linking both genders, members of the family, and the inhabitants of the coffeehouse. The two characters deliberate on how one garners meaning from text. Ester is illiterate but deliberates about how very much, in spite of being illiterate, she "reads." She cannot transcribe into meaning the written code, as denoted in the translation from Arabic of Qur'an "to read / recite," but as the one carrying mail between Black and Shekure, she finds deep insights from fragrances sprinkled upon the letter, insights in what she detects as incongruities between what Shekure says and means, and insights from how the missive is fondled. Such contextual signs convincingly argue that not being able to decipher script is but another aspect of one comprehending a social act. Ester values the contexts and trappings, more in the tradition of McLuhan's credo that the media is the message. Acknowledging the influence of sufism on his art, Pamuk has populated this work with many voluble, figuratively and literally blinded, characters monologuing about the essence of the elephant.

The White Castle

Set a century later, Pamuk's *The White Castle* layers another text of the Ottoman palimpsest.[15] In the first chapter a Venetian ship carrying the narrator relies on enslaved Moors and Turks to row an escape from a Turkish man-a-war. Failing, the attacking Ottoman frigate captures and inverts power relations among those aboard. The Christians, previously either passengers or crew, are now enslaved, though the narrator, feigning medical knowledge, serves to minister the medical needs of his Ottoman captors. This delineation within slavery now pits embittered fellow religionists against those viewed as comprador, e.g. the narrator.

For the next nine chapters the enslaved protagonist negotiates with representatives of Ottoman hierarchy, especially the *hoja,* who except for his beard resembles the speaker. The *hoja* teaches and serves his superiors, first the pasha and, ultimately, the young Sultan.[16] The speaker and the *hoja* engage in series of scientific feats for the aristocrats, achievements which result in fused identities of the two principals. By novel's end, the reader experiences a kind of auditory vertigo: is the narrator in the last chapter the Italian or the *hoja?* The two have appropriated and accommodated each other to a point of interpenetration that make identity in terms of religious convictions, utterances, and social class indistinguishable. Both principal characters are localized intellectuals, the narrator, a university student from Renaissance Florence and the Republic of Venice, learned enough to feign mastery of Western science and technology, and the *hoja,* one schooled in not only Islam but also its ancient Hellenic cosmological underpinnings. For the pleasure and glory of the Sultan, the two first create a display of fireworks, then models of the universe, followed by cures for the plague, and, finally, they construct the ultimate weapon for the sultan's army to conquer Vienna and Poland.

Pamuk's two novels are palimpsests of the Ottoman Empire, narratives set in the past that display symbols of how diversity coexisted among ethnicities to foster open-mindedness, tolerance, pragmatics, and reciprocity of evolving identities. An aspect of this Turkish identity is diminishing ego and subjective individualism for the greater good of the community. The reader of *The White Castle* may be reminded of a quote by Thomas Jefferson:

> "He who receives an idea from me, receives instruction himself without lessening mine; as he who

lights his taper at mine, receives light without dark-
ening me."[17]

Each of Pamuk's principal characters possesses localized knowledge but complementing expertise; the episodes of the novel deal
with how difference tapers illuminate universals.[18] However, consumption of material objects like gold, books, tables, mirrors, etc.,
are different from ideation in that such objects are desirable or
repugnant and influences motives. The two characters respond to
such material obstacles giving rise to tensions in ego, in possessive-
ness, yet progressively, to revelations and heuristics that ultimately
achieve fused identities. For example, when the narrator constructed
a Venetian table for the *hoja,* such western furniture repels the recipient who soon unconsciously adapts, for the table facilitates writing.

Further and more important to how diversity melds collaboration,
it situates *hoja* directly opposite the slave, an innovation that at once
overcomes the limitations of reclining on cushions to compose and,
more pointedly for theme, fosters mutuality and reciprocity. Facing
one another across the table, the two proceed to write about feelings,
sins, and dreams. The *hoja's* power wanes as the slave waxes, the two
approaching fusion. They meld their earlier contrasting fear of the
plague and notions of death, and soon *hoja* filches the other's dream
and then dreams they are brothers and eventually elicits realizations
that they have become one.[19]

Pamuk seems to have appropriated Tzvetan Todorov's axes of
relations to the Other to fuse these identities, as the postmodern-
ist argues in Conquest of America.[20] During the beginning chapters of The White Castle, each possesses self-esteem and judges the
Other inferior. The protagonist has arrived in Istanbul an enslaved
guest fearful of the Other's culture; the *hoja,* valuing his new slave
for service as property, appropriates ideas and claims authorship
of all that pleases pasha and sultan. Each character experiences the
novelty of the Other, judging customs, possessions, and habits as
inferior or superior. Like a husband of an enterprising marriage,
the *hoja* claims before the sultan total credit for what the narrator's
taper has contributed. Eventually, the two, overcoming reactions to

differences, realize how in each case, the Other has illuminated each life. Each approximates a rapprochement, which advances toward an assimilation in which what was imposed upon the slave or given by the master eventually results in a kind of love. At this level of relations, a pragmatics results in identity exchanges. By novel's end both value the Other as equal by expanding identity of each to entail both similarity and difference without connotations of inferiority or superiority.

Cityscapes of Gülersoy

No less manifestly, but more tangibly, Çelik Gülersoy, as director from 1974 until his death in 2005, channeled earnings of the Türkiye Turing ve Otomobil Kurumu to transform into modern structural palimpsests that signified periods of Anatolian history. From archeological remnants of the Ottoman past, Gülersoy restored thirty-four sites that a traveler can visit from the Turkish / Bulgarian border to nearly the capital, Ankara. A lawyer by training with expertise in building and refurbishing, Gülersoy grounded upon ruins of the Ottoman culture modern hotels, pensions, pavilions, parks, kiosks, library, musical halls, and convention centers that can be admired by today's wayfarers, each a vestige of continuity from a multicultural past.

Today, Turkish and international sojourners can have lunch in an Ottoman neighborhood adjacent to the Christian Orthodox church, the Kariye, with its fabulous thirteenth century mosaics; they can observe ancient crafts in a folk bazaar, transformed from classrooms of a fifteenth century *madrasah;* and they can dine at a restaurant in a Roman cistern, excavated and furbished from a 1950's auto repair garage. The next day, they might stroll past the Turing restored façade of the Sublime Porte on the way to attend concerts of Western and Eastern music at pavilions of tulip hues in Emirgan Park, which dates back to the reign of Murad IV. Anyone can lodge at the eighteenth century apartments abutting the Topkapi walls and lounge in tearooms of konaks, serras, or pavilions in palaces or enjoy the verdure of the Sultans' hunting grounds at Yeşil Park. They can take a boat to visit an Italo-Greecian palace, now a Culture Center, on the

Princes' island of Büyükada or ferry up the Bosporus to visit the early twentieth century Art Nouveau summer palace, the Khedive Kasrı, on the Asian side near the Black Sea. Gülersoy restored the Ottoman past for the present with transformations that hundreds of Turkish entrepreneurs have emulated over the last twenty-five years.

With the exception of the British Museum, the Gülersoy Library includes the greatest collection of books and engravings on Istanbul and Turkey in the world. Gülersoy constructed the library that carries his name at the end of a street upon which Turing restored eighteenth century dwellings that lie alongside Topkapi walls, buildings designed after the mid-nineteenth century engravings of Fossati during the time the Italian was restoring the Aya Sofya. The oldest manuscript in the collection dates from 1551. Pierre Giles' original essay on Istanbul of 1561 is another rare document of the Ottoman past, one in which this French diplomat describes an early palimpsest of the Topkapi. In addition to Fossati's art representing the time of Abdul Mecit in the mid-nineteenth century, other library illustrations capturing the past include an original 1492 map of Istanbul and an array of paintings and photographs of foreign authors dating from a drawing of Lady Montagu during the reign of Sultan Ahmed Üç to Pierre Loti at the turn of the last century. All of the authors depicted and celebrated Turkey in their writings.

While harkening back to the Ottoman past, Gülersoy operationalized modern Turkish values of gender equity and commerce with three important innovations. First, he recruited from rural Turkey youth of superior talent and then arranged for them to apprentice in the hospitality industries in Europe, such as Claridges Hotel in London. These Janissaries were trained for future management in the newly restored Turing enterprises. Second, Gülersoy transformed the ancient concept of the caravanserai as an inn that provided free lodging only to males into suitable accommodations for both females and males. Moreover, young women who apprenticed in Europe often managed these Turing caravanserais. Traditionally, only male travelers anywhere in Islam could find free lodging at a caravanserai, but not women. Third, Gülersoy introduced capitalism into the system of the caravanserais so that those benefiting would pay for services

rendered. Each of these three innovations hastened the establish-
ment in Turkey of the present tourist industry, one in which today's
Istanbul, for example, is both an Ottoman capital and a modern
Turkish metropolis.

In addition to Pamuk's literature and Gülersoy's restorations,
other Turkish artists meld Ottoman past with Kemalist present. The
successful "Sultans of the Dance," or as it was known when it toured
the United States in 2005, the "Fire of Anatolia," celebrates in dance
and music a Turkish multicultural heritage. In each performance the
mythic god Prometheus choreographs an ensemble of Turkish and
other minorities who have thrived in Anatolia. These artistic representations in the symbolic code of print, the icon code of design, and
of the enactive code of performance provide a means to return to the
past and experience momentarily the life of the Ottomans.

Most importantly, the representations expunge for all but the
lazy and bigoted any visions of an inherent "clash of civilizations"
between East and West. In each case, these palimpsests of texts, per-
formances, and cityscapes illustrate how the Ottomans celebrated
commonalities that undergird diversity and that deny a polarization
of "Us" versus "Others." Art is a powerful facet of the Turkish genius
to resolve both internal and external stresses. Pamuk, through his
fiction, and Gülersoy, through his physical restorations, herald for
the world how good will and understanding of the Ottomans can
model solutions for stresses caused by the racial, ethnic, ideological,
and gender differences found in many modern multicultural societies. The importance of these artistic representations is that they
exhort our polarizing world to look and listen deeply to the Ottoman
past and to present-day Turkey. By doing so, citizens throughout the
globe can reduce, if not nullify a suicidal, global momentum toward
violent confrontation.

Chapter Nine

**Analysis of the Millet System
in Light of Contact Theory**

by Dr. Yetkin Yildirim and Dr. Maria Curtis

Introduction

INCREASING GLOBALIZATION AND THE RECENT ACTS of terror in the US and Europe make the need for dialogue between religious and cultural groups more pressing. Indeed, the concept of dialogue has become increasingly popular as individuals from both the East and West have sought answers and explanations for world events. Some look to examples from the past for inspiration in coping with current events. One such example is the millet system employed by the Ottoman State.

This chapter explores the history of the Ottomans as a relevant example of a peaceful multicultural society. The first section will be a description and analysis of the Ottoman millet system of law. In the second section, the millet system will be compared to contact theory, another framework for coping with ethnic tensions. This contemporary theory of multicultural existence was being practiced in many ways by the Ottomans. The third section of the chapter will delve deeper into the Ottoman example by showing how contemporary individuals, such as the Turkish writer and scholar Fethullah Gülen, perceive Ottoman society as setting an early precedent of coping with religious tensions and providing a possible example for contemporary interfaith models.

The Millet System

The term *millet system* refers to the legal system in the Ottoman State, in which communities of religious minorities were granted autonomous rule with minimal interference from the Ottoman government.[1] The system first arose during the reign of Sultan Mehmet II in the mid-fifteenth century upon the conquest of Istanbul and the expansion of the Ottoman State, in order to incorporate the ethnically and religiously diverse region of the Balkans.[2]

Under this system, non-Muslims enjoyed a large degree of religious and cultural freedom and had great administrative and legal autonomy through leaders appointed from within their communities.[3] Non-Muslims, or *Dhimmis*, consisted of three main groups: Orthodox Christians, Catholic Christians, and Jews.[4] They were recognized as fellow "Peoples of the Book" and were not forcibly converted.[5] Instead, this system allowed religious minorities "to retain their traditions and legal systems."[6] Groups of non-Muslims were granted a legal designation separate from the Muslim population.[7] All non-Muslim groups were autonomous millets represented by their own leaders, who reported directly to the Ottoman Sultan.[8] In a written acceptance of Crimean Jews seeking refuge in the Ottoman state, Sultan Abdülmecid shows the importance of distinct groups electing their own leaders in order to avoid potential conflict. He writes, "The Jews migrating from Kerc, the Crimea, and applying for taking refuge have been accepted to Ottoman territories on the condition that their rabbi is appointed from them, for there are differences [between them and] . . . the Jews [currently] living in the Ottoman state."[9]

In return for declaring loyalty to the empire, millets were granted autonomy, not only over religious matters, but over everyday legal matters, including education, marriage, health, communication, and the collection and distribution of taxes.[10] All millets were subject to the penal code of the empire and were responsible for paying taxes to the empire; otherwise, most legal matters were under local jurisdiction.[11]

The empire, in turn, was responsible solely for providing protection to these areas and collecting taxes from them.[12] Surviving historical documents suggest that Ottoman leaders exhibited a strong ethic of justice and fairness concerning both the protection of lands and peoples under Ottoman control and concerning the collection of taxes from people living under Ottoman rule. Over Ottoman history, several sultans have issued reassurances to various minority millets that their people would be protected under Ottoman rule. A *ferman* issued by Sultan Mehmed the Conquerer in 1478 regarding a group of Bosnian Priests reflects this. It reads:

> With my beneficence, I, Sultan Mehmed Khan, order the Bosnian priests to pray in your churches and to live in our country without fear. No person, either from my viziers or my citizens, shall ever hurt you.[13]

Similarly, Ottoman authorities offered protection from discriminatory taxing practices as well. Many surviving documents reflect this desire for justice, which can be seen most clearly in a *ferman* in which Sultan Selim III boldly writes, "My *ferman* has been issued not to let anyone ask for any excessive taxes illegally from the Greeks and Armenians living in Istanbul and its surroundings."[14]

Autonomy granted to millets by the millet system included local governance over finances and welfare institutions, local control of educational systems, collection of taxes by locally appointed collectors, and the ability of community leaders to negotiate taxes with the central government.[15] Millets were allowed to maintain a separate court system where legal disputes not pertaining to matters with the central government could be decided.[16]

Millets were granted a great deal of cultural and religious freedom: communities were allowed to establish and maintain their own places of worship and decide the language used locally in government and schools, and local laws were mainly based on local religious beliefs.[17] Many everyday decisions were made by local community leaders who were more familiar with the needs of the small communities than the patriarchs of the millets.[18] While each millet was largely responsible for the creation and inner-workings of their own institutions, historical evidence shows that many groups received assistance from the central government in establishing these institutions. One letter from Sultan Abdülhamid II declared the opening of a synagogue for Jews living in Darülaceze. In this letter, Abdulhamid writes that "a room has been arranged as a Synagogue . . . until a [permanent] Synagogue is built there. . . . A rabbi, a servant, and a cook have been appointed to the Synagogue. Necessary attention has also been paid to the days of Jews and their foods."[19] In another instance, a letter written by a group of Christian inhabitants of Princan to Sultan Abdülaziz expresses gratitude to the central government "concerning the assistance by the Ottoman Treasury to complete the construction of the church."[20]

The millet system was developed to enable the peaceful coexistence of highly diverse populations over a widespread geographic area during a time when today's technologies for administration, communication and control did not yet exist.[21] The empire took a laissez-faire approach to local affairs, not even attempting to change the local political order if there was no pressing need for it, while still maintaining centralized control through a strong hierarchical administrative structure to which local leaders were accountable.[22] As time went on, the millet system was strengthened by legal recognition and regulation of millets. Leaders of local communities gained increasing control over the educational, cultural and religious institutions and the local court system.[23]

In some cases, hostility and prejudice existed among different ethnic groups.[24] Nonetheless, the atmosphere in the Ottoman State was mainly one of tolerance and religious co-existence.[25] The "normal state of relations" between Christians, Jews, and Muslims was one of reciprocity and cooperation.[26] Evidence indicates that Christians and Jews seldom exhibited protest that they were being treated unfairly. For instance, there is no evidence of complaints by Jewish and Christian guild members of unfair treatment from their Muslim guild masters. Also, even though Jewish and Christian communities had their own courts, they frequently took their cases to

Sharia courts, thus exhibiting their confidence in their fair treatment by the court system.[27]

Christians and Jews were awarded a separate and inferior status under Ottoman rule, but this very policy allowed for the diversity in the empire that was one of its greatest strengths. The state obtained a compartmentalized structure of *umma* communities.[28] The system created a prevailing state of peaceful coexistence among these disparate communities without homogenizing them; by identifying with their communities first, Christians and Jews were able to maintain their distinct religious traditions. That subjects were generally content under Ottoman rule and that Muslims and non-Muslims were able to coexist in relative peace for five centuries is a testament to the satisfaction of various ethnic groups with their treatment under the policy and the effectiveness of the policy toward promoting peaceful interrelations among a highly diverse population.[29]

The Millet System and Contact Theory

For the most part, the millet system effectively enabled diverse groups to coexist peacefully without an active effort to assimilate and subjugate minorities.[30] In fact, the number of religious minorities constantly increased with time.[31] The millet system resembles contact theory in its promotion of peaceful contact between diverse groups.

Contact theory is based on the idea that contact between members of different groups under certain conditions can improve intra-group relations. As derived from George W. Allport's 1954 study, there are four basic conditions for positive interaction between groups:

1) Group members must perceive one another as equals.
2) Groups must be focused on a common goal;.
3) Groups must cooperate to obtain a common goal without competition.
4) Peaceful contact between groups must be supported by laws and customs.[32]

The laws of the millet system essentially created conditions in which peaceful interaction among diverse groups could occur. In line with contact theory, equality was a crucial condition for keeping the diverse communities within the Ottoman State content. Christian, Jewish, and Islamic millets possessed equal rights to govern themselves locally. So, each community enjoyed many of the same freedoms, and all groups had the same access to the government within their respective communities.

Though different religious communities were kept separate and allowed to maintain their distinct identities, the millet system also provided ways of uniting communities under federal control and enabled them to perceive of themselves as a part of the empire, working toward the goals of the empire. Community leaders were made accountable to the sultan and were given access to the government to influence its policies. Taxes were collected for the government by these community leaders, who also had the opportunity to gain great power and status within their communities through working with the central government. Hence, leaders of communities were unified under a hierarchical system of government and were invested in working for the overarching goals of that government.

This system promoted cooperation among its diverse communities. Particularly, through setting super-ordinate goals and limiting competition between groups, cooperation is important for creating peaceful contact between groups.[33] By allowing religious enclaves to operate autonomously, the empire kept economic competition among Christians, Muslims, and Jews to a minimum. Meanwhile, a court system to which everyone had access and central government united citizens under super-ordinate goals and a common identity.

In fact, identity is an important factor in contact theory. Samuel Gaertner and John Dovidio discuss the importance of both a common group identity and individual identity to the generalization of a positive experience with members of an out-group.[34] Norman Miller recognizes the near contradictory requirements of these two types of identity for promoting peaceful inter-group relations.[35] Group members must at once perceive of themselves and the others as members of a common group in order to commence interaction, but should, in the end, perceive one another as "typical" members of an out-group in order to generalize their experience and feel friendly toward the group as a whole.[36]

In other words, in a single interaction, individuals' identities as members of a common group and as members of an out-group must be salient in order for the experience to create pleasant feelings towards out-groups. The millet system created just such a situation: citizens were primarily members of their communities, but their identity as citizens of a common empire was also salient. By recognizing and supporting subgroup identities, the empire in effect created more positive interactions between groups. It reduced the tensions created by competition and enabled individual communities to retain their distinct religious identities.

It is also clear that the Ottoman example matches contact theory in the requirement that "peaceful contact between groups must be supported by laws and customs."[37] There is evidence that over the course of Ottoman history, government leaders often issued official decrees in which the establishment or maintenance of peaceful interaction between groups was an explicit goal. A *ferman* written by Sultan Abdülaziz regarding the establishment of an independent Bulgarian Exarchate provides a clear example of this. Abdülaziz writes, "We require that everyone living in our dominions . . . get on with each other in a safe and comfortable way in terms of religion, sects . . . etc. and to work for the progression of the country."[38]

Thus, through the creation of conditions similar to those specified by Allport, the Ottoman State united its citizens in working together peacefully for the goals of the empire. Though segregation seems to have played a large role in keeping communities separate, there is evidence that interaction between communities flourished; there were residential quarters where the population was allowed to mix, there was considerable mobility from one quarter to another and there was profuse contact in public spaces outside of residential areas.[39] The millet system enabled a diverse population to coexist, flourish and intermingle in relative harmony.

The Ottoman Example as a Model for Tolerance
and Dialogue in the Contemporary World

While the Ottoman system is historic and cannot be directly copied and applied to contemporary society, it does include relevant examples of tolerance and dialogue that can inspire people, such as Fethullah Gülen, to foster similar principles in their work. Fethullah Gülen is a prominent Islamic scholar who promotes interfaith understanding. He has been called "one of the most serious and significant thinkers and writers, and among the wisest activists, of twentieth century Turkey or even of the Muslim world."[40] Gülen writes: "Tolerance is something that has always existed."[41]

The notion of a tolerant society is essential for understanding and connections to develop across cultures. According to Gülen, this concept was exemplified during the prominence of the Ottoman State and the millet system, which "organized the Ottoman State according to religious adherence."[42]

Gülen believes that a key element of the Ottoman State was the extent to which the state mixed cultures. He writes that the multicultural nature of the Ottomans has "been passed on to us by speech and writing, [and it] has made our nation a distinct society," and furthermore, "this cultural richness should be used and evaluated in the future as an unmatched treasure and source of strength."[43] Here, he stresses the influence of a multicultural society on the formation of cultural and religious tolerance.

When discussing the model of the Ottoman State, Gülen aptly points out that the greatness of the Ottomans was often looked upon as a model by counterpart nations of its time, asserting that the strength and success of the Ottoman state was actually due to the tolerant, multi-ethnic culture of the Ottomans. Gülen writes: "The golden pages of our history bear witness that our ancestors always carried tolerance to the regions where they were in control of their destiny."[44] The ancestors of the Ottoman State established a "multinational, multicultural and multi-religious system...[and] ensured tolerance and harmony among its peoples."[45] Gülen frequently invokes the role of the Ottomans as a positive ancestral and cultural artifact, the aspects of which are engrained in the fiber of the individual, community, state, and society. In an interview with Nevval Sevindi, Gülen describes the continued legacy of the Ottoman tradition as exhibited by contemporary Turkish attitudes toward other cultures:

> The Ottomans, who lived in lands totaling twenty-two million square kilometers, were in touch with all cultures. While this enriched them, it also led to modernization. Turks have never regarded any other culture as being above or below them at any time. The result of this has been tolerance.[46]

He observes that the Ottomans had "prestige" and "authority in the balance of power," such that they became a model for the rest of the nations and states in the world, who "looked to them and adjusted themselves and their affairs accordingly."[47] He further asserts that tolerance "for religious and ethnic minorities" was embedded in the fabric of the Ottoman State to such an extent that it "amazed visiting Europeans."[48] In light of on-going interfaith and interethnic conflicts around the world, such a system of smooth multicultural interaction in the time of the Ottomans is indeed amazing. Gülen reflects upon the unique nature of the Ottoman case, writing:

> The secret of Ottoman magnificence that enabled the Ottomans to govern a huge, cosmopolitan population, of which only 1 / 20 was Turkish, in an area that stretched over three continents for many centuries and that enabled them to maintain security in the best possible way lies in the Ottoman's tolerance of all faiths; that is, they practiced real laicism, as it is understood by some.[49]

Here, Gülen notes the political advantage that the state gained from its policy of tolerance, supporting the idea that the Ottomans' tolerance towards non-Muslims was the key to their long, successful rule over a highly diverse empire.

Part of the success of tolerant multiculturalism in Ottoman society was the fostering of effective dialogue and interchange between different groups. This necessary connection between positive, public discourse and the ethic of tolerance is an idea toward which Gülen often directs his attention. He states:

> If Ottoman tolerance existed today in the world, I believe there would be a very good basis for dialogue not only among Muslims but also humanity. In a world that is becoming more and more globalized, being open to dialogue is very important.[50]

Today's advances in technology have helped generate global communication on an unprecedented level. The global communication environment leaves an opening for individuals and communities from a multitude of cultures to participate in public discussion and dialogue. However, Gülen stresses that public conversation must be combined with tolerance in order to have positive effects on humanity. Without this notion of tolerance, which Gülen bases on the Ottoman social order, the potential for dialogue is lost, and groups resort to violence and destruction. Gülen points to the Ottomans' ability to create a society in which multiple religious groups lived side by side as an example of successful dialogue for today's society.

"Dialogue-oriented practices," which contrast with Samuel Huntington's concept of the "clash of civilizations," guide Gülen's work.[51] Gülen uses the Ottoman model of tolerance to confront the "discourse of conflict" and provide to "the idea of dialogue" to a global audience.[52] Gülen has been able to sustain interfaith communication through the promulgation of the "pillars of dialogue: love, compassion, tolerance, and forgiving."[53] Also integral to Gülen's definition of tolerance is the idea of acceptance: "Gülen understands tolerance as cooperation among different societal groups and as cooperation on the international level, based on shared values," and further, he "encourages dialogue with others and acceptance of their differences."[54] For Gülen, Ottoman tolerance combined with dialogue has the potential to facilitate interfaith communication.

Gülen believes that the Ottomans' approach to tolerance has relevance to today's world as a "basis for dialogue not only for Muslims but for humanity."[55] He therefore advocates it as a model for dialogue and peace among people of different religions. He urges people to live up to the Ottomans' example of tolerance and to use it to promote the effort towards peaceful dialogue across religions:

If people of today, who are civilized, enlightened and open to the world, are going to fall short of those who lived in that period, then this means they have not understood this age. In this respect, as individuals, as families and as a society, we have to speed up this process that has been begun. I personally believe that even the people who do not share our feelings and thoughts will soften when we go to see them. Thus, in the name of dialogue we can unite on common ground and shake hands with everyone.[56]

An important part of Gülen's definition of tolerance is the acknowledgement that tolerance does not require individuals to relinquish their own views on religion, society, or culture. He relates: "The Ottomans were faithful both to their religion and to other values and, at the same time, they were a great nation that could get along with other world states,"[57] a truth clearly exhibited in the millet system. For Gülen, tolerance is an ideal that may be sought after without compromising one's religious beliefs. Dialogue guided by tolerance is not rigid or stifling but instead empowering for those involved. Hence, Gülen believes that the precedent of tolerance set by the Muslims of the Ottoman State has the potential to influence even non-believers, and that this history-based definition of tolerance has the ability to create dialogue among different cultures and religions. Filiz Baskan notes that "according to Fethullah Gülen, the problems of difference among people can be solved by means of tolerance."[58] Gülen promotes dialogue based on this historical-cultural definition of tolerance, showing that it was foundational to the success of the Ottoman State during a time in which Islam was envisioned "as a flexible and tolerant belief system."[59]

This idea of Islam as "flexible and tolerant" points to the possibility of rethinking Islam in light of the Ottoman example. In his writings, Gülen attempts to mitigate violent stereotypes of Islam and to revive an ethic of tolerance in Islam. He believes that tolerance has been a fundamental value for Muslims throughout history, and he looks to the Ottoman example as a historical basis for this belief:

> [I]n our world, the Companions and the two gen-
> erations following our Prophet up to the Seljukis,
> Ottomans and the present day all accepted toler-
> ance as a basic principle in their relationships with
> others."[60]

Gülen continues in this line of thought, writing of the Ottoman State as a historical example of a powerful Islamic nation, whose strength was its multiculturalism and its ethic of tolerance. In partic- ular, according to Nevval Sevindi, Gülen's affinity for the Ottoman legacy of tolerance is demonstrated by his observations of four specific characteristics of Ottoman practice, namely: "the spirit of dialogue that existed there, the fact that the Ottoman state was a multilingual, multiethnic, and multireligious society, the role of women and their place in Ottoman culture, and great intellectual and cultural rap- prochement between Ottoman society and the West."[61]

In this light, Gülen also sees the heritage of the Ottoman State as a model of well-practiced Islam. When an interviewer posed the question, "Islam is a universal religion. Are there also Turkish traces in it?" Gülen responded, "Islam is universal with respect to its principles. Details can be interpreted differently. It's my humble opinion that the Turkish nation has interpreted those interpretable matters quite well."[62] Here, Gülen is referencing the impact that the Ottoman State has had on the way that Islam is practiced in Turkey. He believes that Anatolia has practiced a different sort of Islam than other places in the world based on its Ottoman heritage. To demonstrate such diversity in Islamic practice, Gulen invokes an example of the role of women in Islamic societies, an issue of much contemporary debate, and further illustrates the distinctiveness of the Turkish experience:

> Despite the enormity of the significance of women
> and their place in the main sources of Islam, the
> Qur'an and the sayings of the Prophet, there are

feudal, macho Islamic types who regard women as second-class citizens; they have never understood our Prophet. To my mind, it was the Turks who understood him best. The value placed on women in Anatolian Islam, the equal place of women in the Turkish tradition, the motif of women who fight alongside men and share the throne with men, these are elements of Turkish Islam.[63]

He refers to the practice of Islam in Turkey as "Anatolian Islam," and one of his major goals is to spread the tolerance that is a part of Anatolian Islam beyond the boundaries of Anatolia. It is also important to note, however, that despite his admiration of Ottoman tradition, he does not promote the reinstitution of the caliphate, an issue of contention in contemporary Turkish politics. Gülen seeks only to emphasize the endurance of "religious, cultural, and historical" features of the Ottoman caliphate in contemporary Turkey.[64]

In emphasizing significant Ottoman legacies, particularly that of tolerance, Gülen suggests that tolerance itself is actually based on Qur'anic teachings. The definition of tolerance that Gülen presents is one that moves beyond the Western concept of simply tolerating others, and instead proposes one based on the Turkish word *hoşgörü*, which means "to see something as pleasant and amiable." This word is generally simply translated as "tolerance." Gülen states, "One who does not embrace humanity with tolerance and forgiveness will not receive forgiveness and pardon."[65] Gülen's perspective is imbued with the belief that while all people are compelled to practice tolerance, Muslims are spiritually compelled not simply to tolerate other groups, but to act with warmth and compassion toward them. Gülen writes, "tolerance should be so broad that we can close our eyes to others' faults, show respect for different ideas, and forgive everything that is forgivable," a profound call to acceptance.[66] Mucahit Bilici has summed up Gülen's desire to redefine Islam in this positive light, writing, "The Gülen movement has a vision of reviving a faithful and tolerant Turkish-Islamic tradition as exemplified in the Ottoman Empire."

Consistent with this vision, a product of the Gülen movement has been the construction of several educational institutions. Through his educational mission, Gülen is attempting to reinvigorate Turkish society with the many valuable legacies of Ottoman history and understand the possible utility of such a history in light of contemporary global challenges.[67]

Gülen-inspired schools that promote science, universal values, and the same interfaith understanding that existed under the Ottomans have been established throughout much of the world.[68] Asma Afsaruddin indicates the similarity in the concept of tolerance to the understanding of the Ottomans:

> Gülen often quotes Mevlana Rumi's comment to the effect that the individual should be "like a pair of compasses, with one end in the necessary place, the center, and with the other one in the 72 nations [millet]," referring to the different *millets* or religious communities which co-existed peacefully under the Ottomans. Gülen schools, whose curricula are not specifically religious, are open to students of any faith background.[69]

So, in addition to preaching about the tolerance of the Ottomans, Gülen has taken action and tried to mimic some of the elements of the Ottomans that led to such tolerance.

At the same time, however, Gülen is not attempting to recreate or copy the Ottoman system through these schools, but rather to put the lessons learned from the Ottoman system into practice: "For [Gülen], the schools are not about a reviving of an Ottoman Islamic past but entering the future." Gülen clarifies that his goal is to "integrate [students] with their past and prepare them intelligently for the future."

It is necessary to teach students about this past because modernization in Turkey led to a breaking away from many Ottoman ideals that Gülen believes are important for "the development of the whole person i.e. the spiritual person." Part of this development must include the tolerance for other religions that Gülen so admired in the Ottomans.[70]

These efforts are all the more significant given contemporary discussions of Islam as being engulfed in "crisis," which further promulgates misguided, at times vicious, ideas both within and outside Islamic communities. The multicultural and multireligious circumstances that guided the actions and practices of the Ottomans are analogous to the diversity experienced through contemporary globalization, as Gülen himself recognizes:

> As time passes, the world is coming more and more to resemble a global village, different beliefs, colors, races, customs, and traditions will continue to live in this village. For this reason, the peace of this (global) village lies in recognizing all differences, accepting them as natural, and not treating anyone differently because of them, which means global tolerance and dialogue.[71]

The Educational projects undertaken by the Gülen movement offer students in their ever increasingly diverse environment the opportunities to confront challenges that are unique to their generation. For example, issues surrounding tenuous relationships between the Middle East and Europe or the United States and the miss representations of Islam are addressed by reiterating the precedent of tolerance and dialogue exemplified by the Ottomans. The focus of this educational philosophy is on constructive ideals that will enable this generation to be successful where previous ones failed, rather than solely promoting material success.

Conclusion

There are many contemporary models for approaching peaceful interfaith, interethnic relations. As this chapter has demonstrated, the history of the Ottomans provides a relevant example of the existence of a peaceful Islamic multicultural society. This analysis has outlined the specifics of the millet system in which outside groups were granted a great deal of autonomy. The Ottomans succeeded in uniting diverse communities under a common identity and promoting peace and cooperation among them through common goals and minimizing competition between groups, while simultaneously enabling these communities to maintain distinct identities.

As such, the millet system stands as an inspiring historical example of the effectiveness of contact theory principles for creating peaceful interaction between Muslims and other religious groups. The Ottoman Turks followed many of the basic tenets of the contemporary Contact Theory long before it was ever introduced. Moreover, the model of tolerance in the millet system brings a valuable new perspective to contact theory by demonstrating that among highly distinct groups it is possible to create peace and cooperation without the need to assimilate and compromise distinct identities.

Finally, this study has shown how these points are echoed by contemporary scholars, such as Gülen, who have sought to understand and outline the principles beneath the Ottoman system—those principles of tolerance and dialogue that make the Ottoman example so relevant to contemporary struggles of globalization and multiculturalism. Gülen's writings and the activities of the Gülen movement have also sought to analyze the foundations of Ottoman society in order to bring this relevant history to the fore and to take guidance and inspiration from Ottoman methods of tolerance and dialogue. From many different perspectives, the example of the Ottomans provides a much-needed model for peaceful coexistence in a diverse society.

Chapter Ten

Multicultural Science in the Ottoman State: Examples from Medicine and Astronomy

by Salim Aydüz

THROUGHOUT THE SIX CENTURIES OF OTTOMAN HISTORY, science in the Ottoman Empire displayed a unique course of development. Although the Ottomans shared heritage and traditions with the other Islamic societies situated outside of the Ottoman State, their geographical location affected the administration of their state and the dynamism of their society. Thus, Ottoman science was unique and innovative in its developments, even though it shared common sources with the rest of the Islamic world. In its beginning, Ottoman scientific tradition was influenced by the older Islamic centers of science and culture. However, after a short period, Ottoman science reached a point at which it could influence the old centers of science and culture and serve as an example to them.[1]

The great changes in the scientific and educational life of the Ottomans were achieved over an extensive period of time. Consequently, it is difficult to connect the radical changes in Ottoman history to specific events or to picture their exact beginnings. In general, the "old and new" existed side by side. To substantiate such a claim, I will focus on the formation and development of the classical Ottoman scientific tradition that was based on the Islamic classical scientific tradition, including the heritage of the

Seljuks and other Muslim and Turkish states.[2] I will also touch on the impact that the Ottoman State's multicultural structure had on the development of its sciences.

"Ottoman Science" will be used in this article to describe the scientific and educational activities that occurred throughout the Ottoman period in the territories where the empire extended. The Ottoman State was established as a small principality at the turn of the fourteenth century and gradually expanded into the Byzantine Empire and other Muslim and non-Muslim states. Its authority reached the Arab world after 1517, and it became the most powerful state of the Islamic world. The Empire extended from Central Europe to the Indian Ocean and lasted for many centuries by keeping the balance of power with Europe.[3]

Ottoman science emerged and developed in Anatolian cities from the scientific legacy and institutions of the pre-Ottoman Seljuk period and benefited from the activities of scholars who came from Egypt, Syria, Iran, and Turkestan—that is, from the most important scientific and cultural centers of the period. The Ottomans, at least partly due to their close contact with other cultures, such as those of Jews from Spain and of Christians in the conquered Balkan territories, brought a new dynamism to cultural and scientific life in the Islamic world and enriched it.[4] Thus, the Islamic scientific tradition reached its zenith in the sixteenth century. Alongside the old centers of Islamic civilization, new centers such as Bursa, Edirne, Istanbul, Skopje, and Sarajevo flourished. The developments of this period formed the heritage that constitutes the cultural identity and scientific legacy of present-day Turkey, as well as several Middle Eastern, North African, and Balkan countries.

The Ottomans also benefited greatly from their non-Muslim subjects and European neighbors. Early on, the Ottomans had also gained knowledge from the Balkan and East European neighbors, who had information regarding the new developments in firearms.[5] The Ottomans provided very favorable working conditions for scientists from many different fields, including medicine, astronomy, and mathematics, by inviting them to conduct their studies at the important centers of science and culture in the Islamic world. Engaging the services of scientists and artists from either the west or the east as needed without regard to religion or nationality was an established and advantageous practice in the Ottoman State.[6]

In this article, I will provide an overview of the formation and development of Ottoman science in Anatolia and the scientific activities, especially in astronomy and medicine, which later expanded from the capital of the Empire, Istanbul, to all Ottoman lands. During the classical period, Ottoman scientists and scholars had remarkable success in developing Islamic science and were able to produce many works in various branches of science.

I. The Ottoman *Madrasahs*

In the Classical period, the *madrasah* was the source of science and education and the most important institution of learning in the Ottoman State. The Ottoman *madrasahs* continued their activities from the establishment of the state until approximately the turn of the twentieth century. The basic structure of the *madrasahs* remained the same within the framework of the Islamic tradition, but in terms of organization, they underwent several changes during the Ottoman period. Starting with the first *madrasah* established in 1331 in İznik (Nicaea) by Orhan Bey, the second Ottoman sultan (1326–1362), all *madrasahs* had *waqfs* (public foundations) supporting their activities.[7]

Shortly after Mehmed II conquered Istanbul, he built the Fātih *Külliye* (complex) known as the Sahn-i Samān Madrasahs (Eight Court Colleges) which comprised a mosque located at the center, as well as colleges, a hospital, a *mektep* (elementary mosque school), a public kitchen, and other buildings located around the mosque. It was the first educational complex built in Islamic civilization which contained all religious and social components of city life. It set an example for similar structures built by the sultan's successors and high-ranking members of the ruling class.

The *madrasahs* of the Fatih Complex, comprising sixteen adjacent *madrasahs*, represented the first Ottoman *madrasahs* that had the structure of a university campus. Owing to the political stability and economic wealth of the reign of Mehmed, distinguished scholars and artists of the Islamic world assembled in Istanbul.[8] Scholars from different cultures and religions also came to Istanbul, bringing diversity to the intellectual life of the Empire. As the *waqfs*, which were the financial sources of *madrasahs*, grew rich, scientific and educational life developed further.[9]

Ottoman science developed owing to the personal interest of Mehmed II and the educational institutions that he established after the conquest of Istanbul. Consequently, some brilliant scholars emerged and made original contributions to science in this period. Mehmed patronized the Islamic scholars and at the same time made use of scholars of other nationalities by ordering a Greek scholar from Trabzon, Georgios Amirutzes, and his son to translate Ptolemy's *Geography* into Arabic and to draw a world map. Mehmed also encouraged the scholars of his time to produce works in their special fields.[10] For example, for the comparison of al-Ghazali's criticisms of peripatetic philosophers (*meshshâiyyûn*) regarding metaphysical matters, which appear in his work titled *Tahāfut al-Falāsifa* (The Incoherence of the Philosophers), and Ibn Rushd's answers to these criticisms in his work *Tahāfut al-Tahāfut* (The Incoherence of Incoherence), he ordered two scholars, Hocazāde and Alā al-Dīn al-Tūsī, each to write a work on this subject.11 Foreign experts from all over the world were welcomed into the Empire and made contributions to their special fields. [12]

Without a doubt, the most distinguished scientist of Mehmed II's reign was Ali Kuşçu (d. 1474), a representative of the Samarkand tradition. He wrote twelve books on mathematics and astronomy. [13] One of them is his commentary on the *Zīj-i Ulug Bey* in Persian. His two works in Persian, namely, *Risāla fi'l-Hay'a* (Treatise on Astronomy) and *Risāla fi'l-Hisāb* (Treatise on Arithmetic) were taught in the Ottoman *madrasahs*. He rewrote these two works in Arabic with some additions under new titles, *al-Fathiyya* (Commemoration of Conquest) and *al-Muhammadiyya* (The Book dedicated to Sultan Mehmed), respectively. [14]

A remarkable scholar of Bayezid II's reign (1481–1512) was Molla Lūtfi (d. 1494). He wrote a treatise about the classification of sciences entitled *Mawdūāt al-Ulūm* (Subjects of the Sciences) in Arabic and compiled a book on geometry titled *Tadʿīf al-Madhbah* (Duplication of the Cube), which was partly translated from Greek. Mirim Çelebi (d. 1525), a well-known astronomer and mathematician of this period and the grandson of Ali Kuşçu and Qādī Zādeh, contributed to the establishment of the scientific traditions of mathematics and astronomy and was renowned for the commentary he wrote on the *Zīj* of Ulugh Beg.[15]

In medicine, the works of Sabuncuoğlu Şerefeddin (d. ca. 1468) were particularly important in the development of Ottoman medical literature and their influence on Safavid medicine. The first book on surgery that he wrote in Turkish entitled *Jarrāhiyāt al-Khāniyya* (Treatise on Surgery of the Sultans) comprises the translation of Abu'l-Qāsim Zahrāwī's *al-Tasrīf*, a self-contained handbook of the medical arts, and the three sections that he himself wrote. This work is renowned in the history of Islamic medicine in that it illustrates surgical operations with miniatures for the first time. Besides the classical Islamic medical information, this work draws from Turco-Mongolian and Far Eastern practices as well as the author's own experiences. [16]

The establishment of the Süleymaniye Külliye (complex) by Süleyman the Magnificent (1520–1566) in the sixteenth century marked the final stage in the development of the *madrasah* system where, besides the conventional *madrasahs,* a specialized one called Dar al-Tib (Medical College) was founded. Thus, for the first time in Ottoman history, in addition to the *sifahanes* (hospitals), an independent institution was established to provide medical education. [17]

Scientific literature developed considerably during the reign of Süleyman the Magnificent. Two major Turkish mathematical works in this time period are *Jamāl al-Kuttāb wa Kamāl al-Hussāb (Beauty of Scribes and Perfection of Accountants)* and *Umdat al-Hisāb (Treatise on Arithmetic)* by Nasûh al-Silâhî al-Matrâqî (d. 1564). Another one of al-Matrâqî's books worthy of mentioning relates to geography; it is entitled *Beyân-i Menâzil-i Sefer-i Irakeyn* (Description of the Encamping on the Campaign to the Two Iraqs). [18] Mûsâ ibn Hâmûn (d. 1554) shows how science benefited from diversity in the Ottoman State. One of the most famous Jewish physicians of Andalusian descent, Mûsâ ibn Hâmûn, was appointed as Sultan Süleyman's physician and wrote the first Turkish and one of the earliest independent works on dentistry which is based on Greek, Islamic, and Uighur Turkish medical sources, and in particular on Sabuncuoglu Serefeddin's works. In the sixteenth century, the representatives of the Egypt–Damascus tradition of astronomy-mathematics wrote important works on astronomy. The greatest astronomer of this period was Taqī al-Dīn al-Rāsid (d. 1585), who combined the Egypt–Damascus and Samarkand traditions. He wrote more than thirty books in Arabic on the subjects of mathematics, astronomy, mechanics, and medicine.

II. Medical Institutions

In addition to the *madrasahs*, which gave basic education, there were the institutions where medical sciences and astronomy were practiced and taught by the master-apprentice method. These were the *sifahanes* (hospitals), which were maintained by a chief physician (*hakimbashi*), the office of the *munajjim-bashi* (chief astronomership),the Istanbul observatory, and the *muvakkithanes* (time keeping houses).[19-20]

II. 1. Hospitals *(Shifâhânas)*

The chief physician who was responsible for palace and state health matters undertook the administration of all *dar al-shifas* (hospitals) among the Ottomans. The chief physician would maintain a register containing the names and other information pertaining to public service doctors. When there was a need for a doctor anywhere, the chief physician would appoint one in the appropriate order—that is, based on the availability of physicians of a particular rank and qualification.[21] *Shifahanas* carried out the same functions as hospitals do today. As *waqf* institutions, they were concerned with the public health of all social strata. They also offered medical education organized along apprenticeship lines. In Ottoman literature, the buildings where health-related activities were carried out were known variously as *Dâr al-Shifâ*, *dârüssihhâ*, *sifâhâne*, *bîmaristân*, *bîmarhâne* and *tımarhâne*.

Beginning in the early nineteenth century under the influence of the new western-style medical institutions that were emerging, the term *hospital* began to come into use. Many hospital buildings constructed in the cities of Konya, Sivas, and Kayseri during the Seljuk years continued to function during the Ottoman period as they had earlier, without any changes in their charter regulations. In this sense, it can be said that the Seljuk hospital and medical tradition had a major impact, first on the Ottomans, and later on the Europeans.[22] Similarly, the Ottomans built several *darüssifas* in cities such as Bursa, Edirne, and Istanbul. Some sources mention that there were a great number in Istanbul in the sixteenth and seventeenth centuries. This indicates the importance that Ottomans attributed to *darüssifas*. The Ottoman *darüssifas* were not constructed as independent buildings, but as part of a *külliye*. There was a hierarchy of hospitals, and the highest-ranking hospital was the Süleymaniye *Dâr al-Shifâ*, which of course was the most important medical institution in the Ottoman State.[23]

There were a large number of hospitals founded during the Ottoman period, particularly in Istanbul. The first of these was the *Dâr al-Shifâ* in the Fâtih complex (1470). This hospital contained 70 rooms and 80 domes and had separate sections for female patients. Music was used in the treatment of mentally ill patients, who were being burned or tortured in Europe during the same time period. There are few traces left of this hospital, which continued to function until 1824.[24]

The Bâyezîd *Dâr al-Shifâ* constructed by Sultan Bâyezîd II in Edirne in 1488 was well known for the treatment of the mentally ill and the victims of optometrical diseases. The building, which is really an historical monument, is especially notable among Turkish hospitals in an architectural sense. The structure was designed in an especially attractive way and had an impact on the design of European hospital buildings. Evliyâ Çelebi, in his *Seyahatnâme* (Travels), discusses how mentally ill patients were treated with music.[25]

II. 2. Medical Institutions: Suleymaniye Medical College

The Süleymaniye Complex (*külliye*), sponsored by Süleyman the Magnificent and built from 1550 to 1557 in Istanbul by the great architect Sinān (1489-1588), is the largest of the Ottoman building enterprises.[26] It is a rationally planned socio-religious complex with geometrically organized dependencies consisting of the monumental Suleymaniye Mosque, *madrasahs*, and other components.[27] It follows the example of the Fatih Complex, but Sinān made its architectural qualities vastly superior. The courtyard was surrounded by streets where *madrasahs* for different levels of education, a medical school, a large hospital, and other social buildings were set up on the slopes of the terrain.

Architecturally, the Medical Madrasah was planned as a component of the multi-functional Süleymaniye Complex.[28] The Medical Madrasah, with a perpendicular floor plan, was composed of twelve domed cells lined up next to the shops on Tiryakiler Street, which was located in the south-western part of the Süleymaniye Mosque.[29] The Medical Madrasah was related to the other components of the complex: the *dar al-shifā*, (hospital), the *dar al-akakir* (drugstore), the *tabhane* (the place where patients stay during their convalescence period), and the *imarethane* (public kitchen). In terms of handling the medical students, a kind of division of labor shows itself with respect to these components. The medical students depending on the Madrasah used the cells as a dormitory, had free meals cooked in the kitchen, used the hospital for practicing the theoretical lessons they learned in the Medical Madrasah, received their medicine from the drugstore, and, after being cured in the hospital, they would stay in the *tabhane* for the period of convalescence.

The construction of this *madrasah* is considered to be a new stage in the history of Ottoman medical institutions. The Süleymaniye Medical School was the first formal teaching institution for Ottoman medicine. Unlike the previous traditional medical schools, which were just components of hospitals, Süleymaniye was the first medical school in the Islamic civilization to have a deed of trust (*waqfiyya*) that mentioned its character as an institution for medical learning.[30] The Medical Madrasah was described in the charter as "the good *madrasah* which will house the science of medicine." It was established to train specialized physicians and occupied a very important place in the field of Ottoman medical education in terms of medical specialization.[31] Medical education acquired an independent institutional structure with the founding of this school.[32] The entrance to the medical school, which was located across from the hospital, of which only the southwestern wing has survived to this day, opened out onto Tiryâkiler Market. The northeastern wing of the structure was located above the arches and shops of the market.

The Süleymaniye Medical Madrasah was the first institution to be built next to the *Dār al-Shifā*, in Istanbul. Süleyman the Magnificent ordered the establishment of a medical *madrasah* in his complex to educate highly skilled physicians for the needs of both the public and army. The Medical Madrasah and the *Dār al-Shifā* buildings were built side-by-side to provide both a medical education and a public health service. This is very similar to contemporary university hospitals. Sinān placed the school and the hospital parallel to each other in a separate block in one corner of the very large complex, next to two rectangular courtyards. The idea of two buildings together, a Medical Madrasah and the *Dār al-Shifā*, is considered superior in application and was ahead of its time. After a lesson in medical theory, the medical student would go the *Dār al-Shifā*, straight away to put into practice what he had learned. Hence, the Süleymaniye Medical School and *Dār al-Shifā*, have a very important place in the history of medical education and its application to hospitals.

II. 3. Staff of the Medical Madrasah

According to the deed of the complex, the Medical Madrasah had a very basic and small staff. One *muderris* (lecturer), eight *danişmends* (students), and three auxiliary staff—the *noktaci* (assistant), *bevvab* (doorkeeper) and *ferrash* (cleaner)—were assigned.[33] There was a *muderris* as head of the *madrasah*, just as at the other *madrasahs*. However, there were some special conditions for a *muderris* of a medical *madrasah*: they had to be well educated on the medical sciences and be able to direct the students through the medical sciences.[34]

The first teacher at the Süleymaniye Medical School was Tabib Ahmed Çelebi b. İsa Çelebi, who received sixty *akças* per day.[35] The deed mentioned the daily wage of the *muderris* was twenty *akças* per day, but he received a higher salary due to his high skill level in medicine. Some of the Medical Madrasah *muderrisses* were appointed to other medical institutions as a *shagird*.[36] As we see from the documents, some famous physicians were appointed as *muderrisses* at the medical *madrasahs*, such as chief physicians Büyük Hayatizâde Mustafa Feyzi, Ayaşlı Şaban Şifai, Ömer Efendi, and Gevrekzâde Hasan Efendi.[37]

II. 4. The Education at the Medical Madrasah

Although we have no sources available that fully explain the teaching and educational methods followed in the Süleymaniye Medical Madrasah, it is understood from its deed, from the constitutions for courts and *madrasahs* (*ilmiye kanunnameleri*), and from primary sources belonging to the classical period (1300-1600), that the school was formerly taught and carried out along the lines of the master-apprentice method. This practical method also used to be popular among other medical and social institutions, such as the trade market system and *ahl-i hiraf* (artisans) organizations. This system was also common before the Ottomans, in the Seljuk period. The textbooks used in the Süleymaniye Medical Madrasah are only generally mentioned in the deeds and other sources. They taught the famous medical text books at the Medical Madrasah. Although the deed does not mention the names of the textbooks, we do have a list of books which were given to the head physician to teach. In the list, we find sixty-six famous medical books, of which eighteen were written by Ibn Sīnī.[38] Although there is no indication that these books were given for Medical Madrasah teaching purposes, we know that at that time, these books were circulating among physicians for educational purposes. According to the deeds, in addition to medical textbooks, courses on logic (*ilm-i mizan*), medicine (*ilm-i abdan*), and rational sciences (*fenn-i hikmet, ulum-i akliye*) were also somehow taught at the School.

In the deeds, there is no clear statement about the days and hours of the courses. In general, we know that that Süleyman the Magnificent stipulated the teaching of five courses a day on four weekdays. It is thought that pre-Ottoman practices were followed by taking Tuesday, Thursday, and Friday as holidays. Festival days were also holidays, but these holidays could be decreased accordingly.[39] The rest of the days were for teaching.

The Medical Madrasah was under the administrative control of the Chief Physician's Office (*Hekimbaşı*).[40] The chief physician was responsible for the health of the sultan and that of the personnel of the palace, as well as for managing all state health institutions. His office monitored all appointments and any other studies at the Medical Madrasah. All students with diplomas from medical *madrasahs*, medical schools (*Mekteb-i Tıbbiye*), and hospitals would register with the chief physician upon graduation and would then await appointment to a medical institution.[41] The chief physician would appoint new doctors to vacant posts and would approve the promotion of those recommended for such. As a medical institution, the staff of the *madrasah* was under the aegis of the general Ottoman appointment system.

Unfortunately, there is no exact information on how many years medical education lasted at this *madrasah*. Ahmed b. ibrahim, author of *Tashil al-Tadâbir*, mentioned that he himself graduated from the Süleymaniye Medical School after fifteen years and then became a physician at the palace. From his case, we understand that the educational process was very long.[42] Most of the physicians appointed to the palace as palace physicians were selected from physicians who graduated from the Süleymaniye Medical School, and, of course, suitability was a very important point for appointments.

Abbé Toderini, who lived in Istanbul between 1781 and 1786, provides information on the teaching method in the Medical Madrasah of Süleymaniye in a chapter of his famous book, *De La Littérature Des Turcs*. According to Toderini, Turkish medical lecturers taught courses in general pathology and surgery in Süleymaniye for four days per week. In addition to medical students, the courses were open to those who wished to attend. There was no barrier to Franks (Europeans) attending these courses. Ubezio, a European physician, said that he followed the courses many times as a listener. The teaching method consisted of reading medical books, studying diseases and medicines through clinical observation, and learning from the physicians' knowledge and advice.[43]

The Süleymaniye Medical School offered medical education for about three centuries and was the institution which provided doctors for almost all of the Ottoman medical institutions, and mostly for the Fatih Hospital in Istanbul. Süleymaniye Medical Madrasah's graduates and students, such as Osman Saib Efendi, Abdülhak Molla, and Mustafa Behçet Efendi were among the founders and teachers of the modern medical school in Istanbul in 1827. Thus, they pioneered the modernizing of medical education in Turkey.

The School most likely continued to train students until the middle of the nineteenth century—that is, until sometime after the new medical school (*tıbbiye*) opened.[44] After the Second Constitutional Period (*II. Meşrutiyet*), the Süleymaniye Madrasah was included in the body of "Dâru'l-hilafeti'l-aliyye Medresesi," which was a plan to assemble all the *madrasahs* of Istanbul under one roof. It is understood that the Medical Madrasah was out of use and needed restoration during the year 1914. It also seems that on 21 December 1918, people who had lost their homes during a fire used this *madrasah*. Since 1946, after a full restoration, the building has been used as a maternity clinic (Süleymaniye Doğum ve Çocuk Bakımevi).

III. Astronomical Institutions:
The Istanbul Observatory (*Istanbul Rasathanesi*)

In addition to medical institutions, other science related institutions were established for astronomical matters, such as the chief astronomership, time keeping houses and the Istanbul observatory. The first Ottoman observatory was also the last big observatory of the Islamic Civilization. It was established in Istanbul during the reign of Sultan Murad III (1574-1595) by Taqi al-Din al-Râsid. Taqi al-Din, who was born in Damascus in 1526, worked for a time as a *kadi* and a teacher after completing his education in Damascus and Egypt. During his time in Egypt and Damascus, he produced some important works in the fields of astronomy and mathematics. In 1570, he came to Istanbul from Cairo, and one year later (1571-2) was appointed chief astronomer (*Munajjimbashi*) upon the death of Chief Astronomer Mustafa b. Ali al-Muvaqqit. Taqi al-Din maintained close relations with many important members of the *ulema* and statesmen (chief among them was Hoca Sâdeddin), and was presented to Sultan Murad by the Grand Vizier Sokullu Mehmed Pasha.[45]

Taqi al-Din informed Sultan Murad, who had an interest in astronomy and astrology, that the *Ulug Bey Astronomical Tables* contained certain observational errors, resulting in errors in calculations made on the basis of those tables. Taqi al-Din indicated that these errors could be corrected if new observations were made and proposed that an observatory be built in Istanbul for that purpose. Sultan Murad was very pleased to be the patron of the first observatory in Istanbul and began construction immediately. He also provided all the financial assistance required for the project. In the meantime, Taqi al-Din pursued his studies at the Galata Tower, which he continued in 1577, at the partially completed new observatory called *Dar al-Rasad al-Jadîd* (the New Observatory).

The observatory, consisting of two separate buildings, one large and one small, was constructed at a location in the higher part of Tophane in Istanbul. Taqi al-Din had the instruments used in the old Islamic observatories reproduced with great care. In addition, he invented some new instruments, which were used for observational purposes for the first time. The observatory had a staff of sixteen people—eight "observers" (*râsid*), four clerks, and four assistants.[46] The observatory was designed to provide for the needs of the astronomers and included a library largely consisting of books on astronomy and mathematics. This institution, completed in 1579, was conceived as one of the largest observatories in the Islamic world. It was comparable to Tycho Brahe's (1546-1601) Uranienborg observatory built in 1576. The two observatories used instruments that were striking in their similarity. His astronomical tables, called the *Sidratu Muntahal-Afkâr fî Malakut al-Falak al-Davvâr (Lotus of Culmination of Thoughts in the Kingdom of Rotating Spheres)*, Taqi Al-Din states that he started activities on astronomy in Istanbul with 15 assistants in 1573.[47] The observatory continued to function until 22 January 1580, the date of its destruction. Religious arguments were put forth to justify this action, but it was really rooted in certain political conflicts.[48]

Taqi al-Din invented new observational instruments that were added to the array of those already in use for observation in the Islamic world. Among the instruments invented by Taqi al-Din in the observatory were the following:

The Sextant (*mushabbaha bi-'l manâtiq*)

This is used to measure the distances between the stars. Taqi al-din's *mushabbaha bi'l manâtiq* and Tycho Brahe's sextant should be considered among the great achievements of the sixteenth century astronomy. A *mushabbaha bi-l manâtiq* is composed of three rulers. Two of them are attached as the rulers of triquetrum. An arc is attached to the end of one of the rulers. Previous astronomers had not made an instrument like this. Taqi al-Din made this instrument to observe the radius of Venus that was mentioned in the tenth book of *Almagest*.[49]

The *Dhât al-Awtar*

This designates the spring and autumn equinoxes. Some astronomers set up a ring, which was not divided, parallel to the equator to designate this. The instrument was composed of a base in the form of a rectangle and four columns. The two columns were set on this base so that a string was stretched between them. One of them was equal to the cosine of the latitude of the country and the other to the sine. A hole was made on each of these parts according to this proportion. A rope was hung from these holes with a plumb.[50]

The Observational / Astronomical Clock

Taqi al-Din used a mechanical clock, which he made himself for his observations, and a wooden wall dial, which he set up in the observatory. The following is said in The *Astronomical Instruments for the Emperor's Table*:

> The ninth instrument is an astronomical clock.
> The following statement recorded from Ptolemy.
> "I would have been able to establish a great

regularity in method if I was able to measure the
time precisely."

Now Taqi al-Din planned, with the help of God, the astronomical
clock by the command of Sultan, God perpetuates his ruling days.
Thus, he was able to do what Ptolemy had failed to do. In addition,
in *Sidra al-Muntaha*, he says, "we built a mechanical clock with a
dial showing the hours, minutes and seconds and we divided every
minute into five seconds." This is a more precise clock than clocks
used previously and is, as a result, considered to be one of the more
important inventions in the area of applied astronomy developed
during the sixteenth century.[51]

When we compare the instruments which Taqi al-Din used in his
observatory with those used by Tycho Brahe, they are mostly similar,
but some of Taqi al-Din's are larger and more precise. For example,
they both used a mural quadrant (*libna*) for the observations of the
declinations of the sun and the stars. It is said that Taqi al-din preferred a mural quadrant instead of the *suds-i Fakhrî* and two rings
used by the previous astronomers. Taqi al-Din's quadrant was two
brass quadrants with a radius of six meters, placed on a wall, erected
on the meridian. The same instrument used by Brahe was only two
meters in diameter.[52]

Taqi al-Din integrated the Damascus and Samarkand traditions of
astronomy. His first task at the observatory was to undertake the cor-
rections of the *Ulug Bey Astronomical Tables*. He also undertook various observations of eclipses of the sun and the moon. The comet that
was present in the skies of Istanbul for one month during September
of 1578 was observed ceaselessly day and night and the results of the
observations were presented to the sultan. Taqi al-Din was, as a result
of the new methods he developed and the equipment he invented,
able to approach his observations in an innovative way and produce
novel solutions to astronomical problems. He also substituted the
use of a decimally based system for a sexagesimal one and prepared
trigonometric tables based on decimal fractions. He determined the
ecliptic degree as 23° 28' 40", which is very close to the current

value of 23° 27'. He used a new method in calculating solar param-
eters. He determined that the magnitude of the annual movement of
the sun's apogee was 63 seconds. Considering that the value known
today is 61 seconds, the method he used appears to have been more
precise than that of Copernicus (24 seconds) and Tycho Brahe (45
seconds). Taqi al-Din also wrote the first Ottoman book on auto-
matic machines, titled *el-Turuq al-Saniyya fi'l-âlât al-Rûhâniyya*.[53]

The observatory was witness to a great deal of activity within a
short period of time. Observations undertaken there were collected in
a work titled *Sidratu Muntaha'l-Afkâr fi Malakut al-Falak al-Davvâr*.
When compared with those of the contemporary Danish astronomer
Tycho Brahe, who also built an observatory, Taqi al-Din's observations are more precise. Furthermore, some of the instruments that
he had in his observatory were of superior quality to Tycho Brahe's.[54]

Discussion and Conclusion

The Ottomans added to their repertoire of knowledge, many subjects from the accomplishments of earlier Turkish and Islamic nation.
They also gained knowledge from their close involvement with the
Balkan and European states due to the close proximity of the countries. The Ottomans made good use of their close relations to other
ethnic groups and benefited greatly from their non-Muslim subjects
and neighbors. During the early years of the Empire, the Ottomans
had also utilized these relationships to keep up with new firearms
technology as it developed. In turn, they provided assistance and
encouragement to scientists from many fields, including medicine,
astronomy, and mathematics, by allowing them to conduct their
studies at the important centers of science and culture in the Islamic
world. This was a mutually beneficial arrangement. Engaging the
services of the best scientists and artists in every field from both the
west and the east without discriminating against those of a different
nationality or religion was an established and advantageous practice
in the Ottoman State.

Artists of many different ethnicities who worked in the palace
and other branches of government were eventually organized into
groups as their numbers grew. For example, in the art of painting

and decoration, the Anatolian Turkish group was designated *Tâife-i Rûmiyân*, the Persian group was called *Tâife-i Acemiyân*, and the European group was known as *Tâife-i Efrenciyân*. The physicians of the court were divided into two groups called *etibba-i Hassa* and *etibba-i Yahudiyân*. There were also Frank masters and other technicians among the civil servants who were employed as and when necessary. The Europeans in *Taife-i Efrenciyân* had a particularly important place in the Empire, for they served as a bridge between two worlds by introducing new technological advances from Europe into the Ottoman world and facilitating the exchange of ideas.

Especially after the second half of the fourteenth century, the Ottomans benefited greatly from their ties to the non-Muslim masters and technicians because of the role these outsiders played in the transfer of European firearms to the Ottoman State. In order to take full advantage of the technical knowledge of those outside the Empire, the Ottomans used the gunsmiths in workshops they had conquered in the Balkans to produce new firearms and instructed their subjects in firearms production. By assigning Muslim apprentices to the non-Muslim masters already working there, they encouraged learning and spread the new technology amongst their own subjects. Furthermore, prisoners of war and Christian cannon makers of *dhimmî* status were employed in different units of the government without being forced to convert.[55]

Since there was no close-mindedness about the transfer of new sciences and technologies from outsiders, debates on keeping out the foreign influence never occurred between statesmen, scholars, or the people.

Due to the Ottoman social structure, the Sultan had supreme power to decide what was beneficial for the state and people. Therefore, his methods of acquiring new technologies incited no criticism. Persons skilled in any art were rewarded by the Sultan, seemingly with no regard to their status as a Muslim or non-Muslim. A clear example of this is Mehmed the Conqueror giving four times as much, as had been expected, to Urban, a cannon maker.[56] In conclusion, non-Muslim subjects, as well as Muslims, played an important role in the advancement of Ottoman science and technology.

Other than those non-Muslims employed for military purposes, many were also employed in civil architecture and construction. These people usually worked on grand-scale projects, like mosque, palace, bridge, or castle construction,[57] as technicians and architects. Furthermore, non-Muslims often worked in translation, printing, painting, and decoration.[58]

The above is merely a brief outline of some of the Turkish scientific activities and related institutions that brought about the revival of culture, science, and learning in civilizations throughout the world. Many excellent works exist that can serve future researchers interested in this subject. Opportunities for further study abound, as the examples presented in this chapter could certainly be extended to cover a larger percentage of the vast contributions the Ottomans made over six hundred years. The classical scientific tradition that produced its finest works in the most magnificent period of the Empire was set forth in the scientific and educational institutions that are briefly mentioned above, in the scholarly circles established, and developed around these institutions. Still, the Ottoman classical tradition was preserved during this second phase of Ottoman science, when many more translations and transfers were made from European languages, and was able to survive with some of its basic elements until the second half of the nineteenth century.

Notes

Chapter Two
The Roots of Religious Tolerance in the Ottoman Empire
[1]The Seljuks' domination over the Abbasid caliphate began when Tughrul, the real founder of the dynasty, entered Baghdad in 447 AH / 1055 AD, putting an end to the Buwayhid authority there, and lasted until the year 590 AH / 1194 AD. Ali Ibn al-Athir, Al-Kamil fi al-Tarikh, vol. 9 (Leiden, 1853), 609; Ibn al-Athir, vol. 12, 106.
[2]Ibn al-Athir, vol. 10, 65-67; Steven Runciman, *The Fall of Constantinople* (Cambridge: Cambridge University Press, 1990), 25; Philip K. Hitti, *History of the Arabs* (London: Palgrave Macmillan, 1970), 475.
[3]Hitti, 475-476.
[4]Ibid., 476; Runciman, 27.
[5]Yaqut al-Hamawi, *Mu'jam al-Buldan*, vol. 4 (Beirut, 1990), 471.
[6]Ibn al-Athir, vol. 10, 67; Ibn al-Imad al-Hanbali, *Shadharat al-Dhahab*, vol. 2 Beirut, 311.
[7]Thomas Walker Arnold, *The Preaching of Islam* (London: Constable, 1913), 96.
[8]Runciman, 27.
[9]The early Seljuks established the Nizamiyya schools throughout their dominions at the hands of Nizam al-Mulk (d. 485 AH / 1092 AD) for the purpose of propagating Sunni Islam. Ibn Khallikan, *Wafayat al-A'yan*, ed. Ihsan Abbas (Beirut, 1977).
[10]Ahmad Abd al-Rahim Mustafa, *Usul al-Tarikh al-Othmani* (Cairo, 2003), 22-23.
[11]Stanford Shaw, *History of the Ottoman Empire and Modern Turkey*, vol. 1 (Cambridge: Cambridge University Press, 1976), 13.
[12]Lord Eversley, *The Turkish Empire: Its Growth and Decay* (London: T.F. Unwin, 1917), 14-15.
[13]Shaw, 11; Franz Taeschner, "Anadolu," in vol. 1 of *The Encyclopedia of Islam*, 2nd edition, ed. P.J. Bearman et al. (Leiden : Brill, 2005), 467.
[14]After the death of "Ala" al-Din Kayqubad in about 1307, the Seljuk Sultanate of Konya ceased to exist. Taeschner, 467.
[15]The Paulicians were an anti-Catholic Christian sect, and hence were condemned by most of the Christians. The Paulicians reject the worship of the Virgin and

deny that she is the Mother of God. Their name is derived from a certain Paul of Samosata, and their first appearance goes back to the first quarter of the eighth century. Paulicianism was propagated mainly in Armenia, Mesopotamia and N. Syria. C. A. Scott, "Paulicians" in vol. 9 of *The Encyclopedia of Religion and Ethics*, ed. James Hastings (New York: Scribner, 1961), 695-698.

[16]Taeschner, 470.

[17]Ibid. For more details on the millet system see: Yavuz Ercan, "Non-Muslim Communities Under the Ottoman Empire (*millet* system)," in vol. 2 of *The Great Ottoman-Turkish Civilisation*, ed. Kemal Çiçek et al. (Ankara: Yeni Turkiye, 2000).

[18]Eversley, 17.

[19]Colin Imber, "Othman," in vol. 8 of *The Encyclopedia of Islam*, 2nd ed., 180.

[20]Eversley, 18.

[21]Ekmeleddin İhsanoğlu, ed., *Al-Dawla al-Othmaniyya: Tarikh wa Hadara* trans. Saleh Sa'dawi (Istanbul, 1999), 291.

[22]Franz Babinger, "Orkhan" in vol. 3 of *The Encyclopedia of Islam*, 1st edition, ed. H.A.R. Gibb et al. (Leiden: Brill, 1938).

[23]Tash Kopru Zade, *al-Shaqa'iq al-Nu'maniyya fi Ulama' al-Dawla al-Othmaniyya* (Beirut, 1975), 8; Colin Imber, *The Ottoman Empire 1300-1650: the structure of power* (London: Palgrave Macmillan, 2002), 226.

[24]Ibn Khaldūn, *al-Ibar*, vol. 5 (Beirut, 1992), 664.

[25]Siam Savas, "The Role of Dervish Lodges in the Development of Turkish Culture," in vol. 4 of *The Great Ottoman-Turkish Civilisation*, 70.

[26]Ibid.

[27]R. Tschudi, "Bektashiyya," in vol. 1 of *The Encyclopedia of Islam*, 2nd ed., 1161.

[28]Ibid., 1162.

[29]Runciman, 44, note 2.

[30]Tschudi, 1162.

[31]Lord Kinross, The *Ottoman Centuries: The Rise and Fall of the Turkish Empire* (London: Morrow Quill Paperbacks, 1977), 31.

[32]Shaw, vol. 1, 15.

[33]There is another view, however, that emphasizes the Turkish origin of this word which means a noble man. Mustafa, 28; note 2.

[34]Ibn Battuta, *Tuhfat al-Nuzzar fi Ghara'ib al-Amsar* (Beirut, 1992), 285.

[35]Ibid., 287 .

[36]Ibid., 290 .

[37]Ibid., 285-320.

[38]Georgije Ostrogorsky, *History of the Byzantine State* (Oxford: Blackwell, 1968), 519 – 520; Elizabeth A. Zachariadou, "Orkhan," in vol. 8 of *The Encyclopedia of Islam* 2nd ed., 175.

[39]Babinger.

[40]İhsanoğlu, 156.

[41]J. Schacht, "Abu-Hanifa al-Nu'man," in vol. 1 of *The Encyclopedia of Islam* 2nd ed., 123-124.

[42]On the role of the Hanafite school in the legal system of the Ottoman state see: İhsanoğlu, 471-477.

III. Chapter Three
"Upon Them be Peace:" The Ottoman Spirit, Early Modern Models of Toleration, and Contemporary Debates over Multiculturalism

[1]The Ottoman Empire dates from 1299–1923 CE. The apogee of the Ottoman Empire in a political sense, which concerns us here, commenced with the conquest of Constantinople (Istanbul) in 1453. The expansion of the empire came to a halt in the late seventeenth century with the Treaty of Karlowitz (1699), which followed the first significant military defeat of the Ottomans and the loss of a large portion of their European territories.

[2]For instance, Emrah Ulker, "UN Uses Ottoman Tolerance as a Model" and Suat Kiniklioglu, "The Return of Ottomanism," in *Today's Zaman* (September 12, 2004, and June 1, 2008, respectively). *Zaman*, one of the major newspapers in Turkey, is associated with the Gülen movement, on which see M. Hakan Yavuz, "The Neo-Nur Movement of Fethullah Gülen," in *Islamic Political Identity in Turkey* (Oxford: Oxford University Press, 2003), 179-205. Also see: M. Hakan Yavuz, "Turkish Identity and Foreign Policy in Flux: The Rise of Neo-Ottomanism," *Critique* 12 (1998), 19-42, and "The Enduring Ottoman Legacy," in *Islamic Political Identity*, 37-58.

[3]Edward Said, *Orientalism* (1978) (New York: Vintage Books, 1994), 3.

[4]Gerald MacLean, "Writing Turkey: Then and Now," in *Writing Turkey: Explorations in Turkish History, Politics, and Cultural Identity* (Middlesex: Middlesex University Press, 2006), vii-xiii, citing ix. MacLean references Dennison Rusinow, "Yugoslavia's Disintegration and the Ottoman Past," in *Imperial Legacy: The Ottoman Impact on the Balkans and Middle East*, ed. Carl L. Brown (New York: Columbia University Press, 1996), 78-99.

[5]Vernon Van Dyke, *Human Rights, Ethnicity, and Discrimination* (Westport, CT: Greenwood Press, 1985), 74-75.

[6]Bhikhu Parekh, *Rethinking Multiculturalism: Cultural Diversity and Political Theory* (Cambridge, MA: Harvard University Press, 2000), 7; cf. 62.

[7]Milton J. Esman and Itamar Rabinovich, "The Study of Ethnic Politics in the Middle East," in *Ethnicity, Pluralism, and the State in the Middle East*, ed. Esman and Rabinovich (Ithaca, NY: Cornell University Press, 1988), 3-24, citing 16, 21. The latter quote continues, "as in the Ottoman *millets* and the South African homelands." The linguistic parallelism of this phrase nevertheless insinuates an insupportable link between the classical Ottoman Empire and the twentieth century South African apartheid regime. On the Ottoman millet system, see: Benjamin Braude and Bernard Lewis, eds., *Christians and Jews in the Ottoman Empire: The Functioning of a Plural Society*, 2 vols. (New York: Holmes & Meier, 1982).

[8]Christopher Hill, *The Century of Revolution, 1603–1714* (New York: Norton, 1980).

[9]Here "tolerance" is used in the modern sense of "freedom from bigotry or undue severity in judging the conduct of others" (*Oxford English Dictionary*, 2nd ed., 1989). For earlier meanings of "tolerance" and "toleration," see note 25 below.

[10]Samuel P. Huntington, "The Clash of Civilizations?" *Foreign Affairs* 72, no. 3 (1993), republished in *The Clash of Civilizations?: The Debate* (New York:

Foreign Affairs, 1996), 1-25, citing 16. For a survey of challenges that move beyond the scripted confines of this "debate," see: Engin I. Erdem, "'The Clash of Civilizations': Revisited after September 11," *Alternatives: Turkish Journal of International Relations* 1, no. 2 (2002), http://www.alternativesjournal.net/volume1/number2/erdem.htm.

[11]John L. Esposito, *Islam: The Straight Path,* 3rd ed. (New York: Oxford University Press, 2005), 269, groups Gülen with Tareq Ramadan in Europe, Seyyed Hossein Nasr in America, Yusuf Qardawi in Qatar, and Faysal Mawlawi in Lebanon. Also see: M. Hakan Yavuz and John L. Esposito, eds., *Turkish Islam and the Secular State: The Gülen Movement* (Syracuse, NY: Syracuse University Press, 2003).

[12]Peter Kivisto, *Multiculturalism in a Global Society* (Oxford: Blackwell, 2002), 37.

[13]Kivisto, "Canada and Australia: Ethnic Mosaics and State-Sponsored Multiculturalism," in *Multiculturalism,* 84-101, and "The United States as a Melting Pot: Myth and Reality," in *Multiculturalism,* 43-83.

[14]Kivisto, "Germany, France, and Shifting Conceptions of Citizenship," in *Multiculturalism,* 155-85.

[15]For a balanced assessment, see John L. Esposito, *The Islamic Threat: Myth of Reality,* 3rd. ed. (New York: Oxford University Press, 1999).

[16]Roger Hewitt, *White Backlash and the Politics of Multiculturalism* (Cambridge: Cambridge University Press, 2005), 1-17.

[17]John Lichfield, "Liberté, egalité, fraternité; The cry for redress among France's poor is constant — and familiar," *The Hamilton Spectator,* October 28, 2006, D09.

[18]Huntington, "The Clash of Civilizations?," 1, 16, 3.

[19]Ibid., 10. Huntington reiterates his anti-Islamic stance in *The Clash of Civilizations and the Remaking of the World Order* (New York: Free Press, 2002), 209-18.

[20]Huntington, "The Clash of Civilizations?," 8-9.

[21]Huntington underscores his rejection of "domestic" multiculturalism in *The Clash of Civilizations* (318). Parekh, *Rethinking Multiculturalism,* identifies the fallacies endemic to critiques such as Huntington's (77-78).

[22]Nushin Arbabzadah, "Multiculturalism in Medieval Islam," *openDemocracy* (Dec. 13, 2004), http://www.opendemocracy.net/arts-multiculturalism/article_2263.jsp#.

[23]Kemal Karpat, "The Ottoman Ethnic and Confessional Legacy in the Middle East," in *Ethnicity, Pluralism, and the State in the Middle East,* 35-53, citing 40.

[24]Suraiya Faroqhi, *Subjects of the Sultan: Culture and Daily Life in the Ottoman Empire* (London: I. B. Tauris, 2000), 25. On the uneven reception of non-Muslims in the region, see: Gerald MacLean, "The English Abroad: Travellers, Traders, Captives and Colonists in the Ottoman Mediterranean," in *Looking East: English Writing and the Ottoman Empire Before 1800* (New York: Palgrave Macmillan, 2007), 62-96. For a contemporary discussion, see Esposito, *Islamic Threat,* 246-48.

[25]James Ellison, *George Sandys: Travel, Colonialism and Tolerance in the Seventeenth Century* (Cambridge: D. S. Brewer, 2002), 2-7, and John Coffey, *Persecution and Toleration in Protestant England, 1558—1689* (Harlow: Longman, 2000), 1-20.

[26]John Marshall, *John Locke, Toleration and Early Enlightenment Culture: Religious Intolerance and Arguments for Religious Toleration in Early Modern and "Early*

Enlightenment" Europe (Cambridge: Cambridge University Press, 2006), 549-50.

[27]Norbert Rehrmann, "A Legendary Place of Encounter: The *Convivencia* of Moors, Jews, and Christians in Medieval Spain," in *The Historical Practice of Diversity: Transcultural Interactions from the Early Modern Mediterranean to the Postcolonial World*, ed. Dirk Hoerder (New York: Berghahn Books, 2003), 35-53.

[28]Ellison, 2.

[29]Henry Kamen, *The Rise of Toleration* (New York: McGraw-Hill, 1967), 211.

[30]On "the intolerance of the English Restoration," see Kamen, 201-15, and Marshall, 17, 94, passim.

[31]P. J. Vatikiotis, "Non-Muslims in Muslim Society," in *Ethnicity, Pluralism, and the State in the Middle East*, 54-70, citing 68-69. Cf. Said, *Orientalism*, 312-14.

[32]This is a phrase popularized by Richard Knolles in *The Generall Historie of the Turkes, from the first beginning of that Nation to the rising of the Othoman Familie* (London, 1603), which went through six editions, with successive additions, during the seventeenth century.

[33]Aslı Çırakman, *From the "Terror of the World" to the "Sick Man of Europe": European Images of Ottoman Empire and Society from the Sixteenth Century to the Nineteenth* (New York: Peter Lang, 2002), 111-12.

[34]Ellison, 57-59, referring to Edwin Sandys, *Europae Speculum or A View or Survey of the State of Religion in the Westerne parts of the World* (The Hague, 1629).

[35]Ellison, 3.

[36]Anthony Pagden, *Lords of All the World: Ideologies of Empire in Spain, Britain and France c. 1500 – c. 1800* (New Haven, CT: Yale University Press, 1995), 1-10, citing 4.

[37]The Acts of Union, 1707, joined the formerly autonomous realms of Scotland and England into the Kingdom of Great Britain. On the resurgence of Scottish nationalism in the late twentieth century, see: Kivisto, "John Bull's Island: Britain in a Postcolonial World," in *Multiculturalism*, 116-54.

[38]Gerald MacLean, "Ottomanism before Orientalism?: Bishop King Praises Henry Blount, Passenger in the Levant," *Travel Knowledge: European "Discoveries" in the Early Modern Period*, ed. Ivo Kamps and Jyotsna G. Singh (New York: Palgrave, 2001), 85–96, citing 86-87. Also see: MacLean, *Looking East*, 20-23, passim.

[39]Ellison, 1.

[40]Çırakman, 54, 59, 82.

[41]Ellison, 50.

[42]George Sandys, *A Relation of a Journey begun An: Dom: 1610* (London, 1615), 81.

[43]Ibid., 56.

[44] Ibid., 249.

[45]Ibid., 57.

[46]Ibid., 83.

[47]*Qur'an, Sura* 2: 256.

[48]Samuel C. Chew, "The Prophet and His Book," in *The Crescent and the Rose: Islam and England during the Renaissance* (New York: Oxford University Press, 1937), 387-451.

[49]Çırakman, 64-65.

[50]Sonia P. Anderson, *An English Counsel in Turkey: Paul Rycaut at Smyrna, 1667–1678* (Oxford: Clarendon Press, 1984), 20. Also see: Linda T. Darling, "Ottoman Politics through British Eyes: Paul Rycaut's *The Present State of the Ottoman Empire*," *Journal of World History* 5.1 (1994), 71-97, and MacLean, *Looking East,* 191-96.

[51]For an influential duplication of Rycaut's views, see Aaron Hill, *A Full and Just Account of the Present State of the Ottoman Empire in all its Branches* (1709); for a widely read refutation, see Mary Wortley Montagu, *Letters . . . Written during Her Travels in Europe, Asia and Africa*, also known as *The Turkish Embassy Letters* (composed 1716–18; published posthumously 1763).

[52]Paul Rycaut, "Epistle Dedicatory," *The Present State of the Ottoman Empire* (London, 1668), sig. A3.

[53]Ibid.

[54]Ibid., 98.

[55]Ibid., 99-102.

[56]Rycaut, *The Present State of the Greek and Armenian Churches* (London, 1679), 13, 21.

[57]Ellison, 2.

[58]Rycaut, *Ottoman Empire*, 127, cf. 135. I have modernized spelling in this passage.

[59]On the supplicant status of the English vis-à-vis the Ottomans, see MacLean, *Looking East,* 76, passim. On early modern English anxieties about their racial inferiority vis-à-vis the classical Mediterranean-centered theory of climatic zones, see Mary Floyd-Wilson, "The Marginal English," *English Ethnicity and Race in Early Modern Drama* (Cambridge: Cambridge University Press, 2003), 1-19.

[60]MacLean suggests, but does not develop, this point in *Looking East*, 245-46.

[61]John L. Esposito, in *Unholy War: Terror in the Name of Islam* (Oxford: Oxford University Press, 2002), considers Khatami as one of many "voices of reform and dialogue" in the Muslim world today (133-41). Concomitantly, Esposito challenges Huntington's proposal of "an inevitable clash of civilizations" (126-33), which he frames as a question.

[62]Thomas Michel, Forward to *Toward a Global Civilization of Love and Tolerance*, by M. Fethullah Gülen (Somerset, NJ: The Light, 2004), i-iii, citing i. Michel is identified as "director of the Jesuits' office for interreligious dialogue" in "Jesuit Expert Sees Hope in Catholic-Muslim Relationship," *JesuitUSA News* (March 19, 2003), http://www.companysj.com/sjusa/030319.htm.

[63]Gülen, "The Necessity of Interfaith Dialogue," in *Essays—Perspectives—Opinions*, rev. ed. (Somerset, NJ: The Light, 2004), 35. This essay was first presented at the Parliament of World Religions, Cape Town, December 1-8, 1999; it was first published in 2000.

[64]Ibid., 36. The first expulsion of Muslims, along with Jews, occurred immediately after the 1492 conquest of Granada; the final expulsion of the Moriscos, who were of Muslim provenance, was propelled by state decree in 1609.

[65]Gülen, "True Muslims Cannot Be Terrorists," in *Essays—Perspectives—Opinions*, 100.

[66]Gülen, "A Comparative Approach to Islam and Democracy," in *Essays— Perspectives—Opinions*, 19.

[67]Gülen, "Interfaith Dialogue," 37, cf. 42.

[68]Gülen, "A Comparative Approach," 15.

[69]Gülen, "Interfaith Dialogue," 41.

[70]Thomas Michel, "Gülen as Educator and Religious Teacher," in *Essays— Perspectives—Opinions*, 106-7.

[71]Ibid., 107-8, cf. 111. For a fuller view, see: Sabrina Tavernise, with Sebnem Arsu, "Turkish Schools Offer Pakistan a Gentler Islam," *The New York Times*, May 4, 2008, A1.

[72]Elisabeth Bumiller, "21st-Century Warnings of a Threat Rooted in the 7th," *New York Times*, December 12, 2005, A19, reports on the propaganda use of the "restoration of the caliphate" catch-phase by the Bush administration. Also see: Esposito, *Unholy War*, 62, 90.

[73]M. Fethullah Gülen, "Regarding the Information Age and the Clash of Civilizations," in *Toward a Global Civilization of Love and Tolerance*, 254-57, citing 256.

[74]Ali Ünal and Alphonse Williams, *Advocate of Dialogue: Fethullah Gülen* (Fairfax, VA: The Fountain, 2000), 8, n12.

[75]Edward W. Said, *The World, the Text and the Critic* (Cambridge, MA: Harvard University Press, 1983), 29, where he continues, "its social goals are noncoercive knowledge produced in the interests of human freedom." For an *apropos* analysis of Said's "secular criticism," see Aamir R. Mufti, "Auerbach in Istanbul: Edward Said, Secular Criticism, and the Question of Minority Culture," *Critical Inquiry* 25.1 (1998), 95-125. Mufti observes that "Said most often opposes the term secular not to religion per se, but to nationalism" (107).

[76]Edward Said, "The Clash of Definitions," in *Reflections on Exile and Other Essays* (Cambridge, MA: Harvard University Press, 2003), 569-90, citing 580. Said, a literary critic, focuses on Huntington's "managerial poetics" (582). For a related sociological analysis, see: Esposito, "Islam and the West: A Clash of Civilizations," in *The Islamic Threat*, 212-89.

[77]Said, "The Clash of Definitions," 585; cf. 577-78 and 585-86.

[78]Ibid., 587.

[79]Gülen, "Interfaith Dialogue," 43.

IV. Chapter Four
Diversity, Legal Pluralism and Peaceful Co-Existence
in the Ottoman Centuries

[1]John Griffiths, "What is legal pluralism?" *Journal of Legal Pluralism and Unofficial Law* 24 (1986): 8.

[2]Peter Fitzpatrick, *The mythology of modern law* (London: Routledge, 1992), 3.

[3]Griffiths, 7-8.

[4]Roger Cotterell, *The politics of jurisprudence* (Austin: Butterworths, 1989), 124.

[5]Robert S. Summers, "Naive instrumentalism and the law," in *Law, morality, and society*, ed. P.M.S. Hacker and J. Raz (Oxford: Clarendon Press, 1977), 122.

[6]Griffiths, 34.

[7]Alan Hunt, "Law and the condensation of power," *Law and Social Inquiry* 17 (1992): 59.

[8]Antony Allott, *The limits of law* (London: Butterworths, 1980), 45-46.

[9]For details: Ihsan Yilmaz, *Muslim laws, politics and society in modern nation-states* (Oxford: Ashgate, 2005), 9-30.

[10]For details: Anthony Bradney, "The Legal status of Islam within the United Kingdom," in *Islam and European Legal Systems*, ed. Silvio Ferrari and Anthony Bradney (Dartmouth: Ashgate, 2000), 181-198.

[11]Jean Jacques Waardenburg, "Muslim associations and official bodies in some European countries," in *The integration of Islam and Hinduism in Western Europe*, ed. W.A.R. Shadid and P.S. van Koningsveld (Kampen: Kok Pharos Publishing, 1991), 36.

[12]Ihsan Yilmaz, *Muslim laws, politics and society in modern nation-states* (Oxford: Ashgate, 2005), 49-82.

[13]Werner F.Menski, "Asians in Britain and the question of adaptation to a new legal order: Asian laws in Britain," in *Ethnicity, identity, migration: The South Asian context*, ed. Milton Israel and Narendra Wagle (Toronto: University of Toronto, 1993), 241.

[14]Richard Jones and Welhengama Gnanpala, *Ethnic Minorities in English Law*, (Stoke-on-Trent: Trentham Books, 2000), 103-104.

[15]Yilmaz, *Muslim laws*, 66-81.

[16]*Marriage Act*, 1949, s. 46(2); Qureshi v Qureshi [1972] Fam 173.

[17] Yilmaz, *Muslim laws*, 71-72.

[18]Carolyn Hamilton, *Family, law and religion* (London: Sweet & Maxwell, 1995), 42.

[19]Sydney Collins, *Coloured minorities in Britain: Studies in British race relations based on African, West Indian and Asiatic immigrants* (London: Lutterworth Press, 1957), 160.

[20]Yilmaz, *Muslim laws*, 74.

[21]See also: Dilip Hiro, *Black British, white British: A history of race relations in Britain* (London: Grafton Books, 1991), 159; Hamilton, 74.

[22]Yilmaz, *Muslim laws*, 73.

[23]Family Law Act, 1986, s. 44(1); *Matrimonial Causes Act*, 1973, s. 1.

[24]*Domicile and Matrimonial Proceedings Act*, 1973, s. 16; also: Family Law Act, 1986, s. 44(1).

[25]Yilmaz, *Muslim laws*, 77.

[26]Ibid., 80.

[27]See: Bernard Berkovits, "*Get* and *talaq* in English law: Reflections on law and policy," in *Islamic family law*, ed. Chibli Mallat and Jane Connors (London: Graham & Trotman, 1990), 119-146; Alan Reed, "Extra-judicial divorces since Berkovits," *Family Law* 26 (1996): 100-103; Rhona Schuz, (1996) "Divorce and ethnic minorities," in *Divorce: Where next?*, ed. Michael Freeman (Aldershot: Dartmouth, 1996), 131-157; Menski, "Asians in Britain," 9; Hamilton, 118-120; Lucy Carroll, "Muslim women and 'Islamic divorce' in England," *Journal of Muslim Minority Affairs* 17 (1997): 100; Werner F. Menski and Prakash Shah, "Cross-cultural conflicts of marriage and divorce involving South Asians in

Britain," in *Cross-cultural family relations: Reports of a socio-legal seminar*, ed. Fons Strijbosch and Mari-Claire Foblets (Onati: International Institute for the Sociology of Law, 1996), 167-184.

[28]Yilmaz, *Muslim laws*, 150-151.

[29]See: Bernard Berkovits, "Get and *talaq* in English law: Reflections on law and policy," *Islamic family law*, ed. Chibli Mallat and Jane Connors (London: Graham & Trotman, 1990), 119-146; Reed; Hamilton.

[30]Yilmaz, *Muslim laws*, 150-151; Hamilton, 118-120; Rhona Schuz, "Divorce and ethnic minorities," in *Divorce: Where next?* ed. Michael Freeman (Aldershot: Dartmouth, 1996), 150; Carroll, 100.

[31]For details: Sonia Nurin Shah-Kazemi, *Untying the Knot: Muslim Women, Divorce and the Shariah* (London: Author, 2001). On 11 April 1986, the *Guardian* reported that there were more than 1000 Muslims limping marriage cases, in Britain. Zaki Badawi, "Muslim justice in a secular state," in *God's law versus state law: The construction of Islamic identity in Western Europe*, ed. Michael King (London: Grey Seal, 1995), 80 reports that in Amsterdam there were 750 Moroccan women in a position between marriage and divorce. The same problem also occurs among Jews (Berkovits, 138-139; Reed).

[32]Badawi, 77.

[33]Hamilton, 121.

[34]Reed, 103.

[35]Schuz, 141; Carroll underlines that the council claims to have dealt with more than 1150 cases (115); Badawi, 73-80; David Pearl and Werner F. Menski, *Muslim family law*, 3rd ed. (London: Sweet & Maxwell, 1998).

[36]For details: Yilmaz, *Muslim laws*, 171-173; Carroll, 97-115; also Shah-Kazemi.

[37]John L. Esposito with Natana J. DeLong-Bas, *Women in Muslim family law*, 2nd ed. (New York: Syracuse University Press, 2001), 9.

[38]Yilmaz, *Muslim laws*, 16-17.

[39]Justin McCarthy, *The Ottoman Turks – An Introductory History to 1923* (London: Longman, 1997), 128.

[40]Count Leon Ostrorog, *The Angora reform* (London: University of London Press, 1927), 79.

[41]Norman Itzkowitz, *Encarta Online Encyclopedia*, s.v. "Ottoman Empire," http://encarta.msn.com/text_761553949___3/Ottoman_Empire.html.

[42]Gulnihal Bozkurt, "The Reception of Western European Law in Turkey (From the Tanzimat to the Turkish Republic, 1839-1939)," *Der Islam* 75 (1998): 283.

[43]Ibid., 284.

[44]For details: Ali Bulaç, *İslam ve demokrasi*. 3rd ed. (Istanbul: Iz, 1995), 161-167; Ali Bulaç, *Din ve modernizm* (Istanbul: Iz, 1995), 82-87.

[45]Serhat Gürpınar and Seref Malkoç, "Anayasa-uzlaşma belgesi önerisi: Yeni bir Medine vesikası taslağı üzerine tartışma," *Bilgi ve Hikmet* 7 (1994): 169-172. It is also well known that a huge body of literature exists regarding human rights in Islam. In that context, the *millet* system, the Medina Constitutional Charter and the situation of non-Muslim minorities in Muslim countries have been continuously referred to and discussed. This issue at times constitutes an important section in contemporary books about Islamic law and society in Turkey. For such an

example: Mehmet Akif Aydın, *İslam ve Osmanlı hukuku araştırmalari* (Istanbul: İz, 1996), 229-236.

[46]Bahri Zengin of the Welfare Party is the champion of these ideas. For example: *Milli Gazete*, November 14, 1995, 12. Taha Akyol, *Medine'den Lozan'a* (Istanbul: Milliyet Yayınları, 1996), 12 strongly criticises Zengin's views and asks what will be the law of this co-ordinatorship, and who would produce it. In the end he seems to conclude that an apparatus, whether the state or not, will have to be in the role of ultimate authority of producing or enacting laws and of being a co-ordinator.

[47]Ali Ünal and Alphonse Williams, *Advocate of Dialogue: Fethullah Gülen* (Fairfax: The Fountain, 2000), 256-258.

[48]Ibid., 243.

[49]Ibid., 67.

[50]Ibid., 67-70. I discuss Gülen's discourse and practice vis-à-vis diversity, Muslim legal pluralism and acceptance of the Other elsewhere in detail: Ihsan Yilmaz, "*Ijtihad* and *Tajdid* by Conduct: Gülen and His Movement," in *Turkish Islam and the secular state: The Gulen movement*, ed. John L. Esposito and Hakan Yavuz (New York: Syracuse University Press, 2003); Ihsan Yilmaz, "Inter-Madhhab Surfing, Neo-*Ijtihad*, and Faith-Based Movement Leaders," in *The Islamic School of Law: Evolution, Devolution and Progress*, ed. Frank Vogel, Peri Bearman and Ruud Peters (Cambridge: Harvard University Press, 2005); Ihsan Yilmaz, "State, law, civil society and Islam in contemporary Turkey," *Muslim World* 95 (2005).

[51]M. Fethullah Gülen, *Toward a Global Civilization of Love and Tolerance* (Somerset: Light, 2004), 249-250.

[52]Ibid., 58-59.

[53]Peter Mandaville, "What does progressive Islam look like?" *Isim Newsletter* 12 (2003): 33-34 states that "in the case of Turkey's Gülen movement... we find elements of Sufi spirituality fused with socio-economic liberalism in a highly successful transnational educational project. Dozens of Gülen-sponsored schools, emphasizing a modernist curriculum against a backdrop of 'non-invasive' Islamic morality, now operate throughout much of the Balkans and Central Asia."

[54]Thomas Michel, *Said Nursi's Views on Muslim-Christian Understanding* (Istanbul: Soz, 2006), 70.

[55]Elsewhere I tried to show that it is more proper to call Al Qaeda terror, "neo-assassin terror" rather than mistakenly calling it "Islamic terror". I attempted to justify this new term by comparing general characteristics and roots of Al Qaeda terror and assassin (*Hashshashin*) terror of medieval Nizari Isma'ilis & Hassan Sabbah that existed at the time of Seljuk Turks. For details: Ihsan Yilmaz, "Panacea to Neo-Assassin Terror: Nursi's Discourse & Praxis" (paper presented at "Islam in Contemporary Turkey: Perspectives of Bediuzzaman Said Nursi" Conference, Cleveland, Ohio, November 5-6, 2006).

[56]Selçuk Gültaşli, "Prince Hasan: Turning the Page on 1916," *Today's Zaman*, March 21, 2007, Interviews Section, http://www.todayszaman.com/tz-web/detaylar.do?load=detay&link=106062.

V. Chapter Five
Christian-Muslim Interaction on the Ottoman Frontier:
Gaza and Accommodation in Early Ottoman History

[1]Leopold von Ranke, *The Ottoman and the Spanish Empires in the Sixteenth and Seventeenth Centuries,* trans. Walter K. Kelly (Philadelphia: Lea & Blanchard, 1845), 7.

[2]Paul Wittek, *The Rise of the Ottoman Empire* (London: Royal Asiatic Society, 1938), 14-51; quotation on 43.

[3]Halil İnalcık, "The Question of the Emergence of the Ottoman State," *International Journal of Turkish Studies* 2 (1980): 71-79.

[4]Cemal Kafadar, *Between Two Worlds: The Construction of the Ottoman State* (Berkeley: University of California Press, 1995), 66-72.

[5]Kafadar, *Between Two Worlds,* 63-65, 73-80; see also Linda T. Darling, "Contested Territory: Ottoman Holy War in Comparative Context," *Studia Islamica* 91 (2000): 139-41.

[6]Kafadar, *Between Two Worlds,* 138-54.

[7]Heath W. Lowry, *The Nature of the Early Ottoman State* (Albany: State University of New York Press, 2003), 38-42; see also Feridun M. Emecen, "Gazâya Dâir: XIV. Yüzyıl Kaynakları Arasında Bir Gezinti," *Prof. Dr. Hakkı Dursun Yıldız Armağanı* (Ankara: Türk Tarih Kurumu Basımevi, 1995), 195-96.

[8]Lowry, *The Nature of the Early Ottoman State,* 49-54.

[9]Lowry, *The Nature of the Early Ottoman State,* 86-109.

[10]Lowry, *The Nature of the Early Ottoman State,* 115-29.

[11]Lowry, *The Nature of the Early Ottoman State,* 55, 64-65, 78, 140-43.

[12]Emecen, "Gazâya Dâir," 191-97; Şinasi Tekin, "XIV. Yüzyılda Yazılmış Gazilik Tarikası 'Gaziliğin Yolları' Adlı bir Eski Anadolu Türkçesi Metni ve Gazâ/Cihâd Kavramları Hakkında," *Journal of Turkish Studies* 13 (1989): 139-204.

[13]For the comparisons on which these conclusions are based, see Darling, "Contested Territory," 133-63.

[14]This tactic was previously used by Wittek and Speros Vryonis to dissect the Seljuk conquest of Anatolia, but they did not apply it to the Ottoman conquests; in addition to Wittek's book in n. 2, see Speros Vryonis, *The Decline of Medieval Hellenism in Asia Minor and the Process of Islamization from the Eleventh through the Fifteenth Century* (Berkeley: University of California Press, 1971).

[15]Kerimuddin Mahmud Aksarayi, *Müsâmeret ül-Ahbâr: Mogollar Zamanında Türkiye Selçukları Tarihi,* ed. Osman Turan (Ankara: Türk Tarih Kurumu Basımevi, 1944), trans. Mürsel Öztürk as *Müsâmeretü'l-Ahbâr* (Ankara: Türk Tarih Kurumu Basımevi, 2000); and Anonymous, *Anadolu Selçukluları Devleti Tarihi, III: Histoire des Seldjoukides d'Asie mineure,* ed. F. N. Uzluk (Ankara: Türkiye Yayınevi, 1952).

[16]Linda T. Darling, "Persianate Sources on Anatolia and the Early History of the Ottomans," *Studies on Persianate Societies* 2 (2004): 126-44; see especially 132.

[17]Keith Hopwood, "Tales of Osman: Legend or History?" in XIII. *Türk Tarih Kongresi (1999): Kongreye Sunulan Bildiriler* (Ankara: Türk Tarih Kurumu Basımevi, 2002), 2056. According to the Persian chronicles, all the border tribes were semi-sedentary.

[18]These conditions are well described in Keith R. Hopwood, "The Byzantine-

Turkish Frontier c.1240-1300," in *Acta Viennensia Ottomanica*, ed. Markus Köhbach, Gisela Procházka-Eisl, and Claudia Römer (Vienna: Institut für Orientalistik, 1999), 153-61.

[19]Colin Imber, "The Legend of Osman Gazi," in *The Ottoman Emirate (1300-1389)*, ed. Elizabeth Zachariadou (Rethymnon: Crete University Press, 1993), 68.

[20]Lowry, *The Nature of the Early Ottoman State*, 66, describes these egalitarian relations.

[21]For the dates of these inscriptions see Lowry, *The Nature of the Early Ottoman State*, 42, 64; Irène Beldiceanu-Steinherr, "Analyse de la titulature d'Orhan sur deux inscriptions de Brousse," *Turcica* 34 (2002): 223-40; Ludvik Kalus, "L'Inscription de Bursa au nom du sultan Orhān, datée de 738/1337-38: Comment faut-il la lire?" *Turcica* 36 (2004): 233-51.

[22]Aşıkpaşazâde, *'Āshıkpashazādeh Ta'rīkhī: a History of the Ottoman Empire to A.H. 833 (AD 1478)*, ed. 'Ali Bey (Istanbul: Matbaa-ı 'Amire, 1914; rpt. Westmead: Gregg International Publishers, 1970), 15, 19.

[23]Lowry, *The Nature of the Early Ottoman State*, 73-74.

[24]Mehmed Neşri, *Kitâb-i Cihân-Nümâ*, ed. Faik Reşit Unat and Mehmed A. Köymen (Ankara: Türk Tarih Kurumu Basımevi, 1949), 88-89.

[25]Irène Beldiceanu-Steinherr, *Recherches sur les actes des règnes des sultans Osman, Orkhan et Murad I*, Societas Academic Dacoromana, Acta Historica, 7 (Monachii: Societatea Academica Romana, 1967), docs. 5, 7, 10, 11, 12.

[26]Aşıkpaşazâde, *'Āshıkpashazādeh Ta'rīkhī*, 40.

[27]Aşıkpaşazâde, *'Āshıkpashazādeh Ta'rīkhī*, 20, 38.

[28]Linda T. Darling, "The Development of Ottoman Governmental Institutions in the Fourteenth Century: A Reconstruction," in *Living in the Ottoman Ecume209nical Community: Essays in Honour of Suraiya Faroqhi*, ed. Vera Costantini and Markus Koller (Leiden: E. J. Brill, 2008), 27-28.

[29]Beldiceanu-Steinherr, *Recherches*, docs. 36, 40, 50.

[30]Halil İnalcık, *The Ottoman Empire: The Classical Age*, trans. Norman Itzkowitz (London: Weidenfeld and Nicolson, 1973), 12. For the *pençik* and *kazaskerlik*, see Aşıkpaşazâde, *'Āshıkpashazādeh Ta'rīkhī*, 54.

[31]G. Georgiades Arnakis, "Gregory Palamas among the Turks and Documents of His Captivity as Historical Sources," *Speculum* 26 (1951): 106, 114.

[32]Tijana Krstic, "How to Read Ottoman Soldiers' Stories: 'Syncretism,' 'Anti-Syncretism,' and Conversion to Islam in Fifteenth-Century Ottoman Rumeli," unpublished paper.

[33]On the Ottomans' Christian military forces see Halil İnalcık, *Hicrî 835 Tarihli Sûret-i Defter-i Sancak-ı Arvanid* (Ankara: Türk Tarih Kurumu Basımevi, 1954); idem, "Tımariotes chrétiens en Albanie au XV. siècle d'après un register de tımars ottoman," *Mitteilungen des österreichischen Staatsarchive* 4 (1951): 118-38; Heath W. Lowry, *Fifteenth-Century Ottoman Realities: Christian Peasant Life on the Aegean Island of Limnos* (Istanbul: Eren, 2002).

[34]Lowry, *The Nature of the Early Ottoman State*, 137-38.

[35]Neşri, Kitâb-i Cihân-Nümâ 541-43; Linda T. Darling, "Prolegomena for a Study of Ottoman Administrative Documents and Ilhanid Precedents," in *Enjeux*

politiques, économiques et militaires en Mer noire (XIVe-XXIe siècles): Études à la mémoire de Mihail Guboglu, ed. Faruk Bilici, Ionel Cândea, and Anca Popescu (Braïla, Romania: Éditions Istros, Musée de Braïla, 2007), 465-80.

[36]Anonymous, *Gazavât-ı Sultân Murâd b. Mehemmed Hân,* ed. Halil İnalcık and Mevlûd Oğuz (Ankara: Türk Tarih Kurumu Basımevi, 1978). This book is about the Crusade of Varna, suggesting that Murad may not have won the title of gazi until then.

[37]İsmail Hikmet Ertaylan, *Ahmed-i Dāî: Hayatı ve Eserleri* (Istanbul: İstanbul Üniversitesi Edebiyat Fakültesi, 1952), 3-28, 129, 157-60; Walther Björkman, "Die Anfänge der türkischen Briefsammlungen," *Orientalia Suecana* 5 (1956): 20-29; Çetin Derdiyok, "Eski Türk Edebiyatı'nda Mektup Yazma Kuralları Hakkında Bilgi Veren En Eski Eser: Ahmed Dâ'i'nin *Teressül'*ü," *Toplumsal Tarih* 1, no. 6 (June 1994): 56-59; Şinasi Tekin, "Fatih Sultan Mehmed Devrine âit bir İnşâ Mecmuası," *Journal of Turkish Studies* 20 (1996): 282-90.

[38]For the scholarship on this topic see Oktay Özel, "Limits of the Almighty: Mehmed II's 'Land Reform' Revisited," *Journal of the Economic and Social History of the Orient* 42 (1999): 226-46.

[39]This episode is described in Halil İnalcık, "The Policy of Mehmed II toward the Greek Population of Istanbul and the Byzantine Buildings of the City," *Dumbarton Oaks Papers* 23/24 (1969/70): 231-49, rpt. in idem, *The Ottoman Empire: Conquest, Organization and Economy* (London: Variorum Reprints, 1978), VI.

[40]Franz Babinger, *Mehmed the Conqueror and His Time,* ed. William C. Hickman, trans. Ralph Manheim (Princeton: Princeton University Press, 1978), 462-77, 494-508.

[41]Lowry, *The Nature of the Early Ottoman State,* 115-30.

[42]See Linda T. Darling, "The Renaissance and the Middle East," in *A Companion to the Worlds of the Renaissance,* ed. Guido Ruggiero (Oxford: Blackwell, 2002), 55-69.

[43]Joel Shinder, "Early Ottoman Administration in the Wilderness: Some Limits on Comparison," *International Journal of Middle East Studies* 9 (1978): 503-5; Halil İnalcık, "How to Read 'Āshık Pasha-Zāde's History," in *Studies in Ottoman History in Honour of Professor V. L. Ménage,* ed. Colin Heywood and Colin Imber (Istanbul: Isis Press, 1994), 139-56.

[44]Lowry, *The Nature of the Early Ottoman State,* 40.

VI. Chapter Six
The Role of Ottoman law in the Establishment of Pax Ottomana

[1]Cemal Kafadar, *Between Two Worlds: The Construction of the Ottoman State* (Berkeley: University of California Press, 1995), 11.

[2]"The noble families in the Balkan countries were assimilated to the mass of Ottoman *tımariots* and became Muslim. Islamization was actually a psycho-social phenomenon among the Christian *sipâhîs,* who were definitely the first converts in the Empire. The state did not as a rule seek their conversion to Islam as a necessary prerequisite to enrolment in the Ottoman *'askerî* class, and it did not even attempt to achieve such conversion by indirect methods." Halil İnalcık, "Ottoman Methods of Conquest," *Studia Islamica* 2 (1954): 116.

[3]Caroline Finkel, *Osman's Dream: The History of the Ottoman Empire* (New York: Perseus Books Group, 2006), 59.

[4]See for instance, Akgündüz, II, 67, ar. 187: "*Ve raiyet sipahi öşrünü anbara iletüp ve hisar erenlerinin hisara iletmek reaya üzerine bidan-ı marufedir. Amma mesafe bir günlükten ziyade olsa def'an lil-harac teklif olunmaya deyü emr olunmuştur. Ve ortakçılara hasıl götürmek teklif olunmaya...*"

[5]Ahmet Akgündüz, *Osmanlı Kanunameleri ve Hukuki tahlilleri, İstanbul 1990, I, 368*

[6]Akgündüz, III, 458

[7]Akgündüz, II, 422

[8]Akgündüz, II, 594

[9]Akgündüz, II, 53, md. 98

[10]Paul Wittek, *The Rise of the Ottoman Empire*, (London: Royal Asiatic Society, 1963), 42-43.

[11]Akgündüz, I, 406

[12]See for the imperial edict granted to Genoese Galatians, Akgündüz, I, 477

[13]Haim Gerber, *State Society and Law in Islam, Ottoman Law in Comparative Perspective,* State University of New York Press 1994, 55-57

VII. Chapter Seven
The Turkish Jews

[1]Based on: Naim Güleryüz, *The History of the Turkish Jews*, (İstanbul: Gözlem Gazetecilik Basın ve Yayın A.Ş., 1991); and Güleryüz, *Türk Yahudileri Tarihi –1- 20.yüzyıl başına kadar* (İstanbul: Gözlem Gazetecilik Basın ve Yayın A.Ş., 1993).

[2]Moise Franco, *Essai sur l'histoire des Israélites de l'Empire Ottoman depuis les origines jusqu'a nos jours* (Paris: Librarie Durlacher,1897), 35-37. Original edict at the National Library, Madrid.

[3]Minna Rozen, *A History of the Jewish Community in Istanbul The Formative Years, 1453 – 1566* (Boston: Brill Leiden, 2002), 47.

[4]Abraham Galante, *Histoire des Juifs d'Istanbul, depuis laprise de cette ville en 1453 par Fatih Mehmet II jusqu'a nos jours,* vol. 1 (Istanbul: İmprimerie Hüsnütabiat, 1941),7.

[5]Yusuf Sarinay, ed., *Living Together Under the Same Sky*, Beyhan Haciomeroğlu and Durmus Kandira, trans., (Ankara: Başbakanlık Basımevi, 2006), 170.

[6]Flavius, *Antiquitatum Iudaicum,*12-119.

[7]Franco, 27.

[8]Ibid., 28.

[9]Mark Alan Epstein, *The Ottoman Jewish Communities and their Role in the 15th and 16th Centuries* (Freiburg: Klaus Schwarz Verlag, 1980), 26-27.

[10]Joseph Nehama, *Histoire des Israelites de Salonique*, 7 vols. (Salonica: Librairie Molho, 1978).

[11]Güleryüz, *History of the Turkish Jews*, 7; Bernard Lewis, *The Jews of Islam* (Princeton: Princeton University Press, 1984), 135-136.

[12]*Encyclopedia Judaica*, vol. 16, 1532.

[13]Franco, 38

[14]Güleryüz, *History of the Turkish Jews*, 9.

[15]Franco, 37

[16]Avigdor Levy, ed., *Jews, Turks, Ottomans*, (Syracuse: Syracuse University Press, 2002), xix.

[17]Güleryüz, *History of the Turkish Jews*, 9.

[18]Levy, xix.

[19]Naim Güleryüz, *Toplumsal Tarih*, (Istanbul: Osmanlı'da İlk Basımevi – Yahudi Matbaacılığı, 2006), 46-52.

[20]Levy, xix.

[21]Rhoads Murphey, "Jewish Contributions to Ottoman Medicine, 1450-1800," in *Jews, Turks, Ottomans*, ed. Avigdor Levy, (Syracuse: Syracuse University Press, 2002), 62.

[22]Güleryüz, *Türk Yahudileri Tarihi*, 89-109.

[23]Murphey, 61.

[24]Ibid., 61.

[25]Ibid., 62

[26]Ibid., 63.

[27]Ibid., 64.

[28]Ibid., 65.

[29]Güleryüz, *History of the Turkish Jews*, 11.

[30]Güleryüz, *Türk Yahudileri Tarihi*, 190-191.

[31]Sarinay, 174.

[32]Daniel J. Schroeter, "The Changing Relationship between the Jews of the Arab Middle East and the Ottoman State in the Nineteenth Century," in *Jews, Turks, Ottomans*, ed. Avigdor Levy, (Syracuse: Syracuse University Press, 2002), 89.

[33]Levy, xix.

[34]Sarinay,170.

[35]Naim Güleryüz, *500.Yıl Vakfı Türk Musevileri Müzesi* (Istanbul: Gözlem Gazetecilik Basın ve Yayın A.Ş., 2004), 37.

[36]Stanford J. Shaw, "Roads East: *Turkey and the Jews of Europe during World War II*," in *Jews, Turks, Ottomans*, ed. Avigdor Levi, (Syracuse: Syracuse University Press, 2002), 246.

[37]Güleryüz, 40-41.

[38]Shaw, 247.

[39]Ibid., 247-248.

[40]Ibid., 247-248.

[41]Ibid., 248.

[42]Güleryüz, 42-43.

[43]Sarinay, 102.

[44]The Quincentennial Foundation Museum of Turkish Jews, www.muze500.com.

[45]Ibid

[46]Ibid

VIII. Chapter Eight
Ottoman Palimpsests: The Past Reviewed in Architecture and Literature

[1]Stephen Kinzer, *Crescent & Star: Turkey between Two Wars* (New York: Farrar, Straus and Giroux, 2001), 172.

[2]Daniel Goffman, *Britons in the Ottoman Empire 1642-1660* (Seattle, U of Washington Pr, 1998).

[3]C. A. Bayly, *The Birth of the Modern World 1780-1914: Global Connections and Comparisons* (Oxford: Blackwell, 2004), 213-216 & 398.

[4]Nabil Matar, "To Tom Gage" personal correspondence. The word "slave" suggests in the West a permanent condition of enforced servitude. This misconception is clarified by Matar, who differentiates two categories of slavery: *Abeed*, that is, captives who were to spend the rest of their lives in slavery, and *Asr*, a slavery that could be negotiated by mutual agreement. Both Arab words are translated in Western languages as slavery.

[5]Kinzer, 40-44.

[6]Fatema Mernissi, *Scheherazade Goes West: Different Cultures, Different Harems.* (New York: Washington Square Pr, 2001), 109-111.

[7]Orhan Pamuk, *My Name Is Red*, tr. Erdağ Göknar (New York: Alfred A. Knopf, 2001).

[8]Maria Rosa Menocal, *Writing in Dante's Cult of Writing: From Borges to Boccaccio* (Durham, Duke U Pr, 1991), 11-50.

[9]Pamuk (2001), 235-242 & 252-266.

[10]*Ghazals of Ghalib*, ed Aijaz Ahmad (New York: Columbia U Pr, 1971), 73-79.

[11]Miguel Asin Palacio, *Islam and the Divine Comedy.* tr. Harold Sunderland (New York, E. P. Dutton, 1926), 55-67.

[12]*Surname-İ Hümayun: An Imperial Celebration* (1582) tr. Nurhan Atasoy (Istanbul, Koçbank1997).

[13]Faulkner, William. (1930) *As I Lay Dying* (New York, Vintage).

[14]Pamuk (2001), 321.

[15]Orhan Pamuk, *The White Castle*, tr. Victoria Holbrook (New York: Braziller, 1991).

[16]Pamuk (1991), 48-60.

[17]Thomas Jefferson "to Isaac McPherson" 13 August 1813.

[18]Walter D. Mignolo, *Local Histories/Global Designes: Coloniality, Subaltern Knowledges, and Border Thinking* (Princeton: Princeton U Pr, 2000).

[19]Pamuk (1991), 83.

[20]Tzvetan Todorov, *Conquest of America* tr. Richard Howard. (Norman, U of Oklahoma Pr, 1984).

IX. Chapter Nine
The Analysis of the *Millet* System in light of Contact Theory

[1]Feyzi Baban, "Community, Citizenship and Identity in Turkey," Trent International Political Economy Centre (2004), http://www.trentu.ca/org/tipec/4baban4.pdf; Kemal H. Karpat, "*Millets* and Nationality: The Roots of the Incongruity of Nation and State in the Post-Ottoman Era," in *Christians and Jews in the Ottoman Empire*, ed. Benjamin Braude and Bernard Lewis (New York: Holmes and Meier Publishers, 1982), 142; Avigdor Levy, "Christians, Jews and Muslims in the Ottoman Empire: Lessons for Contemporary Coexistence," The Alan B. Slifka Program in International Coexistance (2000), http://www.brandeis.edu/programs/Slifka/research/sec_4.pdf: 2.

[2]Karpat, 145-8.

[3]Karpat, 142.

Levy, 2.

[4]Berdal Aral, "The Idea of Human Rights as Perceived in the Ottoman Empire," *Human Rights Quarterly* 26 (2004).

[5]Karpat, 149.

[6]Salah Hannachi, "In Search of Dialogue Among Religions in the Middle East," (paper presented at a meeting of the Japan-Middle East Intellectual Exchange Grant Program, Nagoya, Japan, March 21, 2005).

[7]Baban, 10.

[8]Baban, 10; Karpat, 142; Philip Walters, "Notes on Autocephaly and Phyletism," *Religion, State and Society* 30, no. 4 (2002).

[9]Yusuf Sarinay, ed., "Living Together Under the Same Sky" Beyhan Haciömeroğlu and Durmuş Kandira, trans., (Başbakanlik Basimevi, 2006), 174.

[10]Baban, 10; Karpat, 142.

[11]Baban, 11.

[12]Hannachi, 8.

[13]Sarinary, 4.

[14]Sarinay, 88.

[15]Karpat, 145; Levy, 3.

[16]Levy, 3.

[17]Aral, 476; Karpat, 143; Levy, 2.

[18]Karpat, 147.

[19]Sarinay, 102.

[20]Saryinay, 24.

[21]Levy, 2.

[22]Hannachi, 8; Levy, 2.

[23]Hannachi, 8.

[24]Aral, 476; Levy, 4.

[25]Rainer Forst, "Foundations of a Theory of Multicultural Justice," *Constellations* 4, no. 1 (1997).

[26]Charles H. Parker, "Paying for Privilege: The Management of Public Order and Religious Pluralism in Two Early Modern Societies," *Journal of World History* 17, no. 3 (2006), http://www.historycooperative.org/journals/jwh/17.3/parker.html.

[27]Ibid., 23.

[28]Ahmet Içduygu and B. Ali Soner, "Turkish Minority Rights Regime: Between Difference and Equality," *Middle Eastern Studies* 42, no.3 (2006).

[29]Aral, 477; Levy, 6.

[30]Baban, 11.

[31]Aral, 475.

[32]Thomas F. Pettigrew, "Intergroup contact theory," *Annual Review of Psychology* 49 (1998).

[33]Yehuda Amir, "The role of intergroup contact in change of prejudice and race relations," in *Towards the Elimination of Racism* ed. Phyllis A. Katz (New York: Pergamon Press, 1976), 267.

[34]John F. Dovidio and Samuel L. Gaertner, *Reducing Intergroup Bias : The Common*

Ingroup Identity Model (Philadelphia : Psychology Press, 2000), 49-50.

[35]Norman Miller, "Personalization and the promise of contact theory," *Journal of Social Issues* 58, no. 2 (2002): 395.

[36]Ibid., 398.

[37]Pettigrew, 66-7

[38]Sarinary, 52.

[39]Levy, 3.

[40]Ali Ünal and Alphonse Williams, *Advocate of dialogue* (Fairfax: The Fountain, 2000), 1.

[41]M. Fethullah Gülen, *Toward a global civilization of love and tolerance* (Sumerset: The Light, Inc., 2004), 43.

[42]James R. Payton, Jr, "Ottoman millet, religious nationalism, and civil society: Focus on Kosovo," *Religion in Eastern Europe* 26 (2006).

[43]M. Fethullah Gülen, *Love and the essence of being human* (Istanbul: Da Yayincilik, 2004), 36.

[44]Ibid., 42.

[45]Biçer and Sezgin, 412.

[46]Nevval Sevindi, *Contemporary Islamic Conversations: M.Fetullah Gülen on Turkey, Islam, and the West* (Albany: State University of New York Press, 2008), 71.

[47]M. Fethullah Gülen, "What are the Reasons for the Fact that Islam Spread Over Such Vast Territories in Such a Short Time in the Past? What are the Reasons for the Muslim's Defeat and Failure in the Present Time?" Fethullah Gülen (December 5, 2005), http://en.fgulen.com/content/view/2109/6/.

[48]Ünal and Williams, iii.

[49]Gülen, *Love and the essence of being human*, 40.

[50]Ünal and Williams, 56-57.

[51]Bilici, 1.

[52]Ibid.

[53]Ünal and Williams, 253.

[54]Bekim Agai, "Fethullah Gülen and his movement's Islamic ethic of education," *Critique: Critical Middle Eastern Studies* 11 (2002): 43.

[55]M. Fethullah Gülen, "The 'Turkish Islam' Expression," Fethullah Gülen (November 5, 2003), http://en.fgulen.com/content/view/1243/13.

[56]Gülen, *Love and the essence of being human*, 70-71.

[57]Gülen, *Toward a global civilization of love and tolerance*, 43.

[58]Filiz Baskan, "The Fethullah Gülen community: Contribution or barrier to the consolidation of democracy in Turkey?" *Middle Eastern Studies* 41, no. 6 (2005): 853.

[59]Elisabeth Özdalga, "The hidden Arab: A critical reading of the notion of 'Turkish Islam,'" *Middle Eastern Studies* 42, no. 4 (2006): 560.

[60]M. Fethullah Gülen, *Love and the essence of being human* (Istanbul: Da Yayincilik, 2004), 42.

[61]Sevindi, ix.

[62]Ünal and Williams, 56.

[63]Sevindi, 72.

[64]Sevindi, ix.

[65]Ünal and Williams, 256.
[66]Ünal and Williams, 255.
[67]Sevindi, x.
[68]Yetkin Yildirim and Suphan Kirmizialtin, "The Golden Generation: Integration of Muslim Identity with the World through Education," (paper presented at The AMSS 33rd Annual Conference, Arlington, Virginia, September 24-6, 2004).
[69]Asma Afsaruddin, "The Philosophy of Islamic Education: Classical Views and M. Fethullah Gulen's Perspectives," (paper presented at the first meeting of The Fethullah Gülen Movement in Thought and Practice, Houston, Texas, November 12-13, 2005), http://en.fgulen.com/content/view/2131/27.
[70]Dr. Ian G.Williams, "An Absent Influence? The Nurcu/Fetullah Gulen Movements in Turkish Islam and Their Potential Influence Upon European Islam and Global Education," (paper presented at the first meeting of The Fethullah Gülen Movement in Thought and Practice, Houston, Texas, November 12-13, 2005), http://en.fgulen.com/content/view/2199/27/.
[71]Sevindi, 62.

X. Chapter Ten
Multicultural Science in the Ottoman Empire:
Examples from Medicine and Astronomy
*PhD., Senior Researcher at Foundation for Science, Technology and Civilisation (FSTC) in Manchester, Visiting Scholar at the University of Manchester and Associate Professor at Fatih University, Istanbul.
[1]Adnan Adivar, *Osmanli Türklerinde Ilim*, 5th edition, ed. Aykut Kazancigil and Sevim Tekeli (Istanbul: Remzi Kitabevi, 1983), several pages; Ekmeleddin Ihsanoglu, "Ottomans and European Science," in *Science and Empires*, ed. Patrick Petitjean, Catherine Jami and Anne Marie Moulin (Dordrecht: Kluwer Academic Publishers, 1992), 37–48; Ekmeleddin Ihsanoglu, "Ottoman Science in the Classical Period and Early Contacts with European Science and Technology," in *Transfer of Modern Science & Technology to the Muslim World*, ed. Ekmeleddin Ihsanoglu (Istanbul: The Research Centre for Islamic History, Art and Culture, 1992), 1–48.
[2]Ekmeleddin Ihsanoglu, "Ottoman Educational and Scholarly-Scientific Institutions," in vol. 2 of *History of the Ottoman State, Society and Civilisation*, ed. Ekmeleddin Ihsanoglu (İstanbul: IRCICA, 2002), 361-512.
[3]Halil Inalcik, *The Ottoman Empire: conquest, organization and economy*, (London: Variorum, 1978).
[4]Ihsanoglu, op. cit.
[5]Salim Aydüz, *Tophâne-i Âmire ve Top Döküm Teknolojisi*, (Ankara: Türk Tarih Kurumu, 2006).
[6]Cevat İzgi, *Osmanlı Medreselerinde İlim*, vol. I, (İstanbul, İz Yayıncılık, 1998), 224-226.
[7]For ilm life in the formative period see Arif Bey, "Devlet-i Osmaniye'nin teessüs ve takarrürü devrinde ilim ve ulema [Ilm and *Ulema* in the formation and development of the Ottoman State]," *Darülfünun Edebiyat Fakültesi Mecmuası* 2 (1913): 137-144; İ. H. Uzunçaşılı, *Osmanlı Devletinin İlmiye Teşkilatı*

(Ankara: Türk Tarih Kurumu, 1965); Şahabettin Tekindağ, "Medrese Dönemi," *Cumhuriyetin* 50. *Yılında İstanbul Üniversitesi* (1973): 3–4; Halil İnalcık, "Learning, The Medrese and the Ulema," in *The Ottoman Empire: The Classical Age 1300-1600* (London: Weidenfeld and Nicolson, 1973), 165-178; Mustafa Bilge, *İlk Osmanlı Medreseleri* (İstanbul: İstanbul Üniversitesi Edebiyat Fakültesi, 1984); Cahid Baltacı, *XV-XVI. asırlarda Osmanlı medreseleri: Teşkilat, tarih* (İstanbul: İrfan Matbaası, 1976).

[8]"Fatih reign is not only a turning point in terms of *madrasah* organization but also in terms of perspective or approach. In the famous law regarding organization and protocol there were provisions about *ulema* for the first time. In addition, a clear-cut differentiation was made between *ilmiye, seyfiye* and *kalemiye* occupations, with some preferences with regard to origins, educational backgrounds and formations of the youngsters that would serve in those fields." Mehmet Ipsirli, *"The Ottoman Ulema"*, *The Great Ottoman-Turkish Civilisation* (ed. Kemal Çiçek), (Ankara: Yeni Türkiye, 2002), III, 339-347.

[9]Ahmet Süheyl Ünver, *İstanbul Üniversitesi tarihine başlangıç Fatih, külliyesi ve zamanı ilim hayatı* (İstanbul: İstanbul Üniversitesi Tıp Fakültesi, 1946); Fahri Unan, *Fatih külliyesi: kuruluşundan günümüze* (Ankara: Türk Tarih Kurumu, 2003).

[10]Franz Babinger, *Mehmed the conqueror and his time*, trans. Ralph Manheim, ed. William C. Hickman (Princeton: Princeton University, 1978).

[11]Muhyiddin Muhammed Karabaği, *Ta'lika ala şerhi tehafüti'l-felasife li-Hocazade*, ed. Abdurrahim Güzel (Ankara: Kültür Bakanlığı, 1991).

[12]George N. Vlahakis et al., "Science in the Ottoman World," *Imperialism and Science* (Denver: ABC-CLIO, 2006), 73.

[13]Ekmeleddin Ihsanoglu and others, *Osmanlı Astronomi Literatürü Tarihi*, vol. 1 (İstanbul: IRCICA, 1997), 27–38.

[14]Ahmet Süheyl Ünver, *Türk Pozitif İlimler Tarihinden Bir Bahis Ali Kuşçi, Hayatı ve Eserleri*, (İstanbul: Kenan Matbaası, 1948); George Saliba, "al-Qushjis Reform of the Ptolemaic Model for Mercury," *Arabic Sciences and Philosophy* 3 (1993): 161–203; B.A. Rosenfeld and Ekmeleddin Ihsanoglu, *Mathematicians, Astronomers and Other Scholars of Islamic Civilisation and their works (7th-19th c.)* (Istanbul: IRCICA, 2003), 285–287.

[15]Salim Aydüz, "Uluğ Bey Zici'nin Osmanlı Astronomi Çalışmalarındaki Yeri ve Önemi," *Bilig* 25 (Spring 2003), 139-172.

[16]İlter Uzel, *Amasyalı hekim ve cerrah Sabuncuoğlu Şerefeddin: (1385- 1470?)* (Amasya: Amasya Valiliği, 2004); S. N. Cenk Buyukunal-Nil Sarı, "The Earliest Paediatric Surgical Atlas: Cerrahiye-i Ilhaniye", http://muslimheritage.com/topics/default.cfm?ArticleID=541.

[17]G. Veinstein. "Suleyman," *the Encyclopaedia of Islam*. CD-ROM Edition v. 1.0, 1999 Koninklijke Brill NV, Leiden, The Netherlands; Ali Haydar Bayat, "Osmanlı Devleti'nde Tıp Eğitimi," *Osmanlılarda Sağlık I*, ed. Coşkun Yılmaz and Necdet Yılmaz (İstanbul: Biofarma, 2006), 237–246.

[18]Nasuh b. Abdullah Matrakçı Nasuh, *Beyan-ı menazil-i sefer-i Irakeyn-i Sultan Süleyman Han*, ed. Hüseyin G. Yurdaydın (Ankara: Türk Tarih Kurumu, 1976).

[19]Salim Aydüz, "Osmanlı Devleti'nde Müneccimbaşılık Müessesesi," *TTK*

Belleten, no. 257 (Nisan 2006), Ankara; 167-272.

[20]Salim Aydüz, "İstanbul'da Zamanın Nabzını Tutan Mekanlar," *Istanbul* 51 (September 2004): 92-98.

[21]Ali Haydar Bayat, *Osmanlı Devleti'nde Hekimbaşılık Kurumu ve Hekimbaşılar* (Ankara: Atatürk Kültür Merkezi, 1999).

[22]Arslan Terzioglu, "Die Architektonischen Merkmale der Seldschukischen, Mamelukischen, und Osmanischen Krankenhäuser und ihre Einflüsse auf die Abendländischen Hospitäler," *Fifth International Congress of Turkish Art*, ed. G. Feher, (Budapest: Akademiai Kiado, 1978), 837–856; Aydin Sayili, "Certain Aspects of Medical Instruction in Medieval Islam and Its Influences on Europe," *Belleten* vol. 45, no. 178 (1981): 9–21; Aydin Sayili, "Central Asian Contributions to the Earlier Phases of Hospital Building Activity in Islam," *Erdem* 7 (January 1987): 149–161.

[23]Arslan Terzioglu, "Bîmâristan," *Türkiye Diyanet Vakfı İslam Ansiklopedisi* 6 (1992): 173–178.

[24]Aykut Kazancıgil, *Osmanlılarda Bilim ve Teknoloji* (İstanbul: Gazeteciler ve Yazarlar Vakfı, 1999), 110–115.

[25]Ratıp Kazancıgil, *Edirne Sultan II. Bayezid Külliyesi* (Edirne: Trakya Üniversitesi Rektörlüğü Yayınları, 1997); Özge Gençel, "Müzikle Tedavi," *Kastomonu Eğitim Dergisi* 14, no. 2 (September 2006): 697–706.

[26]Ahmet Süheyl Ünver, "Süleymaniye Külliyesinde Darüşşifa, Tıp Medresesi ve Darülakakire dair (1557–1555) 965–963," *Vakıflar Dergisi*, 2 (1942): 195–196; Ö.L. Barkan, "Süleymaniye Camii ve İmareti Tesislerine Ait Yıllık Bir Muhasebe Bilânçosu, 993–994 (1585–1586)," *Vakıflar Dergisi* 9 (1971): 109–161: 47–50; Mebrure Değer, "Süleymaniye Darüşşifası ve Tıp Medresesi" *I. Türk Tıp Tarihi Kongresi (İstanbul, 17-19 Şubat 1988) Kongreye Sunulan Bildiriler* (Ankara: Atatürk Dil ve Tarih Yüksek Kurumu Türk Tarih Kurumu, 1992), 189–192; Yasin Yılmaz, "Süleymaniye Dârüşşifası ve Tıp Medresesi," *Osmanlılarda Sağlık I*: 285–298.

[27]Gülru Necipoglu-Kafadar, "The Süleymaniye Complex in Istanbul: An Interpretation," *Muqarnas* 3 (1985): 92–117.

[28]Evliyâ Çelebi, *Seyahatnâme I*, ed. O.Ş. Gökyay (İstanbul, 1996), 65; İsmail Hakkı Uzunçarşılı, *Osmanlı Devletinin İlmiye Teşkilâtı* (Ankara: Türk Tarih Kurumu, 1988), 34-35.

[29]Seyyid Lokman, *Hünernâme*. Topkapı Palace Museum Library, Hazine no. 1524, fol. 284b-286b; Ünver, "Süleymaniye Külliyesinde," 199.

[30]For the charter of the Süleymaniye Medical Madrasah, see *Süleymaniye Vakfiyesi*, ed. Kemal Edib Kürkcüoglu (Ankara: Vakıflar Umum Müdürlüğü, 1962), 32-33.

[31]Cevat İzgi. *Osmanlı Medreselerinde İlim: Tabii İlimler*, vol. 2 (İstanbul: İz Yayıncılık, 1997), 24-26.

[32]Nil Sarı, "Teaching Medical History" (paper presented at the 36th International Congress on the History of Medicine, Tunis, Tunisia, September 6–11, 1998).

[33]Ö.L. Barkan. "Süleymaniye Camii ve Imareti Tesislerine Ait Yıllık Bir Muhasebe Bilancosu, 993–994 (1585–1586)," VD 9 (1971): 109–161.

[34]The deed of foundation explains the compulsory conditions for the instructor with this sentence: *They should be intelligent, have strong senses, be logical, educated well on medicine, Plato of the time, Aristotle of age, he should have the reviving effect of*

Jesus, like Galen, selected between physicians, careful about students who wish to learn medicine, and follow the rules of medicine, who continue medical lessons and will be given 20 akças per day. Süleymaniye Vakfiyesi (Ankara: K. E. Kürkçüoğlu, 1962).

[35]Peçuylu, *Tarih I* (İstanbul 1866), 462.

[36]Ünver, "Süleymaniye Külliyesinde," 200-203.

[37]A. Adnan Adıvar, *Osmanlı Türklerinde İlim* (İstanbul: Remzi Kitabevi, 1970), 144. Tuncay Zorlu found 19 names who were the *muderris* at the Medical Madrasah from the beginning until the end. Tuncay Zorlu, "Süleymaniye Tıp Medresesi I," *Osmanlı Bilimi Araştırmaları*, ed. F. Gunergun 3, no. 2 (2002): 79–123.

[38]Topkapi Palace Museum Archive, D 8228.

[39]İnalcık, 165-172; Mustafa Bilge, *Ilk Osmanli Medreseleri* (İstanbul: İstanbul Üniversitesi Edebiyat Fakültesi, 1984).

[40]Ali Haydar Bayat, *Osmanlı Devleti'nde hekimbaşılık kurumu ve hekimbaşılar* (Ankara: Atatürk Kültür Merkezi, 1999); Ünver, "Süleymaniye Külliyesinde," 199.

[41]Ekmeleddin Ihsanoglu and Mustafa Kaçar, "Ayni Münasebetle İki Nutuk: Sultan II Mahmud'un *Mekteb-i Tıbbiye* Ziyaretinde İrad Ettiği Nutkun Hangisi Doğrudur?" *Tarih ve Toplum*, no. 83 (Kasim 1990): 44–48; Ekmeleddin Ihsanoglu and Feza Günergun, "Tip Egitimin Türkcelesmesi Meselesinde Bazi Tespitler," *Türk Tıp Tarihi Yilligi= Acta Turcica Historiae Medicinae. I. Uluslararasi Tıp Tarihi ve Deontoloji Kongresine Sunulan Tıp Tarihi ile İlgili Bildiriler*, ed. Arslan Terzioglu (İstanbul, 1994): 127–134.

[42]Ünver, "Süleymaniye Külliyesinde," 200–202.

[43]Abbé Toderini, *De La Littérature des Turcs*, vol. I (Paris 1789), 119–129.

[44]Aykut Kazancıgil, *Osmanlılarda Bilim ve Teknoloji* (İstanbul: Gazeteciler ve Yazarlar Vakfı, 1999), 120–122.

[45]J. H. Mordtmann, "Das Observatorium des Taqi ed-din zu Pera," *Der Islam* 12 (1913): 93; Ramazan Şeşen, "Meşhur Osmanlı Astronomu Takiyüddin El-Râsıd'ın Soyu Üzerine," *Erdem* 4, no. 10 (1988): 165-171; Cevat İzgi, *Osmanlı Medreselerinde İlim*, vol. 1 (İstanbul: İz Yayıncılık, 1997): 301-302, 327, 192; İzgi, vol. 2, 128-132; Salim Aydüz, "Takiyüddin Râsıd," *Yaşamları ve Yapıtlarıyla Osmanlılar Ansiklopedisi*, vol. 1 (İstanbul: Yapı Kredi Yayınları, 1999): 603-605.

[46]Ahmet Süheyl Ünver, *İstanbul Rasathânesi* (Ankara: Türk Tarih Kurumu, 1986), 43-47.

[47]Topkapi Palace Museum Library, Hazine no. 465/1. In addition look: Sevim Tekeli, "Trigonometry in Two Sixteenth Century Works; The De Revolutionibus Orbium Coelestium and the Sidra al-Muntaha," *History of Oriental Astronomy* (Cambridge: Cambridge University Press, 1987), 209-214.

[48]Sevim Tekeli, "İstanbul Rasathânesinin Araçları," *Araştırma* 11 (1979): 29-44; Sevim Tekeli, "Takiyüddin'de Kiriş 2° ve Sin 1° nin Hesabı," *Araştırma* 3 (1965): 123-127; Sevim Tekeli, "Takiyüddin'in Delos Problemi ile ilgili Çalışmaları," *Araştırma* 6 (1968): 1-9; Sevim Tekeli, "Takiyüddin'in Sidret ül-müntehasında Aletler Bahsi," *Belleten* 30, no. 98 (1961): 213-227.

[49]Sevim Tekeli, "Astronomical Instruments for the Zîj of Emperor," *Arastirma* 1 (1963): 86-97.

[50]Ibid.

[51]Aydin Sayılı, *The Observatory in Islam* (Ankara: Türk Tarih Kurumu, 1991), 289-305; Aydin Sayılı, "Alauddin Mansur'un İstanbul Rasathânesi Hakkındaki Şiirleri," *Belleten* 20, no. 79 (1956): 414, 466.

[52]Sevim Tekeli, "Meçhul bir yazarın İstanbul Rasathesi Aletlerinin Tasvirini veren: Alat-ı Rasadiye li Zic-i Şehinşahiye Adlı Eseri," Araştırma 1 (1963): 12–71.t

[53]Egypt, Cairo National Library, falak no. 3845, miqat no. 557/4.

[54]Sevim Tekeli, "Nasiruddin, Takiyüddin ve Tycho Brahe'nin Rasat Aletlerinin Mukayesesi," *Ankara Üniversitesi, Dil ve Tarih Coğrafya Fakültesi Dergisi* 16, no. 3-4 (1958), 224-259.

[55]Cl. Cahen, "Dhimma," Extract from the Encyclopaedia of Islam CD-ROM Edition v. 1.0, © 1999 Koninklijke Brill NV, Leiden, The Netherlands.

[56]Dukas, *Bizans Tarihi*, (trans. V.L. Mırmıroğlu), (İstanbul: İstanbul Fetih Derneği, 1956), p. 151; Franz Babinger, *Mehmed the Conqueror and His Time*, (translation: Ralph Manheim; ed. William C. Hickman), (Princeton: Princeton University, 1978), p. 78.

[57]*II. Bayezid Dönemine Ait 906/1501 Tarihli Ahkam Defteri*, (Pub. by İ. Şahin-F. Emecen), (İstanbul: Türk Dünyası Araştırmaları Vakfı, 1994), pp. 60-70; Ömer L. Barkan, *Süleymaniye Cami ve İmareti İnşaatı*, (Ankara: Türk Tarih Kurumu, 1972), I, 132 -150.

[58]Salim Aydüz, "XIV.-XVI. Asırlarda, Avrupa Bilim ve Teknolojisinin Osmanlılara Aktarılmasında Rol Oynayan Avrupa'lı Teknisyenler (Tâife-i Efrenciyân)," *Türk Tarih Kurumu Belleten*, LXII/235 (Dec. 1998), (Ankara 1999), pp. 779-830.

The Authors

Chapter One
From the Classical Ottoman Religious
Cultural Order to Nation State
by Dr. Kemal Karpat, Professor Emeritus in History, University of Wisconsin-Madison

Kemal Karpat is a Turkish historian and professor emeritus at the University of Wisconsin-Madison. He received his LLB from the University of Istanbul, his MA from the University of Washington and his PhD from New York University. He has previously worked for the UN Economics and Social Council and taught at Montana State University and New York University. He has written extensively on the history of the Ottoman State in published work that includes *The Politicization of Islam* (Oxford UP, 2001), *The Ottoman Past and Today's Turkey* (Brill, 2000), *An Inquiry into the Social Foundations of Nationalism in the Ottoman State* (Princeton UP, 1973), *Political and Social Thought in the Contemporary Middle East* (Praeger, 1968), and *Turkey's Politics: The Transition to a Multi-Parti System* (Princeton UP, 1959).

Chapter Two
The Roots of Religious Tolerance in the Ottoman Empire
by Dr. Abdel Rahman Ahmad Salem, Cairo University

Dr. Abdul-Rahman Salem is a professor in the Department of History at Cairo University. His research interests include the Ottoman Empire.

Chapter Three
"Upon Them be Peace:" The Ottoman Spirit, Early Modern Models of Toleration, and Contemporary Debates over Multiculturalism
by Dr. Bernadette Andrea, University of Texas at San Antonio

Bernadette Andrea (PhD, Cornell University) is a Professor of English at the University of Texas at San Antonio, where she chaired the Department of English,

Classics, and Philosophy. Her main line of research focuses on women's writing from the sixteenth through the eighteenth century, with emphasis on Western European interactions with the Ottoman Empire. Her recent publications discuss modern Algerian, Egyptian, and Turkish women writers. Her book *Women and Islam in Early Modern English Literature* (2007) is available from Cambridge University Press. Her critical edition *English Women Staging Islam, 1696—1707* is forthcoming from the Center for Reformation and Renaissance Studies / University of Toronto.

Chapter Four

Diversity, Legal Pluralism, and Peaceful Co-existence in the Ottoman Centuries
by Dr. Ihsan Yılmaz, Fatih University

Ihsan Yılmaz received his BA in Political Science and International Relations from the Bosphorus University in 1994 and completed his PhD at the Faculty of Law and Social Sciences SOAS, University of London in 1999. He then worked at the University of Oxford as a fellow between 1999 and 2001. He taught Turkish government and politics, legal sociology, comparative law and Islamic law at SOAS, University of London between 2001 and 2008. He was also the Deputy Chair of the Centre for Ethnic Minority Studies at SOAS (2003-2008) and the director of the London Centre for Social Studies (2003-2008). Currently, he is a professor in the Department of Political Science and Public Administration at Fatih University, Istanbul. His current research interests are Turkish government and politics; political parties; media and politics; Islamism in Turkey, Central Asia and the Middle East; faith-based movements; society-law-politics relations; diaspora studies; elites; centre-periphery relations and sociology of Muslim law in the West. He has been publishing on these issues as well as presenting conference papers at the eminent universities such as Harvard, Georgetown, Oxford, and Cambridge. He has published his work in international scholarly journals such as British Journal of Middle Eastern Studies, the Middle East Journal, Journal of Ethnic and Migration Studies, Muslim World, International Journal of Turkish Studies, Journal for Islamic Studies, Journal of Muslim Minority Affairs, Journal of Caucasian and Central Asian Studies, Journal of Economic and Social Research, and Insight Turkey. Dr Yilmaz is also a regular columnist at *Today's Zaman*, an English language daily published in Turkey.

Chapter Five

Christian-Muslim Interaction on the Ottoman Frontier: *Gaza* and Accommodation in Early Ottoman History
by Dr. Linda T. Darling, History Department, University of Arizona

Linda T. Darling received her PhD in History from the University of Chicago, specializing in the Ottoman Empire, the Ottoman Arab provinces, state formation and governmentality, and socioeconomic history. She is currently researching fiscal administration in the Ottoman Empire and its connections with political legitimation, setting her work on the Ottomans within the wider context of the early modern period in Europe. She is the author of *Revenue-Raising and Legitimacy: Tax*

Collection and Finance Administration in the Ottoman Empire, 1560-1660 and has taught Middle Eastern history at the University of Arizona since 1989.

Chapter Six

The Role of Ottoman Law in the Establishment of Pax Ottomana
by Dr. M. Akif Aydın, School of Law, Marmara University

Dr. Mehmet Âkif Aydın attended the İstanbul High Islamic Institute (Marmara University Faculty of Theology) and graduated from the Istanbul University Faculty of Law in 1974. In 1977, he began working at Istanbul University as an assistant in the Faculty of Islamic Studies Institute. He was appointed to the Marmara University Law Faculty as an assistant professor in 1983, then as a professor in 1993. Dr. Aydın specializes in the History of Turkish Law and Islamic Law and is a member of the Turkish Historical Society. His published work includes *Islamic-Ottoman Family Law* and *History of Turkish Law*. Dr. Aydın also is a member of the Council of Higher Education.

Chapter Seven

The Turkish Jews
by Nisya Ishman Allovi, Manager of the Jewish Museum of Turkey

Born in Istanbul in 1979. Mrs. Nisya İsman Allovi is graduated from the Istanbul Bilgi University, International Relations department.Manager of the 500. Yil Vakfi Türk Musevileri Müzesi (Jewish Museum of Turkey) at Istanbul since 2002, Mrs Allovi is married and the mother of a daughter. For more: www.muze500.com

Chapter Eight

Ottoman Palimpsests: The Past Reviewed in Architecture and Literature
by Dr. Tom Gage, Professor Emeritus in English, Humboldt State University, State University System, California

Dr. Tom Gage, is Professor Emeritus in English at Humboldt State University. He earned all degrees at the University of California, Berkeley. He is the principal architect of Humboldt's Masters degree in the Teaching of Writing at Humboldt, where he founded the Redwood Writing Project, one of the pilot sites of what became the US National Writing Project. Gage has co-authored eight literary anthologies for Scott, Foresman & Co. In classes at Humboldt, he has taught every work by Pamuk, which has been translated into English. A founding member of the Consultants in Global Programs, he has lectured widely, including Turkey, Greece, and China, where he conducted a seminar on William Faulkner. He is a recipient of awards for dedication to international programs, for excellence in classroom teaching, and a Fulbright in Aleppo, Syria. His URL is http://www.humboldt.edu/~teg1/

Chapter Nine

Analysis of the Millet System in Light of Contact Theory
by Dr. Yetkin Yıldırım, the Institute of Interfaith Dialog and
Dr. Maria Curtis, University of Houston

Yetkin Yıldırım, Ph.D., is a researcher at the University of Texas at Austin and the vice president and founding member of the Institute of Interfaith Dialog. He received his MA and PhD from the University of Texas at Austin. His research interests include interfaith dialog, conflict resolution, Islam, and sufism. He has organized several conferences including at the University of Texas at Austin and St. Edwards University including, "Preventing another September 11th", "Living Together through the Legacy of Abraham", and "Clash of Civilizations." His "Islamic Perspectives on Spirituality in Childhood and Adolescence," appeared as a chapter in Nurturing Child and Adolescent Spirituality: Perspectives from the World's Religious Traditions. He has presented papers at the AMSS 33rd Annual Conference at Washington DC, the 2005 Middle East and Central Asia Politics, Economics, and Society Conference, and the American Academy of Religion Conference.

Maria Curtis is an Assistant Professor of Anthropology and Cross-Cultural Studies at UHCL. She has written on medical racism in the United States, and women's spirituality, performance and globalization in Morocco, as well as Turkish and Turkish-American women's experiences in interfaith initiatives. She is currently working on several articles from her dissertation, *Sound Faith: Nostalgia, Global Spirituality, and the Making of the Fes Festival of World Sacred Music*. Her current research interests range from the history of women's roles in the monotheistic religious traditions, to representations of contemporary women in Turkish television serials.

Chapter Ten

Multicultural Science in the Ottoman State: Examples from Medicine and Astronomy
by Dr. Salim Aydüz, Fatih University

Dr. Salim Ayduz is a senior Researcher at the Foundation for Science, Technology and Civilisation (FSTC), UK and Research Visitor at the School of, Languages, Linguistics and Cultures, The University of Manchester. He is also a lecturer at the Fatih University, Istanbul. His research interests include Islamic science and technology and particularly history of Ottoman science and technology. He recently contributed to the "1001 inventions: Discover the Muslim Heritage in our world" book under the editorialship of Prof. Salim Hassani. He is a respected academic who has published and contributed to an array of texts. He is a member of the FSTC and Turkish History of Science Society.

Select Books & Publications

The following books and publications are followed by page numbers that indicate their use in the text and full citations in the Notes. For additional books and publications see the Notes (p197).

Index